£6.99

YO-BUY-507

Schooling the Violent Imagination

Routledge Education Books

Advisory editor: John Eggleston
Professor of Education
University of Warwick

Schooling the Violent Imagination

John F. Schostak

School of Education
University of East Anglia

Routledge & Kegan Paul
London and New York

First published in 1986
by Routledge & Kegan Paul plc

11 New Fetter Lane, London EC4P 4EE

Published in the USA by
Routledge & Kegan Paul Inc.
in association with Methuen Inc.
29 West 35th Street, New York, NY 10001

Set in Times, 10 on 11pt
and printed and bound in Great Britain
by Butler & Tanner Ltd, Frome and London

Library of Congress Cataloging in Publication Data

Schostak, John F.
Schooling the violent imagination.

(Routledge education books)
Bibliography: p.
Includes index.
1. School violence——Great Britain. 2. Violence in children. 3. Child-
rearing——Great Britain. 4. Home and school——Great Britain.
I. Title. II. Series.
LB3013.3.S38 1986   370.19   85—28122
British Library CIP data also available

ISBN 0-7102-0365-9

Contents

Preface

During September and October 1985 British newspapers were again filled with stories of street violence. The images of violence were startling. The centre pages of the *Daily Express* on Monday, 30 September 1985 showed a picture of police in riot gear passing a blazing four-storey building in Gresham Road, Brixton under the headline:

Front-line inferno

These are images of war. These and other media-created images shape our interpretations of what is going on in the world, evoking feelings towards thousands, even millions of people we have never met and will never meet. We will never hear their voices except through newspapers, TV, radio, journals and books.

How are we to respond responsibly, honestly, compassionately and morally to these images? Take, for example, the story of Inspector Lovelock and Mrs Groce as reported by the *Star* on Monday, 30 September:

Inspector Douglas Lovelock, 42, led Saturday's dawn raid of seven men. Mrs Groce was downstairs with her common-law husband, Leon Lawrence, 35, and her three youngest children, Lisa, eight, Lee, 11, and Sharon, 13.

Noise

As police tried to keep them in one room Mrs Groce is believed to have tried to go upstairs where a noise was heard.

She was warned to stay still but kept moving, say police.

Inspector Lovelock fired two shots, one of which hit her in the shoulder and lodged in her spine.

This incident, variously reported, was taken as the cause of the riot that followed. The shooting, according to the police, was an accident – and this was how it was reported by the newspapers. However, on page 4 of the same newspaper, another story is told. This second story provides a key by which the first story may be reinterpreted at the level of imagination rather than fact.

> Inspector Douglas Lovelock would have been gripping his Model 10 Smith and Wesson .38 calibre revolver with both hands as he kicked down Cherry Groce's front door.
>
> But before he even plucked the weapon free from his leather press-stud holster he knew he had only three-eighths of a second to judge whether he could shoot.
>
> Only last Wednesday I faced the same nerve-racking decision. Suddenly in front of me stood a black woman dressed in jeans holding a shotgun.
>
> *I hesitated. And, academically, I was dead.*
>
> Police sergeant David Chambers switched off the slide viewer at the end of the shooting gallery and turned on the lights.
>
> 'It was the fact she was a woman that put you off, wasn't it?' he said.
>
> I should not have hesitated. I should have shot to kill.
>
> That was the chilling message which came through loud and clear at the Metropolitan Police's basic firearms course at Lippitt's Hill, Epping Forest, Essex.

Was it like this as Inspector Lovelock led his men into Mrs Groce's home? How could the story have been told from the viewpoint of Mrs Groce? What kinds of images sympathetic to her could have been found? The images of the above account are drawn from any 'Starski and Hutch' or 'Mike Hammer' story told and re-told in books and on the screen. The macho images, the smell of leather, the tension, the drama is all there. But Mrs Groce was not 'a black woman dressed in jeans holding a shotgun'. Inspector Lovelock is not Mike Hammer. There was not just 'three-eighths of a second to judge whether he could shoot'. Mrs Groce was a black woman at home with her family, unarmed, innocent.

The young people on the streets, too, found their images within which to interpret what they were doing – black resistance against the white police oppressors just as in the current situation in South Africa. This was an analogy drawn and drawn again as black youth spoke about their relationship to the police.

Just a few weeks after the rioting in Brixton, police broke their way into the home of Mrs Cynthia Jarrett. She died of a heart attack. The riots that followed this were described as worse than anything that had happened in 1981. The most terrible incident was when police officer Keith Blakelock was repeatedly stabbed, resulting in his death.

The emotions, the images, the recriminations which follow such events cannot be simply described or analysed. Inevitably there are political responses. But political responses which merely seek to oppose force with even greater force have historically proved totally ineffectual. We need a more radical response. Violence always has a history. We need to understand how the images of violence and counter-violence are created, maintained and justified by the various participants of a drama. It is not a matter of stricter controls, harsher punishments, more effective socialisation, and a return to some golden age of moral values. Young people need to have a stake in the creation of community. By this I do not mean having a stake simply in conformity to rules, norms and values which perpetuate inequality, discrimination and social injustice. Young people, like all others, need to be effective creators of community. And to do that they need to be able to critique prevailing social orders and to act *with* others, rather than *against* others. Here, the role of education is vital. It is through education that the violent images which form and fashion our minds are subjected to a critique radical enough to free us from their conditioning. Throughout the pages of this book, the processes by which the imagination is schooled in violence are discussed with the object of identifying an educational standpoint for those who would wish to take it.

Acknowledgments

I would like to thank members of the CARE study group at the University of East Anglia who discussed with me chapter 3, and Charles Desforges who commented helpfully on the opening chapters of the book.

Chapter 1

Introduction

> I hate school. I hope it burns down and some of the teachers. I
> like some of my lessons. We should be able to wear what we
> like and if we don't like to go in any lessons, we don't have to,
> but we have to. We should be able to smoke in school. I hate
> it. (Written comment, fifth-year girl)

Expressions of hatred, fantasies and acts of violence may often be
attributed to the abnormal, deviant or perhaps immature mind.
Removing violence from the sphere of normality is a typical strategy. Nevertheless, from another perspective it is quite normal, or
typical of human social behaviour. Historians tell us that violence
has been pervasive in society throughout history (Robottom 1976).
Yet the eruption of violence in a supposedly stable society always
comes as a surprise. Consider some of the events of 1981.

During the summer of 1981 street disturbances broke out in
many of our major cities – Liverpool, London, Manchester, were
the headline catchers. The scale and the ferocity of some of these
riots took the authorities by surprise. Reasons had to be found to
explain them; particularly as the participants were predominantly
school age children and recent school leavers. An examination of
the newspaper coverage of the riots reveals a number of simple if
not simplistic explanations. One simple explanation involved the
alleged existence of 'masked men' who went from city to city stir-
ring up trouble (e.g. *New Standard*, 10 July 1981). Another cham-
pioned by Boyson, the then Junior Education Minister, involved
'Poor discipline, lack of moral guidance and the style of religious
education' in schools (*Times Educational Supplement*, 17 July 1981).
Thus 'If we destroy the authority of the staff, society will reap
dragon's teeth in the form of juvenile revolt', he continued. A

1

picture of children as vacuums vulnerable to the anarchistic slogans of ruthless men was painted. Other explanations involved placing the blame upon the parents of the rioters (e.g. *News of the World*, 12 July 1981). Yet others involved trying to shift blame from such contentious issues as unemployment and the economic policies of the Thatcher government. Thus, Peregrine Worsthorne wrote under the headline 'Unemployment is NOT to blame' (*The Sunday Telegraph*, 12 July 1981) that:

> All sections of society today are dangerously prone to lawless violence, and it is the merest cant to blame Mrs Thatcher for a development which is social, even spiritual, rather than economic. When the miners besieged the Saltley coke depot in 1972, under the leadership of Arthur Scargill, driving the police from the streets by brute force, was this because of their material suffering? Then, as now, the miners were the aristocrats of labour, rioting for privilege, not against injustice.

Where Worsthorne found fault was in failing to strengthen the state on law and order. On the same day in the *Sunday Express* essentially the same message was presented by Teddy Taylor, Tory MP for Southend East – 'Violence has soared. Vandalism has become endemic' therefore 'we must impose tough and nasty penalties on vandals, arsonists and looters caught in the act and found guilty by the courts.' There developed the cry for a new Riot Act and the necessity of experience of a 'short sharp shock' for young offenders being sent on remand. However, as the *Manchester Evening News* commented (10 July 1981):

> in all this flurry of belated activity the main root cause of all the troubles must not be forgotten.
> The problems are stark and clear in Manchester. As they are in all inner cities. They are problems that have been vigorously spotlighted in this column over many years. They are problems based on cities deprived of proper support and attention by successive governments – both Tory and Labour – over many years. Bad housing facilities in certain areas, lack of job opportunities, particularly for younger people, lack of social and training facilities. One could go on ad infinitum.

Scarman (1981), when he came to report on the Brixton disorders, highlighted just these problems together with racial disadvantage and poor police and community relations. There were many people who were not surprised by the riots – only that they had not come sooner. Indeed, in the *Guardian* (30 June 1983) it was reported that the '"Disorders of the summer of 1981 we believe were both predictable and predicted," says the all-party committee of MPs from the last Parliament, whose study was completed just before the general election.' The report, it was said, was ignored.

What appeared to capture the imagination of the headline writers and the article writers was that the rioters were so often children, school children. Indeed, rioting took place at St Saviours primary school, Toxteth (see St John Brooks, 1982), Devon's Bideford School, a comprehensive school (*Eastern Evening News* 13 March 1982), and a Durham comprehensive in December 1982, amongst others. In general terms the history of riot and revolution is very much a history of youth rebellion (Heer 1974). In particular, Humphries (1981) has written a history of working-class resistance to schooling during the period 1889–1939 which involved delinquency, school strikes, truanting and so on. Unrest and rebelliousness by school children is no new phenomenon attributable to some breakdown in moral authority or parental care. Such explanations are as old as governmental manipulation and control of the masses. Such explanations imply some golden age which historically has never existed.

If we really want to understand the causes of violence in young people, particularly school children, we must examine carefully our most cherished beliefs, our social practices, and the organisation of schooling. We must learn to listen to the children. Furthermore, we must ask probably the hardest question of all, is the violence justified?

Central to the argument of this book is that violence is more than simply a nihilistic act. Violence has to be interpreted and is thus always ambiguous in meaning because its meaning depends upon context and viewpoint and is thus political in its implications. The difficulty involves trying to define what is to count as normal. Structurally, an act defined as normal may have an identical abstract form to an act defined as abnormal. Indeed, from different perspectives the same act may be defined as 'just' from the one point of view and as barbaric from an alternative point of view. The case of caning in British schools illustrates the point.

The head teacher of a boys' school still using corporal punishment says:

'If [misbehaviour] occurs then I think boys must know where
they are in terms of sanctions and I believe it's important to
have . . . gradation of sanctions. And I think also in school
terms it's important that the teacher is seen to be capable of

3

imposing his own sanctions. To begin with one may refer a child to somebody else for punishment or for correction but in the long term the more you're able to do it yourself successfully the more likely you are for the question of misbehaviour to diminish.'

For this teacher, as for most of his staff, 'most boys naturally will take advantage.' Two or three times a week he could be seen overseeing the movement of boys along the corridor, arms folded, cane erect against his shoulder. The myth at the basis of his 'philosophy of punishment' is that it is in the nature of boys to take advantage. In religious terms this is enshrined in such conceptions as 'original sin'. In clinical terms, as Toch (1972) has pointed out, it has been assumed that man in general seethes with the forces of destruction, such forces only being kept in check by internalised and external social controls. There is also some felt need for punishment – punishment appeases guilt and vengeance. As a senior teacher in another school which had long since given up corporal punishment recalled:

'... sometimes the police would come to me and say look "if he goes to court, he's going to get off, gonna be let off but he's done wrong. He knows he's done wrong. His parents know he's done wrong. And he should be punished. Will you punish him?" And once or twice, I said – I'm very naughty, but I ... I did punish boys, so they didn't have a police record. And the parents were very grateful. The boy as it happens was glad. He hadn't got away with something.'

The distinction between punishment and violence is entirely social; corporal punishment is simply legalised violence. In the above case the corporal punishment meted out in school was simply an extension of other forms of lawful punishment. The internal system of punishment mirrors the punishment structure external to the school. Birching as a punishment for offenders has been given up (although often called for during the 1981 riots), whereas caning has not; school detention may be seen as a watered-down form of prison detention. The seduction toward the use of corporal punishment and forms of detention is great. It is simple and it is cheap. Of the two the following teacher prefers the use of corporal punishment:

'I don't know whether you want me to say this but I shall say it anyway. I'm a great believer in corporal punishment. For that reason I think if a child is asked to do something on at least two or three occasions and he still defies you then that defiance should be, you know, considered insolence and should be corrected for it in a very severe way rather than just this business of detentions which ... just soul destroying for both the boy and the teacher who puts him on. Whereas a short sharp reminder is usually more efficacious I've found.'

Young teachers can find the 'short sharp reminder' almost irresistible, particularly when parents and even pupils appear to favour it. However, the cane brutalises both teacher and pupils:

'... the time did come when we sort of looked at the punishment book and we said "On occasions somebody who is maladjusted is being punished. And it's wrong. You mustn't do that. These names are coming up again and again. It isn't working is it? It's wrong." ... and one of the ... the things that concerned me more than anything else was the fact that it wasn't the boy it was the teacher. That teachers were pushing pupils sometimes a little too far ... provoking them. That sometimes the teacher was bad tempered ... and a boy reacted ... in a way he shouldn't have done. But it didn't always need corporal punishment and yet that was ... for extreme rudeness to a member of staff in front of the class, then that was the accepted punishment. And I had to do it and I, I used to feel sick when I had to do it. I, I always made the person who had made the complaint come along and be the witness. And I was deliberately, you know, I, I would provoke them not to make me have to do this ever again. They could see how upset I was having to do it. And always of course, a letter to the parents explaining exactly what had been done and why, when it was corporal punishment. We looked at these reasons and said "Right, just for six months we'll see if we can do without. . . ." No problems. Even though the school next door, you see, still has corporal punishment. . . . And the six months became a year, and the year became fifteen years. And we still don't need corporal punishment. And we never will.'

The structural habit of corporal punishment can be kicked, even in an area considered tough by tough standards – an area of massive youth and adult unemployment and all the social problems that go with this. Part of the motivation for this senior teacher and his colleagues abandoning the cane was a sense of revulsion and partly a sense of immorality or injustice.

Nevertheless, the structures of violence are deep within society.

Introduction

The images of force are everywhere. The image of manliness is also one of forcefulness, toughness and even violent action. One fifteen-year-old boy who had been expelled from two previous secondary schools equated discipline with physical violence. He respected the teachers of his present school because they were not afraid to use corporal punishment. He gave an example of the educative effect of such discipline from his experience at a disruptive unit:

> *Dave* '... Like when I went to me disruptive unit it was um ex-copper was the bloke who owned it right. There was only two teachers there an' about five kids went there. An' the atmosphere, it was really great. An' you knew if you did anyfink wrong 'e'd just beat you up. An' 'e did like you know, I ...'
> *J.F.S.* 'You mean physically beat you up?'
> *Dave* 'Yeah! 'e used to get 'old of you an' give you a good kickin' y' know 'e'd slap you about. There was one kid there called Joey, an' 'e was, obviously 'e was well backward, you could tell that an' that was why 'e messed around and uh when 'e went there – right next to it was this other school an' we opened the gates an' chucked 'im (laughing) in the other school an' shut the gates. An' like y' know 'e run 'ome this Joey an' the head, the copper, said, "Where's Joey?" So we said, "Dunno, sir," y' know. An' 'e come back the next day an' 'e said, "Where did you go?" He said, "Ah, I went 'ome sir. They frew me in the next school so I run 'ome." And so like 'e got us, 'e took us outside an' 'e just got this big stick an' 'e 'it us. An' 'e said "You won't do that again will you?" You know, you know you wouldn't do it again.'

Dave desired to be controlled, it took away any need for irksome self-responsibility. Dave could continue – and he did – to be a villain where control could not reach him, and a model pupil where it could.

Dave, although his school career is atypical, does not have atypical attitudes towards caning. In a survey carried out for *ITV Times Magazine* (18–24 June 1983) by Audience Selection, following a series on schools, 62 per cent of pupils, 54 per cent of teachers and 81 per cent of parents approved of corporal punishment. STOPP (an anti-corporal punishment pressure group) estimated that there were 238,000 beatings a year (as reported in *TES* 5 August 1983). The question becomes: because a majority appear to support corporal punishment does that make it right?

An answer may be provided by considering a case taken to the Court of Human Rights. The European Convention on Human Rights holds that:

> Protocol 1 Article 2: No person shall be denied the right to education. In the exercise of any functions which it assumes in relation to education and to teaching, the state shall respect the right of parents to ensure such education and teaching is in conformity with their own religious and philosophical convictions.
> Article 3: No one shall be subjected to torture or to inhuman or degrading treatment of punishment.

Two Scottish mothers in 1976 took to the European Commission for Human Rights a complaint concerning the use of the tawse (a strap) in punishment of their children. In March 1982 the court decided Britain was in violation of Article 2 but not Article 3. The decision showed a clear concern for parental rights although curiously no concern for individual rights as implied in Article 3 on punishment. Children were not asked if the punishment was considered inhuman or degrading. As Holt (1974) has written, children have no individual rights which would enable them to lead an independent existence.

The response of the British government to the ruling came in 1983. Parents would be allowed to 'opt out' of corporal punishment for their children. In effect, in a caning school there would be two classes of pupil, those who could be caned and those who could not. This right has become very controversial. It is clear there is a great reluctance to abolish corporal punishment outright in school. Schools, I argue, condition individuals to accept a form of authority which he or she will meet in later business, political and even married life. Without punishments coercive authority ceases. In adult life the cane is substituted by fear of unemployment, prison, loss of earnings – and in extreme circumstances, riot police wielding truncheons.

The boundary between the normal and the abnormal use of violence differs between societies. Children learn to make distinctions. Thus, according to McWhirter, Young and Majury (1983), after a decade or more of 'the troubles', Belfast children accept violence and violent death as normal. Even in the horrific situation of the Nazi concentration camps, the brutality of the guards became normal to the extent that many prisoners modelled their own behaviour upon that of the guards, taking on the guards' attitude (Moore 1978). In our own more 'normal' history, the history of childhood has been assessed as a nightmare, indeed as a history of child abuse (de Mause 1974). It was the norm to consider it right and moral to beat children, even babies (a topic to be discussed in a later chapter). However, we continually forget our history, rewriting it in memory in terms of past golden ages.

Many psychological and social mechanisms aid in the repression of, censorship of, or selective inattention to acts of violence. Redefinition is one means. Where one considers an act of violence just retribution, another considers it a wanton act of destruction. To distance ourselves from acts of violence and the people who commit them we label them bizarre, alien, inhuman, typical only of certain classes of abnormal individuals (cf. Toch 1972) or criminal subcultures (Wolfgang and Ferracuti 1967). We distance them from ourselves and our culture. Where we are civilised they are uncivilised.

It is hard, however, to escape the fact that our civilisation is constructed out of violence. It is a fact we would wish to forget. Freud argued that civilisation is founded upon the violent acts of the sons (or fraternal organisation) against the father (or paternal organisation). Historically, the Western political democracies are founded upon acts of rebellion. Nisbet (1976) has argued that the state emerged as a war between kinship forms of organisation (paternal) and military forms (fraternal) with the military eventually winning. Today, the fragile peace of the world is founded upon opposing military might which threatens all with extinction. Our continued existence depends upon the realisation that annihilation is but a push-button away. Central to the structure of world peace is mutual suspicion, hostility and fear.

There is a kind of equality under the shadow of the bomb. It is the equality of the mass more or less equally likely to be killed. We are all anonymous. We feel our powerlessness. Yet we all work together to maintain our state of being anonymous and powerless. We all do our part in the great division of labour and of power which divides society into military, industry, welfare, government, education.

Children, the most powerless members of society, are born into structures of privilege and deprivation. School does little, if anything, to modify a child's cultural inheritance. Children carry with them their experiences of privilege or deprivation into school; school reinforces such experiences because schools are inadequately and inappropriately organised to cope with the problems children experience. Rod Ling (1984), in a study of the processes of suspensions, cites a headteacher who wrote an account of one counselling session:

> Pupil seen by head and counselled. Boy reported that there
> were domestic problems. Counselled and told to avoid bringing
> his feelings into school.

Problems, however, do not disappear just because one refuses to look at them. Children bring their whole experience into school. School is interpreted by children in the light of that experience. Thus:

> Teachers don't really want to know about problems as far as I
> can see and if I made a complaint about for example my tutor
> (who I don't like very much) the people in the houseblock
> probably have a laugh about it or turn whatever the complaint
> was about into my fault and they are usually hostile
> afterwards. (written comment, fifth-year boy)

Children see quite clearly that they are denied access to any democratic means whereby they can solve their problems. There are areas of secrecy in schools hidden from all pupils – and it is here that the real decision making goes on. School is divided into two broad camps which at one level of experience is mutually hostile. Waller (1932) argued that teachers and pupils were necessarily hostile to one another. Feelings of hostility may be reduced by the actions of some teachers, increased by others. Since much of the task of the teacher in the modern classroom is to exert a censorial control over pupils, some degree of hostility is probably unavoidable. However, hostility can be aggravated by certain kinds of teacher control techniques: sarcasm, shouting, poking, punching, pushing. Thus:

> The worst thing about school is the way the teachers are
> sarcastic and talk down to you. If teachers concentrated more
> on teaching pupils than on picking on them then there would
> be less truanting in school. (written comment, fifth-year girl)

In the following chapters of this book the social structures which create and reinforce such feelings of hostility and lead to expressions of violence (in teacher and pupil) will be explored. It will be argued that in order to interpret any one particular incident as either violence or non-violence, an individual draws upon cultural knowledge, images, opinions, myths. Violence is rarely, if ever, blind, without reason, surprising or arbitrary. Violence is a normal part of the culture and therefore the structure of everyday life. We

9

are all part of the same fabric. We are all implicated in the violent dramas played out in school life, family life, business life - everywhere. No role is ever too small, too insignificant. Violence underlies the political order.

In this book there will be no attempt to portray any single school. The research data was derived from a variety of sources and will be presented anonymously. All names are fictional. The focus of the book is upon the relationships created by acts of violence and experiences of being violated. Each voice, each incident recorded, becomes symbolic of other voices, other incidents wherever violence occurs. The kind of analytic approach and method of generalisation taken in this book I have elsewhere called phenomenological generalisation (Schostak 1984). Those who would wish to know more of the roots of this method may refer to Schutz (1976), Levin (1968-69), and Tragesser (1977) - these give sociological and philosophical justifications of the approach. No such justifications will be attempted here.

The argument to be presented and justified in this book will be founded first upon a critical review of current theories of violence. Thus in chapter 2, in reviewing the theories of violence, it will be argued that it is not instinct as such which produces violence and nor should violence be defined in terms of aggressive forms of norm violation (which leads to notions of 'treatment' for those labelled violent and the problems of adjusting them to society) but rather this notion must be turned on its head. Violence begins as an experienced violation of an individual's sense of individuality and/ or sense of community with others. Each such experience of violation remains as an image in the contents of what will be called a violent imagination - that matrix of images, folktales, myths and so on which an individual can use to interpret any present, future or past act as being, or not being, violent, or as requiring a violent or non-violent response.

To analyse the structure of violence one must focus upon the major social structures brought to bear upon the growing individual. Chapter 3 takes as its theme the first and most general of these: childrearing practices. Schooling, it is argued, has been moulded by the influence of the dominant forms of childrearing practices and that these practices lead to experiences of the violation of individuality and of community. The organisation of the school, it will be argued, is a legacy of outdated (often more brutal) forms of childrearing inappropriate to the realisation of democratic attitudes, behaviours and forms of community.

Chapter 4 widens the discussion to the relationship of schooling to the community and the self. It is argued that the quality of community depends upon the quality of communication between individuals. Based upon the conclusions of the previous chapter, it is argued that at school the self is often inducted into a community of counterfeit relations or a community of lies. Knowledge of and experience of the self as reflected in the voices of the community, it is further argued, for many young people results in a vandalised sense of self.

The next two chapters, 5 and 6, take respectively the themes of racism and sexism as forms of violatory experience.

Chapter 7 will present a more general argument concerning the processes of violence in school. It is argued that the processes of violence are not arbitrary in nature although they may appear as irrational eruptions. Violence may be a means to transform one state of affairs into another and thus create a rational order. Violence and the construction of social reality will be discussed.

Chapter 8 focusses upon what may be called the 'lessons' of violence, identifying the processes which encourage the formation of a curriculum of violence.

Chapter 2

Conceiving violence

There is a dominant view locating the cause or source of violence within the physical nature of the human being. At the same time society is seen as the necessary regulator of the individual's potentially violent and predatory nature. Hobbes spoke for this dominant view when he wrote that without fear of the power of some central agency everyday life would be a war of all against all. Struggle and strife became central images in the evolutionary theories of Darwin which in turn influenced the development of sociology and psychology. However, Harris (1968) has traced the development of the concept of competitive struggle not to biology but to the theories of the classical economists: Indeed, 'Darwin's principles were an application of social science concepts to biology.' The principle of natural selection came from Malthus's *Essay on Population*; 'survival of the fittest' came from Spencer's advocacy of laissez-faire economics and the notion of the 'rugged individual'. At this point, political economy rather than biology underlay conceptions of human violence, aggression, rugged individualism. Such individualism (which is not to be confused with individuality – cf. Schostak, 1983b) required a revolution in moral thought. Macpherson (1973: 17–18):

> Moral and political philosophers had from the earliest times recognised in mankind a strain of unlimited desire, but most of them had deplored it as avarice and had believed that it could, and urged that it should be fought down. What was new, from the seventeenth century onwards, was the prevalence of the assumption that unlimited desire was rational and morally acceptable.

Violence, if placed in the image of rationality, was acceptable. It

became morally acceptable for the competitive individual to appropriate the resources and the products of social activity. The richer
you were the more moral you were and the more society pro-
gressed. The best accumulated the most and this was good for
society. On the one hand was an optimistic belief in the rationality
of the individual as displayed in the works of the utilitarians, but
on the other:

> Underneath the superficial buoyancy and hopefulness and the
> complacent assurance which we tend to identify with the
> Victorian mentality there is nearly always something very like
> fear. This is hardly to be wondered at, for the majestic portrait
> of evolutionary development is also a portrait of the predatory
> struggle for existence. (Aiken 1956: 166)

Such images concerning the predatory nature of people coupled
with religious images of Original Sin could lead one to argue that
the institutions of Victorian society were shaped and sustained by
such theories. Fated to be violent, people therefore required con-
straint through social controls; expressions of violence were thus
attributable to a breakdown or lack of social control. The two
ways of defining individuals in terms of rationality and of violence
may be seen in the kinds of arguments employed to justify the
introduction of mass education. Schooling came to be seen as a
way of revealing to the lower classes the rational value of the
prevailing social order, hence inhibiting revolt, and, to more liberal
thinkers, as a means towards improving the lot of the poor. James
Hole wrote in 1860 (1969 edition: 89):

> What is it but ignorance which deprives the working man of all
> power of raising himself in the social scale, – blots out 'the
> hope to rise, the fear to fall,' and leaves him an easy prey to
> every temptation which his own passions, or the vile cupidity
> of those who batten upon his vices and flourish by his
> degradation, place in his path? If, by any process we could
> secure to every member of the community a superior
> education, it would go a great way to remove many of those
> social evils with which it has apparently little or no immediate
> connexion. It is the ignorant man who unconsciously conspires
> with his equally ignorant landlord, to lower the dwelling-house
> to its meanest standard. It is ignorance of the value of
> education, which leads the parent to keep his child away from
> school, and allows it to run wild in the streets; or which forces
> it prematurely to work, while he riots in drunkenness upon the
> wages which should be devoted to its intellectual advancement.

This reformist view may be contrasted with that of Hannah More (1799, vol. II: 252) the influential founder of a Sunday school who aimed to reconcile the minds of the young to the doctrine of original sin and their station in life. People were to learn of their bestial nature and control it. During her life she had to respond to those who feared her work would make the lower classes dissatisfied with their station in life and rebel. The Silvers' (1974) study of Kensington School illustrates how schools had to justify their existence and quell fears that schooling might lead the poor to become ambitious and discontented. Thus, schooling was ambivalent in nature: on the one hand it was an agent of social control, on the other it introduced the lower classes to ideas 'above their station'. Nevertheless, despite widely spread fears amongst the upper classes that education for the lower classes would lead to discontent and an overthrow of the social order compulsory schooling became law. Its advantages were many. For example, Forster, who introduced the Education Bill of 1870, had, like other politicians, been impressed by the rapidity with which Prussia had defeated Austria in the Seven Weeks War; Prussia had had compulsory education since the 1840s which was widely seen as having an important bearing upon Prussia's triumph. Education had become a military weapon.

There were other motives too in that the increase in franchise, though limited, due to the Reform Bill of 1868 led some to consider how to educate their masters to take the politically right decisions – schooling as a violation of independent thought. For example, Robert Lowe who had been a minister responsible for education opposed extending the franchise, saying 'I believe it will be absolutely necessary to compel our future masters to learn their letters.' Forster who introduced the 1870 Education Bill justified it by saying:

> I am one of those who would not wait until the people were educated before I would trust them with political power. If we had thus waited we might have waited long for education; but now that we have given them political power we must not wait any longer to give them education. There are questions demanding answers, problems which must be solved, which ignorant constituencies are ill fitted to solve. Upon this speedy provision of education depends also our national power. Civilized communities throughout the world are massing themselves together, each mass being measured by its force; and if we are to hold our position among men of our own race

or among the nations of the world we must make up the
smallness of our numbers by increasing the intellectual force of
the individual ... (Hansard, series iii, vol. 199, cols 465-6)

Similarly, a further extension of the franchise in 1918 led Fisher to
introduce his Education Bill by saying 'how can we expect an
intelligent response to the demands which the community propose
to make upon the instructed judgement of its men and women
unless we are prepared to make some further sacrifices in order to
form and fashion the minds of the young ...' (Wardle 1974: 27).
Education was to become a safeguard against 'uninstructed decision making', a means of forming and fashioning minds to make
the right kinds of decisions. At this point it may be useful to make
a distinction between education and schooling. Schooling was what
the formers and fashioners had in mind, but education was what
was feared. Education is taken to be the process of questioning,
reflecting critically upon experience and forming and fashioning the
world towards one's own intentions: premissed on an unconditional
freedom of thought and independence in action. Schooling, as such,
violates the principle of education.

Schooling, by contrast, is premissed upon the inculcation of rules
of conduct. In school the young were to be taught to see the virtues
of society and to appreciate their place in society. A workforce
schooled in the virtues of hard work, obedience, punctuality, basic
literacy and numeracy became the ideal. Indeed, there was some
sense of a civilising mission. Grace (1978) described how Victorian
schools were created as citadels of civilisation amidst the depravity
and ignorance of the masses. Arnold (1973 edition: 204) saw the
danger of the working classes who, being 'raw and half developed'
were asserting 'an Englishman's heaven-born privilege of doing
what he likes' and thus 'beginning to perplex us by marching where
it likes, meeting where it likes, bawling what it likes, breaking
what it likes.' Schooling in Britain was a way of pacifying the
masses.

In America there were similar motives for the introduction of
mass education. Brace, in the mid-nineteenth century, advised 'in
the interests of public order, of liberty, of property, for the sake of
our own safety and the endurance of free institutions here,' there
should be 'a strict and careful Law, which shall compel every
minor to learn to read and write, under severe penalties in case of
disobedience' (source: Platt, 1977). In particular, the childsaving
movement described by Platt (1977: 21, 28) aimed at trying to save
the children of the criminal classes, that is, the lower classes:

The criminal was thought to be morally retarded and, like a small child, instinctively aggressive and precocious unless restrained. It is not difficult to see the connection between biological determinism in criminological literature and the principles of 'natural selection'. . . .

In short,

a basic thrust of nineteenth-century criminological thought in the United States was an emphasis on the non-human qualities of criminals. Darwinist and Lombrosian rhetoric suggested that criminals were a 'dangerous and discredited class who stood outside the boundaries of morally regulated and reciprocal relationships.'

This contextual sketch should provide sufficient background for the task ahead, the contextualisation of the major theories of violence which have emerged in academic culture.

Twentieth-century views of violence

The themes already discussed are still in evidence in modern theories of violence. It will be convenient to examine the various theories under the following broad headings: biological theories; psychological theories; and the criminological and sociological explanations of violence. Finally, the relationship between violence and justice will be discussed.

Biological theories

Biological determinism is not dead, although the notion of an instinct of aggression has received some mortal wounds. In 1904 Kropotkin published his *Mutual Aid*, a work which essentially demonstrated a view of nature contrary to the Darwinian view of struggle. It was a view which emphasised cooperation rather than competition. In distinction to instincts of violence, predation or aggression, he postulated an instinct of cooperation. Rather than struggle and the survival of the fittest, cooperation and mutual aid determined which species survived and advanced along the evolutionary tree. Current views appear to provide more support for Kropotkin than for the Darwinian views of incessant struggle. It is generally accepted that, except for the relationship of predator to prey, overt fighting to the death rarely occurs in vertebrates (Carthy

and Ebling 1964). However, according to Ong (1981: 51) combativeness is 'an advanced rather than a primitive form of behaviour'.
Nevertheless, Carthy and Ebling (1964: 3) maintain:

> Weapons such as teeth, claws, nasal horns and antlers would
> be very dangerous if turned against members of the same
> species; thus fighting is ritualised into display, threat,
> submission and appeasement, and such fights are no more than
> trials of strength followed by disengagement and rapid
> withdrawal by the weaker animals. Even in non-human
> primates, according to Hall, no group engages in fighting with
> other groups and real fighting within a group is of rare
> occurrence even in the most overtly aggressive species. True
> overt fighting in mammals seems to occur when population
> numbers have overtaken the resources of the environment so
> that serious overcrowding is brought about.

Combativeness has, according to this view, social functions in
creating social order in the group rather than leading to group
disintegration. That true overt fighting occurs in situations of
scarce resources has interesting implications, since human social
order is founded upon the allocation of scarce resources and the
competitive acquisition of scarce resources and scarce products.
The richest of countries store up mountains of food or even destroy
superfluous products in order to maintain a desired market price,
while many of their own citizens go without and millions in the
Third World starve. There is the determined maintenance of arti-
ficial scarcity as a basis for social order. Since aggression continues
to have a central role in political economy biologists may be found
who continue to seek explanations in genetics.

This tradition of the genetic basis of aggression and violence is
continued in the ethological theories of Lorenz (1966), Tinbergen
(1951) and Morris (1967) and the sociobiology of Wilson (1978).
For example, Wilson considers that there is no general instinct of
aggression but rather a strong predisposition called into being by
certain stimuli, thus:

> Our brains do appear to be programmed to the following
> extent: we are inclined to partition other people into friends
> and aliens, in the same sense that birds are inclined to learn
> territorial songs and to navigate by the polar constellations.
> We tend to fear deeply the actions of strangers and to solve
> conflict by aggression. These learning rules are most likely to
> have evolved during the past hundreds of thousands of years of

17

human evolution and, thus, to have conferred a biological advantage on those who conformed to them with the greatest fidelity.

The learning rules of violent aggression are largely obsolete. We are no longer hunter-gatherers who settle disputes with spears, arrows and stone axes. But to acknowledge the obsolescence of the rules is not to banish them. We can only work our way around them. To let them rest latent and unsummoned, we must consciously undertake those difficult and rarely travelled pathways in psychological development that lead to mastery over and reduction of the profound human tendency to learn violence. (p. 119)

Wilson's views have received much criticism. Nevertheless, a casual glance at the figures for the war dead of the preceding centuries provide at least circumstantial evidence of his claims. In 1972, Elliot wrote in the introduction to his *Twentieth Century Book of the Dead*: 'The number of man-made deaths in the twentieth century is about one hundred million.' Since then there have been many more wars: in Cambodia, Lebanon, Iran, Iraq, Afghanistan, Nicaragua, the Falklands – and many others. Indeed, such a toll is consistent with the pessimistic views of Freud in the postulation of a death wish which through reason creates the tools and techniques of mutual annihilation.

However, it seems to me that the situation is far more complex than can be explicable through a postulation of some form of predisposition for violence, or innate aggression, or a death wish. That there is some biological element I consider indubitable – we all live as bodies, not in bodies. We are flesh and blood products of the universe. We perceive ourselves and the universe through the senses of our flesh; and work and play are motivated by the desires, ecstasies, fears and anxieties of the body. Nevertheless, Fromm (1974: 177), in a review of anthropological literature, has concluded that:

... the instinctivistic interpretation of human destructiveness is not tenable. While we find in all cultures that men defend themselves against vital threats by fighting (or by fleeing), destructiveness and cruelty are minimal in so many societies that these great differences could not be explained if we were dealing with an 'innate' passion. Furthermore, the fact that the least-civilized societies like the hunter-gatherers and early agriculturalists show less destructiveness than the more-developed ones speaks against the idea that destructiveness is part of human 'nature.' Finally, the fact that destructiveness is not an isolated factor, but . . . part of a syndrome, speaks against the instinctivistic thesis.

If this is correct, explanations of violence must be found elsewhere. Fromm finds them in the conditions of human existence which contribute to the formation of the individual's psychological development. This is not inconsistent with alternative explanations which find genetic or biological pathology, induced by mutation, environmental pollution, drug abuse or disease.

Pathological explanations begin to conjure up the image of the monster. One thinks of the mass murderers such as Charles Manson in America or the Yorkshire Ripper in England. People think of them as abnormal. Indeed, Charles Whitman who committed mass murders at the University of Texas was found to have a malignant tumour in the brain. Studies of violent criminals have provided findings which indicate they have an extra male chromosome thus leading to the speculation that this chromosome abnormality accounts for their over-aggressiveness (cf. Johnson 1972). Such physical abnormalities appear to let normal society off the hook. However, these incidents do nothing to explain the historically pervasive violence in the world. For this attention must return to the physically normal.

To be feared most are those who do their duty, perhaps believing those in authority know best or fearing their wrath. For some, to obey can be a way of shedding irksome responsibility for all kinds of bestial acts. One may set aside the acts of the Nazi concentration camp guards as perpetrated by inhuman monsters, crazed psychopaths. One may set aside the acts of war – fire bombing, napalming, atom bombing – as instrumental in bringing peace; but in setting aside these we are agreeing to ignore the major acts of destruction committed by humans. They cannot be ignored. They were all carried out by individuals – including concentration camp guards – legitimated by their society through their officially appointed superiors just doing their duty for their country, or perhaps worse, fearing to do otherwise. An experiment was carried out by Milgram (1974), who showed the extent to which ordinary citizens would carry out their duty as they saw it, in giving what they believed to be potentially lethal and certainly very painful electric shocks to subjects in what was seemingly a simple test of learning. One subject reported his experience thus:

'Well, I faithfully believed the man was dead until we opened the door. When I saw him, I said, "Great, this is great." But it

didn't bother me even to find that he was dead. I did a job.'
(p. 88)

The experiment was controversial and its interpretations still are.
The matter of duty and the inculcation of obedience will be recon-
sidered later in the context of schooling. At this point psychological
explanations of violence must be considered.

Psychological explanations

Psychological perspectives divide into those which emphasise instinct or biological origins and those which emphasise the environment in explanations of violence. Few take the extreme Freudian
position which posits a death instinct, although echoes of Freud's
views are a feature of many theories. Freud forces attention to the
relation between instinct and the formation of civilisation, the
asocial and the social, the irrational and the rational. In *Civilization and its Discontents* (1963 edition: 49) Freud wrote of *homo
homini lupus* (man is a wolf to man):

> The existence of this inclination to aggression, which we can
> detect in ourselves and justly assume to be present in others, is
> the factor which disturbs our relations with our neighbour and
> which forces civilization into such a high expenditure (of
> energy). In consequence of this primary mutual hostility of
> human beings, civilized society is perpetually threatened with
> disintegration. The interest of work in common would not hold
> it together; instinctual passions are stronger than reasonable
> interests. Civilization has to use its utmost efforts in order to
> set limits to man's aggressive instincts and to hold the
> manifestations of them in check by psychical reaction-
> formations. Hence, therefore, the use of methods intended to
> incite people into identifications and aim-inhibited relationships
> of love, hence the restriction upon sexual life, and hence too
> the ideal's commandment to love one's neighbour as oneself –
> a commandment which is really justified by the fact that
> nothing else runs so strongly counter to the original nature of
> man. In spite of every effort, these endeavours of civilization
> have not so far achieved very much. It hopes to prevent the
> crudest excesses of brutal violence by itself assuming the right
> to use violence against criminals, but the law is not able to lay
> hold of the more cautious and refined manifestations of human
> aggressiveness. The time comes when each one of us has to

give up as illusions the expectations which, in his youth, he pinned upon his fellow-men, and when he may learn how much difficulty and pain has been added to his life by their ill-will.

It is a charge many would rather ignore: it is violence which shapes social relations and forms the political structures of control and justice. The standpoint of the civilised self is that the Other is dangerous and unless controlled through external and internalised norms, structures of surveillance (policing, conscience) and of punishment the Other will act destructively. This is reflected in the psychological structure of the self where the superego is the censor which punishes through guilt. This is elaborated by Ricoeur (1970: 307):

> ... the cultural function of guilt necessarily involves the psychological function of the fear of conscience from the point of view of the psychology of the individual, the sense of guilt – at least in its quasi-pathological form – appears to be merely the effect of an internalised aggressiveness, of a cruelty taken over by the superego and turned back against the ego.

It is an image of the self eating into the self – the ironic structure of the presumed sanity of civilisation where the essential psychic structure of its members is conceived out of violence and maintained by violence.

Freud ends his *Civilization and its Discontents* with the expectation that Eros will assert itself in the struggle with Thanatos: 'But who can foresee with what success and with what result?' This desperate image of life and death struggle is one many have wished to reject, or at least dilute it like Wilson (1978) to more manageable proportions. Within the psychoanalytic tradition Jacoby (1975) has criticised practitioners according to the extent they have made Thanatos anodyne. The individual, in Freud's terms, is the battleground: the battle could be resolved in one of two ways, either by conforming or adapting to society, or by rebelling against it. With the neo-Freudians the emphasis is upon adapting to society rather than resisting it, finding meanings and values which elevate rather than return to the basement, the level of the instincts. Or, in the case of those like Fromm (1974) one adjusts society to the presumed needs of individuals and hence circumvents the need for aggressive solutions. Such a view, however, has to wrestle with what Toch (1972: 36) summed up as the dominant clinical view which assumes:

> that all men are reservoirs of bloody destructiveness. It maintains that civilization equips most people with the means

of discharging their hatred judiciously and selectively –
although there are instances in which this effort fails. Some
people are presumed to remain unchecked in their
aggressiveness, so that they become promiscuously violent
upon slight provocation.

To challenge such a view, alternative assumptions must be found
and found to be at least plausible. Toch, himself, takes the position
that:

> ... if we want to explain why men are driven to acts of
> destruction, we must examine these acts, and understand the
> contexts in which they occur. We must know how destructive
> acts are initiated and developed, how they are conceived and
> perceived, and how they fit into the lives of their perpetrators.
>
> We must also assume that we cannot make sense of violent
> acts by viewing them as outsiders. Ultimately, violence arises
> because some person feels that he must resort to a physical act,
> that a problem he faces calls for a destructive solution. (...)
> Another safe assumption is that violence is at least a two man
> game (1972: 38)

Are these really safe assumptions? The locus of debate is being
shifted from a presumed innate condition of irrationality to a presumed rational context which in being manipulated changes the
individual. There are assumed to be explicable rules which are
context specific and game-like – change the game, change the person.

It is a very popular solution. Change the rules of debate and
many a horrifying problem just vanishes. Nevertheless, the
apparently practical appeal of the game model cannot be ignored.
The image or metaphor of the game is seductive, it promises rational explanation plus a 'pay-off' in terms of finding other grati-
fying games which can wean individuals from destructive to con-
structive games, as in the case of Berne's transactional analysis
(1968) which provides a structure of the psyche influenced by
Freud: the three divisions being the parent, the adult and the child,
paralleling Freud's superego, ego and id. In brief, he argues that
all individuals have some experience of being a child, being an
adult and being and/or having parents or parent substitutes. These
experiences sediment into relatively distinct aspects of the psyche.
Miscommunications arise when one individual, speaking from 'the
parent' position, is answered say, by another's 'child'. The 'child'
or the 'parent' may be playing games with expected pay-offs, sometimes violent games, games learnt from parents. Recently, Renvoize

(1979) has argued that violence in families is passed on from generation to generation, and Pizzey (1982) has argued that battered wives get some thrill out of the violence and are hooked on it as if it were a drug. The general drift of such arguments is that in some way the victim becomes the cause of his or her own misfortune (cf. Von Hentig 1967). Therapy, therefore centres on the patient identifying violence-producing games and substituting other games with other pay-offs (religious games, awareness expansion games, erotic games – see, for example, Berne 1968; Lewis and Streitfeld 1970; Sax and Hollander 1972; Faraday 1974). The emphasis is upon the individual taking control of his or her own inner life which produces the emotional pay-offs. Many such therapies focus on re-designing the individual's self-image and fantasy life, even to the extent of re-designing the individual's self-talk. Zastrow (1979), in his discussion of deviancy and violence, attributes such acts to the kinds of mental talk engaged in just before the act: change the talk and hence change the acts. Without disparaging any benefits to be received from engaging in such therapies, there is the tendency that, in focussing upon the game and hence the individual players, wider contexts as well as that uncomfortable problem raised by Freud recede from the attention. Was Freud right? If he was, then the games take on a more sinister and ironic perspective – the ultimate game is the game of Eros and Thanatos played to the death no matter the variations of games and manipulations of context. Wouldn't it be nice if there were some simple experiment?

Eysenck and Wilson (1973) in their review find little or no support for Freudian theories. Against this there are those who, like Ricoeur (1970) and Freud himself, consider that psychoanalysis can neither be proved nor disproved through such experiments. Psychoanalysis is a work of interpretation and as such is not open to laboratory experimentation. Nevertheless, in support of the death instinct, Freud pointed towards historical evidence of warfare which went beyond mere defensive aggression. Fromm (1974), however, has countered this with anthropological evidence which suggests violence must be categorised into two classes: the benign and the malignant. Benign aggression is defensive and as such is instinctive, the aim being simply to remove danger. It is therefore biologically adaptive. However, in contrast to lower animals, people are capable of forecasting and imagining a wider range of dangers. Fromm considers that to avoid defensive aggression 'full freedom will have to be restored and all forms of exploitative control will have to disappear' (p. 216). The radical social and political changes these entail seem unlikely to be realised, at least in the foreseeable future. Malignant aggression, on the other hand, is not instinctual, but 'is a human potential rooted in the very conditions of human existence' (p. 187). The existential problem is that 'man is the only animal who does not feel at home in nature, who can feel evicted from paradise, the only animal for whom his own existence is a problem that he has to solve and from which he cannot escape' (p. 225). Through culture a relative stability may be found. However, the culture itself may foster the form of aggression which turns life against itself and thus become malignantly destructive. Fromm offers the possibility (although not a probability) of cure through the formation of a utopia; a prospect Freud cannot offer. Essentially the problem remains: although evidence may be presented which sets into doubt Freud's position, the practical accomplishment of change on Fromm's scale remains implausible.

If such large-scale change is not practically foreseeable, what about smaller changes, each contributing to a less-violent society? First, are there causes of (or contributing factors to) violence which may be manipulated or eradicated? It would be useful if one could identify one prime factor as a cause of aggression. Dollard et al. (1939), in postulating that frustration always led to aggression, initially took such a simple view. According to this theory, remove frustration and one removes the need for aggression. However, this did not prove to be the case in any unambiguous sense. By 1972 Berkowitz (p. 80) could say that the link was only tenuous and not the only factor involved:

> Frustration enhances the probability of aggression somewhat, but other factors also help to determine whether any violence will actually occur. These conditions are very important and may even override the influence of the thwarting per se. Frustration is by no means an inevitable precursor to aggression.

The other conditions included 'the presence or absence of aggressive stimuli in the external environment, and the thwarted individual's belief that he has some control over the events happening to him (or that he has some say over what the outcome of his actions will be)' and other factors such as prior learning. He finds it helpful to reformulate frustration as an aversive event so that 'the greater the discomfort or pain' it 'produces, assuming it is not debilitating, the greater is the likelihood of an aggressive reaction. Direct attacks or insults usually create stronger aggressive responses than pure reflections (the blocking of ongoing, goal-directed activity) because they are typically more painful.' In such a behaviouristic account of the genesis of violence, attention becomes focussed upon the environment. Thus, in the behaviourism of Skinner, behaviour is shaped or modified by the pleasure or pain brought about by environmental stimuli. Skinner, by controlling minute units of behaviour, offers us utopia, a fictional account of which he provides in *Walden II*. Desired behaviours, he has shown in his experiments with pigeons, rats and other animals can be produced step by step through rewarding each behaviour which approximates the desired end result, refining each approximation until the exact behaviour has been produced. With human beings the role of such conditioning is complicated through the meaning the mind attaches to stimuli and through the effects of imagination and reason. For these reasons the behaviourism of Skinner which does not allow for the operation of the mind between stimulus and response has received criticisms. Allowing for such factors Bandura, Ross and Ross (1963), for example, develop a theory that behaviour is modelled upon the behaviour of others. When a film was shown to a group of young children, revealing children behaving aggressively to dolls, members of the audience later imitated the filmed behaviour. Recently, the role of imitation and of suggestion have received supporting evidence from studies of the influence of mass media upon other acts of destruction and violence. Phillips (1980) showed that:

(1) After publicized murder–suicide stories there is an increase in noncommercial plane crashes and an increase in airline crashes. (2) This increase in crashes persists for approximately nine days, and then the level of crashes returns to normal. (3) The greater the publicity given by the mass media to a murder–suicide story, the greater the increase in noncommercial plane crashes.

Following Phillips (1982) and Comstock (1978) on the effects of stories on aggressive behaviour, Phillips (1983) made a study of the 'story' of heavyweight prize fighting as presented by the media. He found a peak in homicides after the publicity of a prize fight. He concluded that 'the data presented in this paper indicate that mass media violence does provoke aggression in the real world as well as in the laboratory.' Such stories are only a small part of the cultural repertoire of dramas of violence. It is irrational to study violence in theoretical isolation from this socially constructed imaginative life. For this reason we must look more closely at the social construction of images of violence and their social functions for the reproduction of social forms, identities, roles and personalities. In these imaginative dramas one actor requires detailed attention, the individual defined as dangerous, mad or bad.

Cultural, criminological and sociological explanations

The image of a 'normal society' is potent and dominates explanations of deviance in general and violence in particular. With it one can maintain an imaginative split between deviant violence and normal violence, between military violence and gang violence, madmen and heros. One can divide up the town or the city into good and bad, safe and dangerous areas and peer over the boundaries. Such an image can be seen in the work of Thrasher.

In 1927 he proposed that the gang flourished in the interstices of the city, those areas where there were 'fissures and breaks in the structure of social organisation' (p. 22). There is a sense of the struggle for survival in amidst the crowded, bustling life of the city streets, slums and 'frontiers' residential areas and industrial areas:

> In this ubiquitous crowd of children, spontaneous play-groups are forming everywhere – gangs in embryo. Such a crowded environment is full of opportunities for conflict with some antagonistic person or group within or without the gang's own social mileu. The conflict arises on the one hand with groups of its own class in disputes over the valued prerogatives of gang land – territory, loot, play spaces, patronage in illicit business, privileges to exploit, and so on; it comes about on the other, through opposition on the part of the conventional social order to the gang's unsupervised activities. Thus, the gang is faced with a real struggle for existence with other gangs and with the antagonistic forces in its wider social environment. (p. 26)

In the city slum there is the Darwinian struggle for existence, the violent zoo, its cages the streets, the blocks of flats, the rubbish-filled wastelands. Historically, as earlier described, there has long been an association in the minds of the upper classes, of delinquency with the lower classes.

That the lower classes were the seed-bed of criminality, was a theory asserted by Miller in an influential paper in 1958. His argument was directed against Cohen's (1955) thesis that gang culture was formed through opposition to, and the deliberate negation of, middle-class norms and values. In either case, a group of people are being defined with a variety of qualities including aggression as if other groups were distinguished by not exhibiting those qualities. However, certain individuals or groups are outlawed not because they are violent or destructive but because this violence and destruction is not under the control of, nor does it serve the interests of, those who govern, manage and have the power to appropriate the resources and products of social life to themselves as private property. Aggression alone does not serve as a sufficient condition to distinguish the gang member from the soldier or the police officer, for example. Coercive law enforcement is frequently justified as the only means by which to protect liberty against delinquents, rioters, subversives. Without coercion chaos would erupt as individuals waged wars of self-interest against each other. Thus, for example, Westley in 1953 reported a study on the use and justification of illegal police violence in America. He found that they 'believe that certain groups will respond only to fear and rough treatment' and more generally that:

> The policeman finds his most pressing problems in his relationships to the public. His is a separate occupation but of an incongruous kind, since he must discipline those whom he serves. He is regarded as corrupt and inefficient by, and meets with hostility and criticism from, the public. He regards the public as his enemy, feels his occupation to be in conflict with the community, and regards himself to be a pariah. The experience and the feeling give rise to a collective emphasis on secrecy, an attempt to coerce respect from the public, and a belief that almost any means are legitimate in completing an important arrest. (p. 35)

To deal with the wild and violent criminal a posture of strength is created.

The image of strength has continually to be recreated. Following the 1981 riots in Britain, for example, there was the call to strengthen the police and the demand for the short, sharp shock treatment for the young offenders. Images of chaos and conflict erupting the moment control ceases (or appears to cease from the point of view of one who would maintain a desired form of control for desired purposes) was a much-publicised view together with the demand for increased police powers. There were criticisms of teachers and parents who, it was professed, were losing control. Blame was laid on the 1960s so-called permissiveness and on progressive forms of teaching style.

Loss of control as an explanation for deviance generally can be

seen not only in Thrasher's conceptions but also in the later theories of Matza (1964) and Hirschi (1969). These authors considered
that there is a slide toward amoral self-interest as controls erode or
break; behaviour becomes a function of self-interested pay-offs – a
fundamental tenet of capitalistic individualism, thus:

> In the sociological control theory, it can be and is generally
> assumed that the decision to commit a criminal act may well
> be rationally determined – that the actor's decision was not
> irrational given the risks and costs he faces. Of course, as
> Becker points out, if the actor is capable of in some sense
> calculating the costs of a line of action, he is also capable of
> calculating errors: ignorance and error return, in the control
> theory, as possible explanations of deviant behaviour. (Hirschi
> 1969: 20–1)

Hirschi compares his views with two further theories: cultural deviance and strain.

In cultural deviance theories 'the deviant conforms to a set of
standards not accepted by a larger or more powerful society' (cf.
Miller 1958, and Cohen 1955). The deviant values are therefore
transmitted through the culture of the member. Cohen's views are
more properly called a sub-cultural theory since he sees delinquent
gangs as a sub-set of the larger culture. Specifically, it sets itself
against middle-class values, inverting them so that the delinquent
sub-culture becomes non-utilitarian, malicious and negativistic.
The development of the delinquent attitude he explains in terms of
solving problems within a given social structure. For the development of new solutions there must be a number of others with
similar adjustment problems. The process begins with 'gestures towards innovation' (p. 59) in order to find out whether there will be
a sympathetic audience. In classroom situations a comparison may
be made with Furlong's (1976) notion of interaction sets. These are
ephemeral group organisations which momentarily define a situation and can be the basis of encouraging disruption or conformity.
Cohen explains the further development of sub-cultural delinquency in terms of a reaction-formation, that is, an over-reaction
against middle-class values, the values which schools attempt to
impose.

Miller saw, at the time he was writing in 1958, three major sets
of explanation for delinquency – the physiological (organic pathology), the psychodynamic (emotional disturbance due to a defec-
tive mother–child relationship) and the environmental (disorgani-
sation in the physical or social environment). His own view was

that '"delinquent" behaviour engaged in by members of lower class corner groups involves a positive effort to achieve states, conditions, or qualities valued within the actor's most significant milieu' (pp. 18–19).

Hargreaves (1981) calls both the cultural deviance and the control theories 'input' theories of school delinquency. That is to say, delinquency is considered as arising outside the school in the home or the community and as therefore being a problem imported into school. However, taking a control-theory approach, teachers may contribute to delinquency through their own lack of effective control. Broadly, it seems to me solutions would take a compensatory approach – that is, compensating for the lack of suitable values and parental control – in attempting to provide a stable and disciplined environment and seeking to inculcate teacher-approved values.

Hargreaves further identifies what he calls process theories which include strain, sub-cultural, and labelling theories. Delinquency, according to process approaches, arises as a response to the processes of schooling.

In strain theories Hirschi writes that the 'legitimate desires that conformity cannot satisfy force a person into deviance' (p. 3). He cites Merton (1957), Parsons (1951) and Cloward and Ohlin (1960) as falling under this category, although he allows for some overlapping between categories. He criticises the theory for not being able to explain why an intensely frustrated youth is capable of conforming for days, weeks, months; and for not being able to explain why most delinquent youths become law-abiders as they grow up, yet the conditions which forced them into delinquency have not changed. Hargreaves, referring back to his Lumley study (1967), considered that:

> The streaming system, and its associated mechanisms of regular
> promotion and demotion, ensured that those boys with a
> common problem of adjustment arising from the status
> deprivation found themselves in a common environment in
> which a delinquescent subculture could readily be generated.

The strain arises from status deprivation. This kind of conclusion is reminiscent of Cohen's description of the formation of delinquescent sub-cultures. However, Hargreaves finds a plausible alternative explanation in that the same results could be achieved through cultural transmission plus a 'bad company' theory; or, indeed, through a control theory emphasising the weak control and supervision of the parents.

In the labelling approach an act is committed which is labelled deviant. If the actor is consequently labelled deviant the actor's future acts are interpreted in the light of the label. Through being defined as deviant, the actor becomes deviant. Hargreaves, Hestor and Mellor (1975) have described the processes of labelling pupils as deviant. Once a label has become stable any change of behaviour from the expected is seen as out of character. There is the pressure of expectation to conform with the label.

These various approaches do not exhaust the possible explanations. Indeed, an important class of explanations seems to have been omitted. These are the conflict theories such as Marxism, which sees struggle between the social classes as a necessary relationship in capitalist society. Some such explanation was attempted by Willis (1977). Hargreaves, given his categories, found difficulty in making sense of Willis's approach:

> I can make no sense of Willis's work except as an extremely complex interaction between certain pupils with a particular home background and a certain kind of school experience. I fear we are still a long way from unravelling the complexities of that interaction.

The potential senselessness derives from overlooking the role of social struggle, or the necessary conflict of interests between those who see themselves as benefiting from the capitalistic order and those who do not. Strategies to resolve the conflict may then vary from, say, escapist fantasy to violent revolt. Delinquency thus becomes but one strategy amongst many in a conflict-ridden society. In 1942 Taft, a criminologist, wrote of the inevitability of crime in a society which emphasises competitiveness, acquisitiveness and success. And according to Empson (1966: 20) 'So far as the person described is outside society because too poor for its benefits he is independent ... and can be a critic of society; so far as he is forced by this into crime he is the judge of the society which judges him.' Szasz (1973) takes a similar position in considering the mad and the bad:

> Our adversaries are not demons. We have no enemy that we can fight, exorcise, or dispel by 'cure'. What we do have are problems in living – whether these be biologic, economic, political, or sociopathical ... mental illness is a myth, whose function is to disguise and thus render more palatable the bitter pill of moral conflicts in human relations.

Attention turns towards the moral, political and social dilemmas involved in the physical and mental manipulation and exploitation of the mass who are to be moulded as consumers, and as labour force to be hired and fired according to the rise and fall of prices and profits. If delinquency is defined as the aggressive disregard of the life, property and liberty of others then the proper focus of study must become not a few aggressive youths who displease various authorities but the entire pattern of manipulations, discriminations and prohibitions which prevent the larger proportion of society from obtaining the advantages of the smaller proportion of society. Such an approach can be seen to include many of the foci of control, strain, cultural deviance, sub-cultural deviance and labelling approaches. That is not to say, however, that the assumptions of each are compatible merely that there may be some overlapping in focus.

Moral and political basis of the violent imagination

Barrington Moore (1978) begins his study of the social bases of obedience and revolt with a discussion of moral codes and the sense of injustice. Even in the situation of master and slave, or concentration camp guard and prisoner, there are discernible reciprocal rights and duties which form the basis of distinguishing between fair and unfair. Honderich (1976), in discussing average length of life for different social classes and countries of the world, concludes that 'lifetime-inequalities are consequences of economic inequalities'. One may infer that inequality is a violence against the poor resulting in a shorter life – the rich take away the life of the poor. Violence as a response to such injustice may be morally right.

On the one hand is the individual's sense of justice or injustice and on the other the power which those in authority can bring to bear upon the individual. When the two come into conflict there is a double-structure involving: (1) the individual's sense of justice being violated; and (2) the authority's judgment that the individual has violated the norms of society. The confrontation is made concrete in incidents which each actor in, or witness of, the confrontation can recount from their own perspective and in support of their own interests. Since social and economic inequality is not only in evidence in modern societies but actually justified by authorities and forcefully defended by vested interests (political, commercial, organised labour) occasions for confrontation are plentiful. Such instances become a part of the folklore of the local community, part of the drama as presented by news media, part of the histories written by historians. Moreover, every community and every nation has its myths, stories which seek to explain or interpret the ways people behave, and society works – myths which are conflictual, aggressive, violent.

At the mythic heart of politics is violence. Brown (1966:15, 29) sees 'politics made out of juvenile delinquency', recalling the myth of the sons rising against the father:

> Political parties are primitive secret societies: Tammany's Wigwam; caucus; mafia; cabal. The deals are still always secret, in a smoke-filled room. Political parties are conspiracies to usurp the power of the father, 'a taking of the sword out of the hand of the Sovereign.' Political parties are antagonistic fraternities, or moieties; a contest between Blues and Greens in the Hippodrome; an agon between Leather Seller and Sausage Seller to seduce and subvert Old Man Demos; an Eskimo drumming contest; organised not by agreement on principle, but by confusing the issues to win; in a primitive ordeal or lottery in which the strife is justice, might makes right, and the major is the sanior pars.

Nisbet (1976), in describing the emergence of social philosophy, places it within the context of the search for community and the progressive growth in power of the state/military over – and conflict with – family and the priesthood.

Historically the state has progressively intervened in family and individual life, assuming the rights of the family over the individual in terms of laws, religion and education. Discussions of rights, therefore, have to be set within the context of the individual having no rights unless established and sanctioned by the state. If, within this context, individuals feel an injustice, they can appeal to existing laws or, if appropriate, available conventions to gain retribution. If, however, the laws themselves do not help or even seem in opposition to a felt sense of justice then there is little or no chance for the individual to change the rules of the game or even modify them. Opposition to the laws or to the prevailing conventions may be interpreted by the authorities as rebellion, hooliganism or depravity, but by the individuals as resistance or sticking up for one's rights.

The authors of Unpopular Education (CCCS 1981) have argued that the development of compulsory education was felt by many in the lower classes to be an unjust imposition, a taking away of the family's right to send its children out to work. The loss of the child's income was often a severe blow to the family income. Resistance to schooling, as Humphries (1981) has shown, was widespread, as evidenced by school strikes, truancy and disruptive behaviour – schooling as a violation of family life.

Currently, mass schooling can be seen both as a way of categorising, assessing and controlling children as well as providing the disadvantaged with opportunities for self-improvement. Good intentions aside, modern schooling must be judged by those on the receiving end of it – the children (cf. Schostak and Logan 1984). More and more children are feeling dissatisfied, frustrated or bored with schools (cf. Hargreaves 1982). Many feel that they are a violation of their dignity, independence, age, sex, race, freedom and intelligence (cf. Schostak 1983b, 1984). Many react through disruption, truancy, apathy – the strategies are various. It is not news that schools are failing to meet the needs of large numbers of children, research has been showing this consistently for decades.

One interesting development in response to this failure has been the proliferation of special schools and special units within normal schools. Children defined as having special needs range from those with physical and mental handicap to those who in their dislike of school truant persistently, and those who in their dislike of their classroom experience are deemed unmanageable by teachers and suspended. By defining children as special in these ways they can be ejected from the school. Thus the school itself is spared criticism. Nevertheless, schools have frequently been shown to play a large part in the production of disruption (e.g. Tattum 1982) which leads to suspension (Ling 1984) and then on to special school if this is shown by the school to be necessary.

Every felt sense of injustice contributes to an overall resentment which permeates the developing drama between self and other, between those like Me and those like Them. This is the stuff of the violent imagination – the dramas, the myths, the folktales, the personal anecdotes which tell of the many violations against the self perpetrated by others. Through the contents of the violent imagination an individual recognises incidents as either violatory or non-violatory, justice or injustice. Such images are passed on through the generations by the voices of those who enter into community with each other. It is the developing intelligence of the community – intelligence in the widest sense of practical knowledge, or wisdom, or information concerning the world (cf. Schostak 1984). The violent imagination becomes a way in which people

33

make sense of the world, identifying structures of justice and of injustice, freedom and slavery, creation and destruction, war and peace.

Chapter 3

Rearing children

School is one among many childrearing institutions. Historically, conceptions of childhood and the nature of children are varied. These conceptions influence the childrearing modes of practice for a society or group. However, students of the history of childhood consistently bemoan the paucity of evidence available. Moreover, despite some recent excellent studies, research into the history of childhood, and in particular the history of child experiences of schooling, is seriously neglected. This chapter cannot hope to make good this deficit. It may, however, stimulate some questions which may lead others who are historians by profession and by inclination to enter this important and as yet undervalued field of study. The history of schooling should be founded upon the history of childhood experiences of schooling. If education begins in experience, then necessarily the experiences of children are a fundamental starting point for pedagogy, curriculum development and school organisation. But social experience is largely political, that is, concerned with decision, power, threats of violence and actual violence (Mackenzie, 1975). In the dominant childrearing practices we find varying forms of violence which produce or sustain the familial political ordering.

A useful starting point for this initial study of the relationship between childrearing practices and schooling is de Mause's collection of articles in his *History of Childhood.* De Mause (1974) has identified six such modes in Western history. The further back in history one goes, he contends, then the more brutal are the childrearing practices. Only recently have there been signs of a more democratic helping relationship between parents and their children. The earlier stages currently co-exist with these more modern developments.

Aries (1962) has argued that childhood is a recent invention. De Mause considers this thesis to be:

> ... the opposite to mine: (Aries) argues that while the traditional child was happy because he was free to mix with many classes and ages; a special condition known as childhood was 'invented' in the early modern period, resulting in a tyrannical concept of the family which destroyed friendship and sociability and deprived children of freedom, inflicting upon them for the first time the birch and the prison cell. (de Mause, p. 5)

De Mause and the other contributors to his book offer ample evidence of the thesis that the 'invention of childhood' is both a fuzzy and untenable concept.

In the first of de Mause's categories of childrearing practices is the *Infanticide Mode* (Antiquity to fourth century AD) where 'parents routinely resolved their anxieties about taking care of children by killing them' (p. 51). He refers to the fact that in the London streets of the 1890s dead babies were a common sight, just as they had been when in 1741 Thomas Coram opened the Foundling Hospital 'because he couldn't bear to see dying babies lying in the gutters and rotting on the dung-heaps of London' (p. 29).

The second category de Mause calls the *Abandonment Mode* (fourth to thirteenth centuries AD) where parents would abandon children to wet nurses, monasteries or nunneries, foster families, or be given to nobles as servants or hostages, 'or by severe emotional abandonment at home' (p. 51). The child was still seen as full of evil and thus in need of being beaten. In the next stage, however, though adults still projected their dangerous fears and desires upon children, the moulding of children became a popular image – children were like soft wax. This de Mause calls the *Ambivalent Mode* (fourteenth to seventeenth centuries). Locke, who may be seen as a forerunner of modern behaviourist psychology, for example, advised that:

> It seems plain to me, that the principle of all virtue and excellency lies in a power of denying ourselves the satisfaction of our own desires, where reason does not authorise them. This power is to be got and improved by custom, made easy and familiar by an early practice. If therefore I might be heard, I would advise, that, contrary to the ordinary way, children should be used to submit their desires, and go without their longings, even from their very cradles. The first thing they

should learn to know, should be, that they were not to have anything because it pleased them, but because it was thought fit for them. (Locke 1693; 1880 edition: 103)

Such attitudes seem to pave the way for what de Mause (p. 52) calls the *Intrusive Mode* where:

> The child raised by intrusive parents was nursed by the mother, not swaddled, not given regular enemas, toilet trained early, prayed with but not played with, hit but not regularly whipped, punished for masturbation, and made to obey promptly with threats and guilt as often as with other methods of punishment. The child was so much less threatening that true empathy was possible, and pediatrics was born, which along with a general improvement in level of care by parents reduced infant mortality and provided the basis for the demographic transition of the eighteenth century.

The next stage de Mause calls the *Socialisation Mode* (nineteenth to mid-twentieth centuries). In this attitude childrearing is not so much a battle to conquer the will of the child but a matter of guidance and training towards adult-desired attitudes and behaviours – a matter of bringing the child to conformity, social adjustment.

Finally, de Mause sees evidence of the emergence of what he calls the *Helping Mode* where 'the child knows better than the parent what it needs at each stage of its life, and fully involves both parents in the child's life as they work to empathise with and fulfil its expanding and particular needs'.

These categories provide a means by which to analyse and understand current practices. Although described as historical stages, de Mause makes clear that remnants of preceding stages co-exist with later stages. The sexual exploitation of children is still much greater than imagined, for example. In a letter to the *Sunday Times* (14 October 1984) the Director of the Child Assault Prevention Programme, Michele Elliott, reported studies showing that 46 per cent of children had hidden sexual experiences before 12 years of age, involving older men some of whom were relatives. And '1.2 million children are annually exploited in child prostitution and child pornography'. In addition, according to the National Society for the Prevention of Cruelty to Children, one child a week dies at the hands of parents and 'a further 50,000 suffered the "lesser deaths" of gross neglect, physical and mental torture, sexual abuse or emotional starvation' (*Guardian* 19 October 1983).

However, I do not propose to study such examples but to establish the framework by which to analyse the childrearing practices imposed upon school children. Firstly, I will take an historical perspective on modern mass schooling. Secondly, I will focus more minutely on the experience of school life as a stage for the enactment of a multiplicity of childrearing experiences.

Childrearing and the traditions of schooling

There are three broad traditions of schooling. The first is characterised by an authoritarianism, based upon supposed superiority (whether as parent or as master/ruler) and in itself has many variations; the second is typically referred to as 'progressive' or child centred; the third is the Libertarian tradition which has made little headway in Britain. Each form has its images not only of the child but also of the adult and the adult's relation to the child and each image conditions the childrearing practices employed. More importantly for the argument presented in this book, each image of adult child relations holds the key to the pattern of violations experienced by individuals in their relations with each other. The three traditions of teaching provide a broad initial point of departure for such analyses. Childrearing practices are organised around rights and duties: rights for self, for others, and rights *over* others. Rights and duties may be protective and hence desired or repressive and even provocative and thus unworkable without violatory coercion. I will explore each tradition in turn.

Traditional authoritarianism

There are many forms of authoritarianism, ranging from, say, a ruthless control through to a benign paternalism. Each in their images of the child and the child's relations to the adult invest the final authority in the parent-like adult or member of the ruling class. There was a clear conception early in the history of schooling as to how the education of the poor, for example, should proceed. Hannah More wrote:

> My plan of instruction is extremely simple and limited. They
> learn, on week-days, such coarse works as may fit them for
> servants. I allow of no writing for the poor. My object is not
> to make fanatics, but to train up the lower classes in habits of

industry and piety. I knew of no way of teaching morals but by teaching principles; or of inculcating Christian principles without imparting a good knowledge of scripture. (*William Roberts, Memoirs of the Life of Mrs. Hannah More*, 1836 ed., Vol. II, p. 66, source: Hyndman 1978: 3)

For Hannah More the Christian dogma of Original Sin pervaded her teaching of children. The attitude here is that of forming children according to the definitions or intentions of the adult. In this case, the adult is of a different social class to the child. It is the paternalism of the ruling classes over the lower classes – of master to servant. The lower classes are forever children to the ruling classes, forever kept in a state of dependency; and, as 'children', the ruling classes could project upon them all the attributes of Original Sin:

Industry is the duty to impress upon the lower classes. A little learning makes a man ambitious to rise, if he can't by fair means then he uses foul. . . . His ignorance is a balm which soothes his mind into stupidity and repose, and excludes every emotion of discontent, pride and ambition. A man of no literature will seldom attempt to form insurrections or form an idle scheme for the reformation of the state. (a letter to the *Gentleman's Magazine* 1797, source: Wardle 1974: 88)

The task was to keep them in ignorance. In this instance it was feared education would break the spell and hence unleash the projected terrors. For Hannah More education would reinforce the spell. The argument was about means, not the practical goal: to keep the lower classes dependent and docile. The fear was again echoed in the 1860s by Kay-Shuttleworth before the introduction of the 1868 Bill, predicting a 'destructive revolution' if the working classes took practical control of the House of Commons. Once the Bill was passed, education, through the Education Act of 1870, was pressed into the role of moulding the minds of future voters.

Another source of influence upon modern mass schooling came from the public school system. Rather than teaching pupils to be content with their station in life, the public schools inculcated leadership, ambition, competitiveness – the determination to rise. In the eighteenth century, public schools were heavily criticised for being a corrupting influence upon young people, particularly by Locke and Chesterfield. Nevertheless, as Wallbank (1979) shows, the leading public schools remained popular because of their competitive atmosphere.

Violence, too, was a feature of public school life:

At Eton, in 1768, there apparently took place a major battle, in which (Williams) Windham was a leading light, between the boys and the butchers of Windsor after which a number of the former were able to return across the bridge only by dressing as women. No doubt practice at cudgelling, which seems to have been a favourite pastime at the school throughout the eighteenth century, would have made the Etonians formidable opponents. There are for this period no surviving records so extraordinary as the accounts of the regular battles at Westminster in the first decade of the next century between boys and masters, encouraged it would seem by the head, himself an Old Westminster. Trevelyan has pointed out a letter in the Grenville Papers which recounts how the writer, Thomas Whately, and Lady Mulgrave and her child were riding through Eton when they were mobbed by a crowd of boys from the school and seem only to have been saved from physical assault by the intervention of 'Tom' (Grenville), the son of George Grenville, the politician. Such violence was not reserved for outsiders for Cowper remembered Lord March, later, as the Duke of Richmond, to be one of the leading politicians of his time, setting fire to Vinny Bourne's (a master's) greasy locks and boxing his ears to put it out again. (Wallbank 1979: 7)

Apart from fighting, there were two other elements in the physical component of life at public school according to Wallbank: 'games playing and the ascetic nature of the living conditions'. The formal instruction tended to concentrate upon Latin and Greek language and literature. This, Wallbank argues, prepared the child for a public life in providing 'both as a matter of policy and, in a sense, accidentally, a political education.'

The bias towards classics until the early twentieth century continued together with an emphasis upon sport. The influence of Thomas Arnold's Rugby tended to moderate aspects of public school life towards a nineteenth-century Christian morality:

After Arnold public-school football was transformed into a disciplined and regulated game, amenable to control and direction, and codified to a remarkable degree. Football was converted from its pre-historical turbulence into a quieter, more restrained (though nonetheless tough) team sport, ideally suited to the task of exhausting, controlling and training healthy young boys and men.

Moreover, 'Contemporaries had no doubt that Arnold's boys were quite different from their predecessors; "his pupils were thoughtful, manly minded, conscious of duty and obligation"' (Walvin 1982: 81, 82). Nevertheless, being kicked into conformity was still the rule, whether on the sports field or by bullies off it, a sentiment illustrated by the 'Ten Commandments of the English public school boy':

1   There is only one God, and the captain of football is His prophet.
2   My school is the best in the world.
3   Without big muscles, strong will, and proper collars, there is no salvation.
4   I must wash much, and in accordance with tradition.
5   I must speak the truth even to a master, if he believes everything I tell him.
6   I must play games with all my heart, with all my soul, and with all my strength.
7   To work outside class-hours is indecent.
8   Enthusiasm, except for games, is in bad taste.
9   I must look up to the older fellows, and pour contempt on newcomers.
10 I must show no emotion, and not kiss my mother in public.

(Source: Hyndman 1978: 145: H. B. Gray *The Public Schools and the Empire* 1913: 172–3)

Authoritarianism and conformity, though to different ends, were the hallmarks of school experience for the lower and upper classes. For the working classes the monitorial schools of Bell and Lancaster mechanised the process of schooling to an absurd degree, to the extent that one textbook could serve an entire school. The system was modelled after the conception of division of labour. A teacher instructed a number of monitors who in turn passed on the content to larger numbers of children. However, 'With teachers whose formal training, if they had been lucky, consisted of a three month course at the Borough Road School, and with monitors whose knowledge hardly transcended the contents of the lesson which they were currently teaching, it is not surprising that the slavish conformity to the book was required' (Hyndman 1978: 16). Naturally, the system required organisation and sanctions for the enforcement of rules, especially since the staff–pupil ratio could be 1:500. Discipline measures included having a log tied to the neck, being placed in a sack or basket suspended from the roof, confinement after school hours, ensuring that they stayed by tying them to desks (see Hyndman 1978: 16–17) – old traditions die hard. At Alverton Primary School 'An enquiry had looked into various allegations, including one that a girl of eight was tied to a chair with knitting wool and also had sticky tape put over her mouth on two other occasions' and 'A statement issued by Mr Norman Barr, the county's chief education officer, said the allegations were true. Although they were far from being great outrages, the methods of discipline imposed at the school were unwise and not acceptable' (*Times Educational Supplement* 23 November 1984).

Compulsory schooling, when it came, was not universally applauded by the lower classes for whom it was supposed to be a benefit. By its nature, compulsion is an authoritarian imposition. Working-class resistance to the introduction of compulsory schooling can be seen in terms of truancy, messing about, and school strikes (cf. Humphries 1981). Compulsory education can be interpreted as a way of interfering in working-class lives, a way of regulating or manipulating them physically and mentally. Children in general, and working-class children in particular, were everywhere in Victorian life – the population aged fourteen and under 'never fell below 30 per cent, and for much of the period was closer to 40 per cent' (Walvin 1982: 12). School was one solution to an enormous management problem. However, in de Mause's terms this was a period when the emergent form for childrearing was that of the socialisation mode. Walvin (1982) has characterised the emergent family ideal of the period as that of domesticity for the middle and upper-class family. Working-class family life was regarded negatively in the light of this ideal. Thus (Walvin 1982: 14):

> By the mid-century there were, notably in London, armies of children living beyond the family pale and surviving in wretched groups. When trying to save such childen, and to render them more amenable to training and a useful adult life, reformers created artificial family arrangements. Such waifs were put into 'homes' where they were given foster parents and where they were encouraged to feel part of a wider family group. Even in the proliferating public schools there emerged the concept of '*locus parentis*' to provide those schools with the morally and socially approved sanctions of the family over the pupils.

Moreover, as Walvin later points out, early in the nineteenth century in literary and intellectual circles the belief that children were naturally depraved had given way to the image of innocence

and perfectibility of their nature. Nevertheless, obedience was
the prime virtue to be instilled and corporal punishment the final
resort:

> Bishop Blomfield used to say that if a child were whipped
> before it arrived at the age of three, it would need no floggings
> afterwards.
>   Parents and children themselves when the matter is put
> logically before them, admit the need of corporal punishment,
> and if teachers would only consult the parents before
> administering it to the children, sentimentalists who get so
> much out of this subject would have very little copy to work
> on. As a child, I myself received hidings which I richly
> deserved, and only wonder now that I was so lightly let off.

Swinburne is here reflecting upon his experiences in 1911 (p. 14) of
having been a school inspector for thirty-five years. Of the occurrence of corporal punishment, he wrote that the teachers were
themselves more to blame – for not having kept a proper watch
over the children and hence preventing trouble. He considered that,
'corporal punishment, in any but its justifiable form, has long been
practically dead in the Elementary Schools – and no where more
so, I am proud to say, than in East Suffolk' (p. 19). More than half
a century later corporal punishment is still not dead.

Together with its tendency towards physical punishment, traditional schooling took a subject-centred rather than a child-centred
approach to learning and the curriculum. Dewey described the
subject matter of what he called the traditional approach as
follows: 'The subject matter of education consists of bodies of
information and of skills that have been worked out in the past;
therefore, the chief business of the school is to transmit them to
the new generation' (ibid.: 17). This meant that the main purpose
of school was:

> to prepare the young for future responsibilities and for success
> in life, by means of acquisition of the organised bodies of
> information and prepared forms of skill which comprehend the
> material of instruction. Since the subject-matter as well as
> standards of proper conduct are handed down from the past,
> the attitude of pupils must upon the whole be one of docility,
> receptivity, and obedience. Books, especially textbooks, are the
> chief representatives of the lore and wisdom of the past, while
> teachers are the organs through which pupils are brought into
> effective connection with the material. Teachers are the agents

through which knowledge and skills are communicated and
rules of conduct enforced. (ibid.: 18)

It would be incorrect, however, to view pupils as the passive objects
of teacher dominance. Pupils, as do any individuals, make active
interpretations and assessments of their social situation. Not all
decide on balance that it is best to keep one's head down. Many
react. As we saw in the previous chapter, resistance to the demands
of authorities can be defined as deviance or even as delinquency.
The response by authorities can take the more brutal punishment
forms associated with de Mause's first category of childrearing or
may take more subtle forms of intervention or socialisation. As
Platt has described, nineteenth-century reformists took a child-sav-
ing stance – a matter of bringing the light of Christianity to the
child. In the early twentieth century the model changed to that of
treatment. Burt (1944: 4–5) stressed the need to engage in a scientific investigation of the causes leading to the symptom, that is,
delinquency. Delinquency he saw as a moral disorder analogous to
illness as a disorder of the body. Thus, 'With moral disorders as
with physical, we must find and fight not symptoms but causes.
Not before causes have been discovered can cures be advised.' The
model demands causes to be cured. However, unambiguous causes
are not forthcoming. There are a multiplicity of reasons rather than
causes. These reasons may stand in contradictory relations with
each other and are not reducible to the cause–effect relations which
could be manipulated like so many chemicals. But the model is
appealing. Waller (1932), from a sociological perspective, also
wrote in terms of cure, calling for therapeutic counselling not only
for pupils but also for teachers. The problem was that of adjusting
the individual to the school. However, the adjustment had to take
place within a context of hostility. The essential relation between
teacher and pupil (and also between teacher and parent) was that
of hostility founded upon a conflict of interests. The role of the
teacher for much of the time was to get children to do those things
they did not want to do and to stop them doing those things they
wanted to do.

Trouble in school, however, can be defined as resulting from the
children. Burt saw delinquency 'as nothing but an outstanding sam-
ple – dangerous perhaps and extreme, but nonetheless typical – of
common childish naughtiness' (p. viii). Thus, he hoped a study of
delinquency would throw light upon 'daily disciplinary problems
of the classroom and upon the conduct or misconduct of the difficult child' (p. ix). And the redress of naughtiness was a matter of

character training. In earlier times, instead of naughtiness, one would have talked of Original Sin, the natural sinfulness of the baby. But old superstitions die hard, even in the new science of psychology.

The image of the child held by the educator is a critical factor in the kinds of schools created. Schooling over the last two hundred years developed in a period when the dominant images created by the doctrine of Original Sin were giving way to the image of the child as material to be moulded and finally treated, rather than broken by the will of the adult. Physical punishment, however, has scarcely been out of the imagination of adults. Accounts of floggings are rife in the history of schooling and the treatment of children in Britain generally. Beating, in Britain, is combined with a moral conception of the value of a good hiding. It is perhaps not used as viciously as in the past but still appears to be thought central to educational practice (cf. Schostak 1983b). The *Times Educational Supplement* (8 June 1984) reported, for example, according to a survey held in Salford:

> Mr John Barnes, chief education officer, reported to the education committee that 60 per cent of primary schools supported corporal punishment.
>
> He said: 'The support for its use in secondary schools is even greater – 96 per cent of the schools, 84 per cent of governing bodies and 73 per cent of parents approve of it.'
>
> During the 10 months covered by the survey, only 47 parents asked that their children should not be punished.
>
> The records also show that corporal punishment was used 1,325 times on 1,000 pupils in 65 schools. One comprehensive school used the cane 193 times – an average of more than four times a week.
>
> The list of offences punishable by caning was headed by bullying, followed by gross and persistent bad behaviour, vandalism and confrontations with teachers.

These, of course, are recorded incidents of caning. They do not include the threats, the slaps, the prodding fingers, the cuffings, the verbal abuse which can be found even in schools which have banned corporal punishment.

Traditional authoritarianism is still a major force in teachers' concepts of how to rear children. This approach includes an emphasis on children knowing their place in relation to adults, teacher coercion based upon the final threat of corporal punishment, and children knowing their place in the meritocratic social order. This

meritocracy is still disproportionately influenced by social class origins or home background, race and gender – points which will be
explored in more detail in the coming chapters. Schooling, however, was not exclusively influenced by this viewpoint. It was criticised by both the progressive and libertarian traditions.

The progressive tradition

Progressive educators did not form a unified movement. Rather,
they were more united over their criticisms of mainstream schooling
than in what ought to replace it (Dale 1979a). Dale (1979b: 103):

> Generally speaking, a progressive is one who believes in the
> possibility and desirability of progress, that is of improvement
> in moral, social or rational understanding of the human
> condition, and so he holds a view which implies a certain
> optimism about human nature.

By contrast, therefore, the traditional views hold a certain pessimism about human nature. This is most clearly seen in the respec-
tive roles of punishment in the various alternative views of educational practice and childrearing practices. However, common to
Rousseauian influenced forms of progressive education can still be
seen the kind of pessimism which gives rise to a covert authoritarianism. And Freudian-influenced progressive educationists retain
some degree of Freudian pessimism and certainly a paternalism,
albeit a liberal paternalism largely covert.

Rousseau advocated a form of child-centred education which
located the source of evil not in human nature but in society.
Education was to be paced according to the presumed natural
stages of development of the child. However, the education itself
was far from libertarian, in the sense of letting the child be to
develop according to the desires, needs, curiosities and fancies of
the child without impositions by the adult. Childrearing and education were to take place by methods which were presumed to be
natural. Thus, 'We are working in agreement with nature, and
while she is shaping the physical man, we are striving to shape his
moral being' (Rousseau 1974, p. 278). To accomplish this we must
'surround him with all the lessons you would have him learn without awakening his suspicions' (p. 85) and 'Take care that all the
experiments are connected together by a chain of reasoning, so that
they may follow an orderly sequence in the mind' (p. 140). In the
expressed intentions underlying his philosophy of education the

child is thoroughly, albeit subtly, in the control of a scheming adult. As Smith (1983) has recently pointed out, Rousseau had been criticised by Libertarians since Godwin (1756-1836) who clearly saw Rousseau's authoritarianism, but authoritarianism compounded by deception – and schooling based upon lies is a prime feature of contemporary schooling (cf. Schostak 1983b). Indeed, such schooling which denies the child's own independence of mind, subverts the child's attempts to make the workings of the world conscious and violates the intelligence of the young mind.

It cannot be denied that progressive educators developed a more relaxed relationship between teacher and pupil in practice. It is clear, however, when Dewey (1938: 28-9) writes of progressive education, he intends a subtle authoritarianism, where for the adult 'the central problem of an education based upon experience is to select the kind of present experiences that live fruitfully and creatively in subsequent experiences'. Who is to decide what counts as an educative experience? Who is it that does the selecting? It is most certainly not the child. It is the teachers who should institute 'the conditions for the kind of present experience which has a favourable effect upon the future' (p. 50). The model for teacher-pupil relations is that of the 'well ordered family' (p. 54). Thus:

> in a well ordered school the main reliance for control of this and that individual is upon the activities carried on and upon the situations in which these activities are maintained. The teacher reduces to a minimum the occasions in which he or she has to exercise authority in a personal way. When it is necessary, in the second place, to speak and act firmly, it is done in behalf of the interest of the group, not as an exhibition of personal power. This makes the difference between action which is arbitrary and that which is fair and just.

The interests of the group take precedence over those of the individual. But who is it that defines the interests of the group? How are these values constituted? And why is it that the duty of enforcement falls to the teacher?

The various answers for Dewey depend upon the extent to which the class is a social group engaged in a shared activity:

> When pupils were a class rather than a social group, the teacher necessarily acted largely from the outside, not as a director of processes of exchange in which all had a share. When education is based upon experience and educative experience is seen to be a social process, the situation changes

47

radically. The teacher loses the position of external boss of
dictator but takes on that of leader of group activities. (p. 59)

The teacher is never to lose the central position, that of leader or
director; and if we have understood the intention properly, the
teacher is to be the judge of what is to be the right educative
experience, and of what is the right social process.

The radical-reformist traditions in education gained new impetus
not only from Dewey but also from Piaget and Freud. These influences found expression in Britain in the work of Susan Isaacs
(1930). The image of the parent–child relation can be seen in the
following passage:

It is not what we are to ourselves and in our intention that
matters; but what the children make of us. Our real behaviour
to them, and the actual conditions we create, are always *for
them* set in the matrix of their own phantasies. And what they
do make of us in the years from two onwards is in large part a
function of the already highly complex interplay of infantile
love and hate impulses, and anxiety reactions towards these.
The intensive study of instinct and phantasy in individual
children by the technique of psycho-analysis has shown that,
even at this early age, guilt anxiety and love invest any adult
who has an active relation with the children with a prestige
which he cannot escape. Whether he will or no, he is drawn
into the ambit of the child's intra-psychical conflict. The child's
world is a dramatic world, and the non-interference of the
adult is interpreted in dramatic terms. The adult who does not
interfere cannot be for the child himself a neutral observer – he
is a passive *parent*. And if the parent is passive, one of two
things happens; either the child believes that the grown-up
endorses what he is doing, or he suffers internally from the
tension of guilt which fails to find relief in his being told what
he must *not* do, a tension which issues sooner or later in
actions aimed at provoking anger and punishment. (pp. 8–9)

Isaacs is aware of child projections upon adults. However, it is as
well to consider adult projections upon the child. Typically projected upon the child by progressive, reformist educators are the
educator's own good intentions – the environment is manipulated
in the best interests of the child; that which is in the best interests
of the child is a projection upon the child of the adult's own
paternalistic, or maternalistic attitude and the adult's conceptions
of the child's future and the adult's own ideological concerns to

preserve what is considered as valuable. The violations may be benign in intent but they are nevertheless violations of the child's emergent grasp of the powers which control his or her destiny in the social world. The drama is yet more complex than the drama of paternalism seen by Isaacs. The fantasies played out by adult and child are dialectical; they feed and grow upon each others' energies, each others' conflicts of desire, each others' understanding and misinterpretations. Progressive educationists, for all their liberal humanitarianism, have never quite successfully resolved the confrontation with child freedom, fearing licence and the development of forms of undesirable individuality.

This spirit of liberal paternalism is nicely set out by Nunn (1945: 14) who cannot quite bring himself to confront the free child; he thus forms a strategy of progressive letting go, but a letting go conditioned by adult judgments and environmental manipulations:

> One thing, however, is obvious: namely, that a child cannot at birth be charged with the self-responsibility which he may ultimately claim and must ultimately bear. Family and school are institutions whose existence implies a joint responsibility in which parents and teachers have a share – preponderating at first, then decreasing as the years pass and the lines of the child's individuality form and harden. In the moral sphere the main duty of parents and teachers is to see that the little world in which the child grows up is as rich as may be in those elements that go to the fashioning of the better types of individuality, and that other elements are excluded. Since we here admit a judgement – and it will often be a faulty and mistaken judgement – which is not the child's own, we are, of course, limiting the abstract freedom of his self-creative growth. But such limitations are part of the inevitable conditions of life. An architect can build only with the materials placed at his disposal, but is yet free to make what use of them his genius suggests. Similarly the studies and discipline of a school, while of necessity representing those cultural and moral traditions which authority deems of vital value, should yet leave abundant room for the free development of individuality.

It is like walking along the roadways – you're free to go wherever you want, so long as you keep to the roads and never venture into the free forests and fields.

Recently, the liberal paternalistic view has been developed by the lawyer Freeman who follows Rawls's (1971) *Theory of Justice*. The adult projects upon the child fears of the licence that unlimited freedom evokes in the adult. In short, liberal paternalism 'imposes duties on parents to prepare children for eventual independence' (p. 4). The problem for this approach is that, in shielding children against influences adults imagine they themselves as children would wish to be shielded against, adults are creating webs of projections to be thrown over and imposed upon children; projections which define what children ought to be at any given stage, which evaluate the experiences and wishes of children against criteria imagined as rational by adults, adults who themselves cannot claim to have reached ideal states of rationality and foresight. This approach has not yet reached beyond de Mause's stage of socialisation, the moulding of adults towards some ideologically defined state of what counts as rationality and rational society to the people who have the power to manipulate the resources and influence the institutions of a given society. In the liberal paternalistic version of social reform, progressive child-centred teaching, there is always the assumption that the adult knows best, whether or not it is true. It is a view typically stated without proof but enforced through power. In the liberal view, the role of school is to 'raise the national mind' so that individuals of the lower classes may 'have the capacity to rise' and furthermore to understand the reasons for social arrangements:

> If government be in any sense an arrangement for their benefit and a trustee for their security, it ought to be shown in what manner it acts on their behalf. A foundation should be laid for their confidence. If apparent wrong be done them in any legislative measures, they have a right to be satisfied that it is not real, or that, if real, it is indispensable.

In the above Hamilton (1846) showed the kind of faith in reason typical of the reformist attitude. Nevertheless,

> the children, whose probable lot is labour, are taught how honourable labour is. Betimes they ought to be employed in it, or, if it be suddenly imposed, it will awake an unconquerable dislike. Habits of industry must be formed. The school should be one of industry as well as of general knowledge.

Nothing could be left to chance and free enquiry. A similar difficulty was faced by Mill who being against inequality was faced with the problem of who would do the dirty work in society and who would be free to pursue intellectual interests. Not surprisingly the answer to the dilemma was not to educate the labouring classes so highly but fit them rather for their work. Other reformists were concerned not with raising a nation of free thinkers but rather with raising a nation of fit workers, soldiers, mothers. Such people as Lord Brabazon (1887) saw in the increasing drift to the towns from the countryside cause for fears about the degeneration of the health of the nation. Board School teachers were a source, for him, of advance knowledge concerning the health of town children. The concern was for healthiness rather than a critically reflective population. In this case the image of the child was one which necessitated constant supervision by teachers. Nothing could be left to nature. In support of this Brabazon cited a Dr Fletcher, medical officer:

> It should be remembered that, as regards compulsion in games, bodily exercise should be as carefully supervised by the masters as mental exercise; for it is not wise that boys should be left to manage these physical matters entirely by themselves, thinking that you can trust nature, and all will come right, and that the boy for whom exercise is desirable will be prompted by nature to take just the amount required for his health. No such thing. In the general routine of lessons a boy is compelled to conform to certain rules for the education of his mind; that is not here left to nature nor to the boy's disposition, for, if it were, there would, in most instances, be a miserable deficiency in brain exercises, or, in a few rare cases, a mischievous excess.
> (pp. 68-9)

The emphasis is typically upon boys' education. Although Brabazon, like other reformers, was open to improvement in women's education, he cited the view of Dr Withers Moore, then president of the British Medical Association, to the effect that 'competitive brainwork among gifted girls can hardly but be excessive, especially if the competition be against the superior brain-weight and brain-strength of man.' Thus they have 'to be protected against their own willingness to study' (p. 64).

The broad intention is that of de Mause's childrearing mode of intrusive intervention. The reformist intent is thus compatible with compulsion on the one hand and covert manipulation (de Mause's socialisation mode) on the other. The twin motives continue into the twentieth century where they are finally wedded to the child-centred ethic of progressive education in British infant compulsory schooling. However, as Campbell Stewart (1979) points out,

> from 1889 to 1950, progressive education in England was identified with a minority of middle-class, independent schools,

having the following main features: an interest in child-centred education, a tolerant discipline, frequently a preference for co-education, a readiness to take part in curriculum experiments, in playing down academic and examination demands, generally liberal or left politics, encouragement of the arts and crafts, including dance, music and drama, manual work as an aspect of physical education, an international outlook and anti-military school organisation, simplicity of living (often in boarding schools in the country), and informality of clothes. (p. 105)

Nevertheless, the rhetoric of the child-centred education is a part of the well-rehearsed rhetoric of contemporary mass schooling for the early years age group. Even if, as Sharpe and Green (1975) argue, it is not attained in practice, it is a much-respected ideal. A similar enthusiasm for the adolescent could be found in the writings of social workers working through the clubs for the young. In many ways the atmosphere described in these clubs seems reminiscent of off-site units today (e.g. Hatton 1931).

Libertarian traditions

Libertarian traditions are characterised by a distrust of those who set themselves up as authorities. Taking libertarianism seriously, one is set face to face with freedom. For some this is a terrifying experience, an experience which has been the subject of existentialist writings from Kierkegaard to Sartre. There are as many varieties of libertarianism as there are individuals who seek the experience of freedom – however that experience is defined by them. Some seek freedom from constraints – a negative freedom; some seek freedom to assert themselves – a positive freedom. These freedoms may be thought of as 'freedoms within the law'; or as freedom outside of the law – a freedom to create new domains of experience and rules not subject to previous or current conceptions and rules. For some the mode of achieving such states is through the power of the bomb, for others it is through the power of persuasion. Some are motivated by hatred, some by love, some by ideals, some by greed. The fear most expressed when confronting libertarian ideals is that of fear of chaos, unleashed passions – the rules of greed, and the lust for power. Can people be trusted to act with decency, love, and responsibility in conditions of freedom from compulsion? If the answer is 'yes', then the questions arise: can freedom be achieved without violating the freedoms of others, and without violence in the face of resistance from others?

These are not easy questions to answer. The first depends upon one's conception of 'human nature'. Do people have an unalterable nature which leads them, whether they want it or not, to express themselves violently, without care and concern for others? The earlier chapter on violence should lead to a reasonable doubt concerning inherent violence. Nevertheless, the violence in the world reveals all too clearly that we have not yet learnt to live with each other in a caring, loving, creative way. We have not yet learnt to organise our social life in a way which is cooperative rather than conflictual. And the central assumptions of schooling, as have been earlier described, are based not upon mutual trust, cooperation and freedom from compulsion, but upon an adult (specifically middle- and upper-class adult) distrust of children freely following their own curiosities and developing their powers, upon a need to control the experiences of the young and either to break their will or mould them towards a desired adulthood.

Desiring greater freedom but fearing licence, many have taken the path of a progressive yet paternalistic liberalism as described in the last section. The contribution of this approach can hardly be denied. One only needs to compare descriptions of lessons in the last century (e.g., Swinburne 1911) with experiences of lessons in schools today to be aware of the vast differences in quality. However, desiring greater freedoms, others have sought to create the conditions (in terms of intellectual climate and practical experiment) for a more immediate and radical freedom. Not content with taking pity on the poor and making life a little more comfortable for them, some have sought not only to empower the poor but also to subvert the power of the rich through the education of the poor (cf. Freire 1972).

Individualism has been one solution to the question of how to maximise individual freedom in a manner consistent with doctrines of the pursuit of self-interest, the accumulation of capital and inequality in the distribution of economic and social opportunities. The ideal individualist economy visualised by the classical economists was that of a world of individual producers and consumers. No one was to be able significantly to influence prices and costs and hence could not influence the allocation of goods and services. We live not with their ideal but the consequences of the impossibility of this ideal. Freedom under the shadow of a mysterious economic fatalism is no freedom. There is no natural balance of supply and demand within which the individual may find freedom;

it is the freedom only of the puppet, to dangle upon the whims of those who pull the strings. The powerful hide behind the cloak of invisibility (it is not our fault this high level of unemployment; it is due to the natural forces of supply and demand). Survival of the fittest justifies their wealth, their position, their power – when it suits them.

The libertarian alternative to competitive individualism is that of mutual aid (Kropotkin 1904). It is not necessary to postulate some instinct for cooperation, as did Kropotkin. One requires merely that individuals experience no insurmountable obstacle to the real-isation of cooperation. That individuals do cooperate without con-ditions of coercion is a matter of evidence. That individuals are coerced into relations they do not want, whether competitive or cooperative, is also a matter of evidence. The problem, I suggest, lies with the coercion rather than with the competition or the co-operation.

Libertarians tend to lay a great emphasis upon motivation, the inner drive of the individual and hence upon choice, individuality and responsibility. In 1774 David Williams emphasised that child-ren do not need to be pushed towards education but will themselves pursue it:

> If the subject of education was thoroughly understood, and
> proper people could be always employed in it, punishments
> and even rewards would be as unnecessary to lead a child to
> his business as to his food. The disposition to knowledge is as
> natural to the mind, as the desire of food is to the body. But
> when the taste is vitiated in either, we must have recourse to
> expedients; and among those that offer themselves, chuse the
> least injurious. (Source: Hyndman 1978. David Williams, *A
> Treatise on Education*, 1774: 101)

Williams still has a place for imposing the adults' will on the child to the extent that children should not be left to their own devices, nor obtain information by accident. There was still, clearly, a place left for the teacher as leader, controller, judge.

Godwin (1756–1836), frequently considered the father of English anarchism (although the term itself appeared much later), con-sidered that the initiative should be left with the pupil rather than to the teacher who instead should follow that initiative, building upon it. Smith (1983: 9) characterises Godwin's approach as in-volving:

> a change in the role of the teacher. In essence it would now be
> defined in complementary terms. The teacher's task would be

to stimulate the learner and strengthen his set towards learning; to help him to overcome particular learning difficulties; and to provide the generous and sympathetic support which Godwin believed crucial to the development of the young.

In performing these functions it was particularly important that the teacher should not weaken the pupil's natural drive to learn by substituting his will for his pupil's. He must avoid both the overt direction of the traditional approach and the more subtle assertion of control envisaged by Rousseau. All must be open and above board; and the pupil should have the right to say no.

Yet, in the main, contemporary teachers are concerned to motivate the child towards adult-defined goals rather than be led by the child's motivation towards child-defined goals. Libertarian ideas, however, did not take root in Britain in any substantial way. According to Smith, libertarian ideas and practices were predominantly developed on the continent by people such as Fourier, Robin, Faure, Tolstoy, and Kropotkin. In sum, libertarian education centred around notions of an integral curriculum (education of the whole person), natural motivation and non-directive teaching. From Godwin onwards they criticised non-libertarian schooling in terms of its social control functions, its emphasis upon socialisation and its frequent dependence upon punishment.

Recently, the same themes have emerged in the writings of Neill (1973), Kozol (1967), Kohl (1971, 1974, 1977), Freire (1972), Goodman (1961, 1971) and Holt (1969) – amongst many others. The emphasis is upon returning to individuals a greater degree of power in determining their own educative experiences. Overall, there is a sense of being at the fringe of mainstream schooling, trying to subvert the system, or make spaces for a few children while thinking of the grand educational utopia if only.... But it never seems to happen. In facing the state there is a pessimism which could be overcome if only....

Nevertheless, the experiments continue, the libertarian strategies are ever rediscovered. Smith (1977), in reviewing the underground educational press, found a lively interest in the libertarian stance and its practical successes and failures as radical teachers rediscovered their art. And the pupils of Barbiana wrote their *Letter to a Teacher* (School of Barbiana 1969): 'You won't remember me or my name. You have failed so many of us.' Then the pupils of that school taught themselves to be their own teachers. To rediscover one's own freedom is not easy. The voice of the young, particularly the poor, has not often been heard. Many adults have become raconteurs of the lives of the young, but few young have penned their own experiences. Instead, they are trained to produce prepared answers for expected questions; millions of wasted words disappear on exam scripts, so worthless they are never seen again.

The libertarian image of the child is of a being naturally motivated to learn, essentially good, social and cooperative. Libertarian pedagogy involves being careful not to hinder or pervert the child's natural motivation and inclinations. Such a stance towards child-rearing finds support in the various humanistic psychotherapies which have developed since the 1950s. Goodman, himself, collaborated with Perls, Hefferline and Goodman (1973) to produce such an approach which they called 'Gestalt Therapy' – an approach to re-owning the whole personality, a theme comparable to the libertarian 'integral curriculum', that is, educating the whole person.

The major question for many attracted to libertarian principles is, are they workable in the ordinary state classroom? That the libertarian teacher is faced with immediate practical conflicts when taking a libertarian stance in mainstream schooling is without doubt. The great fear is well illustrated by this account by Andy Cowling:

> Confronted with a room full of rioting 15-year-olds, I tried to be non-authoritarian. 'If you don't want to sit down or do anything then that is fine with me. I'll sit here and read.' Immediately I'm compromising because I have to bawl my head off to make myself heard. I'm also wondering what's going to happen when the teacher next door comes in to complain about the noise. 'I don't like it any more than you do, but if we have to be here then let's work out what we can do together that will be useful to us.'
>
> Then comes the response from amidst the paper darts, flying chairs, thumping dominoes and twenty different arguments: 'You're the teacher, sir. You should make us sit down. You should tell us what to do and make us do it.' I experienced that situation many times ... (Source: Smith 1977: 54)

Pupils, as have frequently been noted, are in the main conservative (MacDonald 1970; Hull 1984). They are active agents in socialising the teacher (Mehan and Griffin 1980). The practice of teaching is very much the art of learning to negotiate work responses, cajoling kids, threatening kids, turning a blind eye, modifying demands (cf.

Woods 1978). If nothing else has been learnt, the child *knows* how teachers ought to behave and is often cruel to those who do not live up to expectations and critical of those who do. The teacher is not expected to be loved, to be human, to be frail, but to be strict and have control. Without control, without strictness, it is implied, the child has total licence to be irresponsible. Adults have taught children an image of themselves which justifies adults in being strict and condemns those who are not. This conservativism has been instrumental in the failure of teacher innovations; such innovations where they have failed have not taken it sufficiently into account. Nevertheless, more and more teachers are questioning their role in relation to children, the relevance (to children-defined interests and needs) of the current curriculum and the practicality of the organisation of schools and schooling. Between the traditional standpoint where all was unquestioned (the teacher knew best and that was that!) and the more libertarian-inspired doubt there is a gap. It is the practical gap of what to do about it. If one wishes to take a more libertarian stance (or at least encourage pupils to initiate their own learning and be self-responsible without all that tiresome 'Oi! You lot, shut up!! And get on with some work!') then one needs tried and tested approaches which will not lead to the dispiriting experience described by Cowling. Again, it is no use looking towards the small experiments say in Summerhill or in the various special schools which deal with those kids mainstream schools don't want. They are special cases. Or at least, so the argument runs. No, few will be convinced until a large-size secondary school, say comprehensive, takes a whole-school approach to individual needs, creating an administrative and organisational structure which satisfactorily resources individuals in the pursuit of their own self-elected education; where pupils do not run amok but can be seen according to acceptable criteria to be acting self-educatively, productively, responsible in ways which do not violate freedoms but which constitute community freedoms. Such a school does not appear to exist. It does not exist, but the schools which do exist are uninspiring, conflict-ridden, production-oriented (some are highly successful crammers; others fail even in this) and anti-democratic. We get the schools and the society we intend.

Concluding remarks

Schools are childrearing institutions. They are currently a battleground of conflicting conceptions of childhood: the demand for caning co-exists (conflictually) with the demand for non-authoritianism. Organisationally schools are still tailored for authoritarian, class-based impersonal forms of teaching, requiring both incentive and punishment as aids to control. The image of the stern and strict teacher forcing his or her will over that of the child is the dominant criterion by which children and teachers judge classroom teacher performance. The classroom exists as a major experience of the violation of individuality in a young person's life, an experience frequently shared also by teachers frustrated that they cannot respond to individual needs, cries for help, interests and moods but must 'lay down the law'. No wonder when, yet again, headteachers still strongly voice their opposition to any move to ban caning or allow parents to have the right of veto on caning (reported by *Times Educational Supplement* 7 July 1984: 3). Alexander Bain's words are as true today, so far as educational practice goes, as they were in 1879 when distinguishing the different practices involved in individual and class teaching:

> The arts of proceeding are not the same for a single pupil and for a class. For the single pupil, individuality may be studied and appealed to; for the class, individualities are not considered. Here, the element of number is an essential feature; carrying with it both obstructions and aids, and demanding a very special manipulation.
>
> It is in dealing with numbers that the teacher stands distinguished from the parent, and it is allied to the wider authorities of the state; exercising larger control, encountering greater risks, and requiring a more steady hand. With the individual pupil, we need only such motives as are personal to himself; with numbers, we are under the harsh necessity of punishing for example. (*Education as a Science*: 108–9)

The form of the organisation of schooling itself defines the kinds of problems and issues pupils and teachers will face each other with. In the history of schooling the forms contributing to the modern organisation of schooling have been largely class-based, punishment-oriented, authoritarian, competitive, and organised on the principle of division of labour. In *School Remembered*, Avery (1967: 7) writes:

> Education is painful. Few people enjoy much of it, still fewer the whole process. Most of us remember it as a period of captivity, of frustration, of boredom; lit, if we were fortunate, by moments of particular happiness. Others recall it with

passionate hatred. 'No power on earth,' said Lord Salisbury who was prime minister in Queen Victoria's reign, when asked to visit Eton, 'would induce me to go back even for a single afternoon to that existence among devils that I remember as a boy.' But he sent his own son to Eton; where else could a Cecil be sent? Besides, one was not supposed to be happy at school.

In compiling her collection of remembrances, Avery found that

> though the country and the century might vary, thousands of miles, and hundreds of years apart, the memories of school remained very much the same. Children were bored, feared their masters and the cruelty of their fellows at all times, it seems. Only in the way they respond do they vary.

Some may put up with it all stoically, others may resist and fight back or run away.

Besides those who saw school as a form of prison, however, there were those, deprived of opportunities, who saw education as a goal and like Booker Washington (1856–1915), a freed slave, despite adversity taught themselves; and there were those who were happy at school because it could be seen to be leading directly towards a chosen career, or social position or because it positively fed some self-image.

It has become commonplace in research literature on schooling to categorise pupil responses towards school in terms of a pro- and anti-school attitude (Hargreaves 1967, Lacey 1970, Ball 1981 – the more famous amongst the many before and after these to have noticed such a polarity). Crudely stated, the division accords to a supposed dichotomy with a working class sub-culture characterised as being anti-school set in opposition to a pro-school middle-class dominant culture as in the case of Willis's (1977) conception. Such a dichotomy is empirically supportable to some degree, but is not entirely satisfactory.

On the one hand, there are the individual cases of education being pursued at great cost to the self by working-class people; and secondly, there is evident support for education being a part of working-class culture rather than being opposed to it or indifferent to it. In a study of late nineteenth century Birmingham, for example, Heward (1981: 39) considered that the lower class's active participation in schooling was curtailed primarily by lack of finances. Indeed:

> The interviews in the Children's Employment Commission suggest that 'getting your letters' was viewed as a long-term

process rather than one to be completed by intensive schooling in childhood. Learning was acquired by a variety of means over a number of years, in Sunday Schools and night schools, with the help of parents, kin or workmates. The values of the children interviewed by Mr White were first of all survival, a roof over one's head and enough food to eat. After that came clothes and lastly schooling.

Moreover, to varying degrees of success the working classes struggled to influence the school boards. Fidler (1980), for example, describes the role of the Liverpool labour movement's attempts to influence school provision in the city aided by the Liberal interest in the working-class vote.

Education is vital. What is at issue is the form that schooling takes. The form can violate and brutalise or it can present resources for freedom. The main thrust of mass schooling has been the question of what to do with the youth of the cities:

> The main purpose of Board schools was to be a 'refuge for the destitute', to bring in the 'street arab' population: 'to pay for education in order to prevent crime, or to pay for the support of criminals educated in the free and popular school of the streets, that is the choice before the ratepayers'. (Fidler: quoting from the *Porcupine* 16 September 1876 and 16 January 1878)

> The relationship between working-class adolescents and middle-class philanthropy has always been one of conflict, characterised as it is by adult suspicion of what is thought to be youthful and, therefore, irresponsible behaviour. During the nineteenth century, however, the adolescent worker, despite being subject to constant and prejudiced criticism, remained more or less at liberty because social reformers concentrated their efforts on the plight of children in factories, workhouses and penal institutions, and on redefining the concept of childhood in terms of compulsory mass schooling. But from the 1880s onwards adolescents were no longer ignored. (Hendrick, 1980)

People such as Bray (1911) and Freeman (1914) proclaimed that adolescents were growing up lacking in the necessary skills to take their place in society. And today, those same cries are heard. Young people leave school – ten years of compulsory schooling – lacking in skills. Factory reared for what? For whom? And to what effect on the young and their teachers?

This is as yet far from de Mause's helping mode of childrearing, particularly in mainstream secondary schooling. In the following chapters the difficulty a child has to influence policy debate concerning his or her future life course will be discussed.

Chapter 4

Schooling, community and the emergence of the vandalised self

Individuals, whether they like it or not, must contend with the actions and interpretations that others make of them. This is a study of such contentions. Parents may or may not have ambitions for their children; may or may not see their children as pleasures or encumbrances. Teachers are paid to care for children; their role demands certain ways of defining children and preparing them to meet school-defined goals. Neighbours may ignore, take pleasure from or fear each other's children. Whatever is the case, the child grows up knowing that others have to be reckoned with in each and every act. The dramatic outcome of this interplay of reckonings is the emergence of the self as both a social and a private experience. There have been many theories of the self. But in the end each of us must look to our own experiences – for one thing is certain, the life of the self is non-transferable. Nobody can live another's life. But many try. Equally, many try to get others to live their lives for them. Total power. Total submission.

Gerth and Mills (1954: 11, 13, 14) express an influential view of the development of the self in the following terms:

> What we think of ourselves is decisively influenced by what others think of us. Their attitudes of approval and of disapproval guide us in learning to play the roles we are assigned or which we assume. By internalising these attitudes of others toward us and our conduct we not only gain new roles, but in time an image of our selves. Of course, man's 'looking-glass self' may be a true or a distorted reflection of his actual self. Yet those from whom a man continually seeks approval are important determinants of what kind of man he is becoming. (...)

The roles allowed and expected, the self-images which they entail, and the consequences of these roles and images on the persons we are with are firmly embedded in a social context. Inner psychological changes and the institutional controls of a society are thus interlinked. (...)

By choosing the social role as a major concept we are able to reconstruct the inner experience of the person as well as the institutions which make up an historical social structure. For man as a *person* (from the Latin *persona*, meaning 'mask') is composed of the specific roles which he enacts and of the effects of enacting these roles upon his self. And society as a *social structure* is composed as roles as segments variously combined in its total circle of institutions. The organization of roles is important in building up a particular social structure; it also has psychological implications for the persons who act out the social structure.

In this view the development of the self is dependent on the views of others. Self and institutional roles become interlinked. Different institutions may prescribe different roles and images of the self. Such roles and images may be inconsistent and the values and beliefs associated with the one may subvert those of the other. The questions may arise, 'Which is my *real* self?' Individuals, thus, may not see themselves as just a composite of roles, an interlacing of masks. Firstly, there may be a sense of the private self or the real self which is not simply a construction of roles. Secondly, individuals may take a moral stance against prevailing social identities and roles or for some other reason may resist them. The self may become a battleground between the private and the public.

To play the pupil role well, this chapter will argue, the child must accept a progressive reduction in spontaneity and autonomy. The process begins from the first day of school. What are the social and personal consequences?

First day at school

The child has to reckon with a crowd of new faces - people he or she has not chosen to be with at a time and place outside his or her control. Reception-class teachers have through experience developed various techniques for dealing with the first days of school. They have an image of the ways in which the child should behave in order to be transformed from so-and-so's child to a pupil. Thus, the teacher has to learn or develop the techniques of transforming the child; an intention very different from the meeting of equals, when adult to adult, individuals have to reckon with each others' opinions and powers; the adult, however, can by and large disregard or dominate with impunity the very young child's opinions and powers. Such relations inevitably affect the kinds and quality of communication that can take place. In attempting to create the pupil identity in another a rough future is being sketched into which the other must fit, or else risk being labelled difficult or maladjusted. It is a future shaped by a multiplicity of past decisions and the conflictual relationships of a multiplicity of alternative conceptions of being a child, being a member of society, being an individual, being a boy or girl, a member of a particular nation, religion, race. From this range of possible meanings and ways of being the child is to be inducted into acceptable forms of being in a relatively well-controlled environment under the supervision of professional teachers trained to believe they know what they are doing and that they are doing it in the best interests for the life of another.

Today's careful and well-trained teachers are gentle with the young children as, anxious and curious, they enter the new place. Kind but firm is the maxim. The children are invited in, shown there is nothing to fear, shown that it is attractive to be in school, that the teacher has kindly intentions, smiles a lot, praises a lot and is calm and comforting.

A dozen children arrive early in the afternoon (the older pupils are still at play), their first experience of school. They are met by the teacher smiling, soft spoken and a welfare assistant in the cloakrooms where they are helped off with their coats. A child edges towards the classroom:

> *WA* (Welfare Assistant):   'And what's your name? (A
> whispered reply. Then to another) And what's your name?
> (Again a whispered reply. Then to another) And what's your
> name?'
> *P*: 'Victoria.'
> *WA*: 'Victoria. Ooh, going to come in and see us?'

With each child entering there is a friendly, 'And what's your name?' One girl says she's got two brothers. The adults appear grateful for any such opening of conversation. The children wander slowly and tentatively through the classroom, past all the polished tables towards the matted area which is divided into a quiet and a play area. Toys have been left out for them. Overall, what is to be communicated? 'We do this the first day' said the teacher to me, 'It gets them into the place and feeling comfortable and safe very quickly. But then we've got to get them used to the routine and settled in.' Safety, comfort, routineness is to be communicated, not expressedly but through a rhetorical climate realised through action and the kinds of communication fostered by the adults.

Soon three boys are playing in the toy area and three girls, in the quiet area, are playing with large chunky jigsaws. A boy and a girl holding hands stand shyly, another girl near them. 'You can walk over, I don't mind.' They walk over the mat to the wall benches and sit quietly. The teacher walks from small group to small group encouraging those who are not doing anything to do something and helping those she thinks are having difficulty. Surveillance and control condition the kinds of interactions and communications which take place.

The children already know how to address these adults, if somewhat formally 'Teacher, the picture is missing' indicating a missing piece in a jigsaw picture. The teacher identity has already emerged, defined by actions and communications.

Noise from the cloakroom indicates the rest of the class is arriving (composed of children who have already been at school two terms). The new children are asked to put away the toys:

T: 'Come on then sit down very, very quietly. Now, here are some more children who are going to be with our class.'

What is the nature, the identity, the requisite activities of a class?

Gradually the children are organised until they are all seated as a collection, facing the teacher, beneath her eye-level, most on the floor, the rest on the wall benches. The register is to be called. The head teacher has entered. 'I'm going to listen to learn the new names as well.' The names are called one by one starting with the old boys, the ones who have already had two terms' experience. Then it is the turn of the new boys:

T: 'Now Brian, Brian (looking around and almost whispering). There he is, do you know what you have to say?'

Brian, like all the other new children, has to learn the formula: 'Yes Mrs Andrews'. Brian whispers a reply. Each new boy who gets the right formula is praised with a 'good boy', a gentle and kindly *training of response*, one example of a gentle but persistent moulding of behaviour towards 'pupil-dom'. When, at last, all the children have been registered, it is found that several have the same Christian names thus:

> *T*: 'Now, you've really got to think hard because, you know, there are two Julias, and two Roberts and four Hannahs.'

Just another Julia, no longer a centre of family attention but another confusing identity, an object of initial curiosity:

> *g*: 'Which is Hannah?'
> *b*: 'That's the Hannah.'
> *g*: 'Where's the other one?'

New people and new things to reckon with, each leads to the experiences by which the social self is constructed: the way the 'I' is responded to and dealt with by others, others who are more powerful, more skilful, more worldly wise. The teacher is the centre and her authority is always apparent: she leads, organises, commands. She creates and holds together the class through the kinds of communication she generates and encourages.

> *T*: 'Now I hope everybody is going to listen because there are some different things to do today (...) Elaine, sit down please (...) Now all those children who've been in school and it isn't their first afternoon this afternoon, have got to listen and ...'
> (she pauses expectantly)
> *Pupils with teacher*: 'Think.'
> *T*: 'The tables are set with quite a few little things. On one table there's this shape. Can anybody put their hand up and tell me what this shape is?'
> *Tony* (a new boy): 'Miss.'
> *T*: 'Thank you Tony but Harry had his hand up so let's hear from Harry what it's going to be ...'
> *Harry* (an 'old' boy): (very quietly) 'A castle.'
> *T*: 'A castle, that's right. They're on the table where you can go. And on the castle ... This is the shape of a castle but it hasn't got any ...' (waits expectantly)
> *Pupils*: 'Windows.'
> *T*: 'And it hasn't got a ...' (waits expectantly)
> *Pupils*: 'Door'

Gradually the children have been sculpted skilfully into an audience. Expressions of the self when a member of an audience must be of a certain kind. The expert 'old' pupils respond on cue, leading the responses of the 'new' pupils. The key classroom control words 'listen' and 'think' have made their appearance. They control not simply overt behaviour like sitting, putting one's hand up, answering; they seek to control the inner realm of acting, the mental acts of listening and thinking. Two months prior to this, in an interview, the headteacher said of the reception class (which she took each morning) that

> 'it's really a case of them getting used to the school, and getting to know them and them getting to know me, getting to know the school routine amongst other things and basically to give them a happy settled start into schooling; without making it become forbidding and yet becoming aware that there are social rules that we have to observe while we are in school, not just for the sake of the teachers but for the sake of all the others in the classroom.'

She continued on to say that their time in the reception class was

> 'usually enough to get them settled in, get used to the idea that the school is completely different from a play group and very much different from a one-to-one relationship – starting them off on the road happily and securely, we hope! I think really and truly those are the sort of main aims, and the fact that we do care for them, we are not here as teachers to tell them off. That is not the idea at all. Although they do have to learn, you know, that when we say something we usually mean them to do it and it is usually for the good of everybody if we say something *isn't* to be done.'

Her view of teaching thus broadly falls into the tradition of liberal paternalism, emphasising caring, rationality ('I find at this level they are usually very receptive if you explain to them *why*'). There is a fundamental rational order and an implied conception of the self which is in everybody's interests to follow or *become* and once explained, every one will naturally be 'receptive' and act or *become* accordingly.

There is an expressed aim of trying to make this rational order and self conscious for the children. But do children interpret their experiences in such a manner? On one occasion the head teacher thought it would be an interesting idea if she asked her class what they thought school was for. Most children made the reply that it was for painting, learning to write, count, read – a couple of boys giggled and instantly said school was 'rubbish'. One girl was certain that she could learn nothing unless there was a teacher to teach her. Another came up with the notion of 'naughtiness'. At school one worked, if one didn't one was naughty. Most children had a well-developed conception not only of naughtiness but of the naughty self – Peter *is* naughty. To avoid naughtiness, one girl made plain, you had not simply to look as if you were working but to think about work all the time. It took further thought and some prompting by the teacher before playtime activities were considered as a part of school. The major factors apparently differentiating school from other contexts were the emphasis upon work (as opposed to play), the naughtiness which results from not engaging (physically and mentally) in work, the indispensability of the teacher in directing learning, and the subject matter of the daily curriculum (counting, reading, writing, painting, etc.).

A pupil mentality or selfhood as being one who is subject to teachers has begun to emerge. The classroom relations being constructed by the teacher impinge upon the child's autonomy and power to negotiate social activities. This is seen already as right. At play, the child negotiates group activities according to his or her power to influence the group. In class, the teacher delimits the kind of negotiation that can take place – in particular that one must work rather than mess about is non-negotiable (the teacher fails as a teacher if this cannot be enforced; the degree to which it can be enforced frequently defines the teacher on a scale from strict/hard to weak/soft from the pupil perspective). How one brings about pupil-work depends upon the temperament, personality and teaching philosophy of the teacher. In this reception class the teacher founded her leadership on building friendly relations and coaxing the children into doing as she wished. In her class there was a tension between treating the group as a whole and thus overlooking or suppressing individualities, as opposed to responding to the individual in disregard of the group. Since friendly relations depended on seeing and responding to individualities there were occasions when both requirements could be satisfied. Teacher and pupils therefore had to reckon with two forms of self-expression demanded in the classroom: the self as a member of the class and the self as an individual.

There is a concern by the teacher that the child learns appropriate roles or patterns of conduct, that self-expression becomes subordinated to the requirements of the classroom. The older children have already been inducted into these and with the coming of the new children become well aware of this. At a nearby table where four children are already painting, one boy says to a girl 'we're old at school now, we're used to school now, aren't we?' They too have found a special social standing in relation to the newcomers. The teacher calls on them to show a new child where the toilet is.

They're used to it all. They can be seen to be the models upon which the others must model themselves – they know where to go, what to do and how to behave in classrooms. These are important ways in which the free interpretations which the child may make concerning the environment are manipulated. The new children have to be continually reminded of their responsibilities, and the expectations laid upon them:

> *T*: 'Right now, I'll tell you what we have to do when we do a
> painting. We have to put an apron on. (. . .) Mummy would
> say "Paint on your jumper and on your very first day at
> school. What was your teacher thinking about?"'

The teacher attempts to legitimise her control by putting words into the mother's mouth, preventing any alternative interpretation: in *locus parentis*. She imagines and projects a drama, a contest of expectations and inferences which is employed to define and communicate relations between ideal mum and ideal teacher.

The teacher is continually watchful: looking for moments when she can praise and say 'Oh, that's super' and for those moments when she has to say 'Barry' in that voice which means 'now don't be silly'. Gradually, the self as seen by and desired by others is delineated in words, actions and interaction. Thus the range of interpretations which may be freely placed on any single instance is being delimited by a generalised notion of 'ideal pupil', 'ideal teacher', 'ideal parent' held by the teacher. The teacher becomes the mediator of a range of possible interpretations of classroom events and inhibits a child's free self-expression and wants:

> *T*: 'Lennie, have you made a castle?'
> *Lennie*: 'No.'
> *T*: 'Come on, you must have one Lennie. (. . .) Billy um,
> Benny I'd like you to do in five minutes time a castle. You
> haven't done one have you?' (. . .)
> *Andrew*: 'I don't want to do one today.'
> *T*: 'Ooh, don't you? Well, what would you think if I said "I
> don't want to do it today?" We wouldn't get anywhere would
> we? No. Two more minutes then you make one for me.'
> *Andrew*: 'I don't want to do one. I don't want to do one.'
> *T*: 'Well, if you don't want to do one today it'll have to be
> done tomorrow. And you won't have a chance to play
> tomorrow will you? It's best if you do it today and then you've
> got more chance to play tomorrow.'
> *Andrew*: 'I don't want to do it today.'

> *T*: 'Well, I'd like you to very much.'
> *Andrew*: 'I don't want to.'

The self of the teacher takes on the attributes of censor, judge and motivator. She must find strategies to inhibit some behaviours, advocate others and gradually bring about the behaviours she desires. The problem was returned to at intervals throughout the following half-hour. Eventually the teacher decided to give up – there was simply too much to do this first day, and Andrew (an 'old' pupil) was a problem at the best of times.

Andrew was expressing his wants, these wants were interpreted as indicating that he was 'an old lazy bones today'. Such a self emerges in relation to the expectations, judgments and demands of the other, the teacher. If the teacher should also express her wants in such a way 'we wouldn't get anything done would we?' There is a moral imperative to 'get things done'. Playing is not getting things done. The castle was to be done for the teacher or for the parent; there was no sense of the castle being done for the child as an expression of the imaginative nature of the child. A distinction was being made between play and work; the distinction was based on whether or not the activity was self-motivated or whether it was teacher-motivated. The teacher too, made a distinction for herself between personal wants and social expectations which override wants. Clearly, the multitude of such incidents act to place limits on the expression of the self of both the pupil and the teacher to realise their own imaginative designs and wants. She is aware of the range of interpretations an ideal representative of society would place upon her children's acts. The ideal classroom relation involves the reduction of self-expression and its transformation into classwork. In short, it is a violation of self-expression, a progressive and persistent influence upon self-expressivity until such expression becomes mediocre or non-exceptional. Those who violate mediocrity become deviants, such deviancy being a control problem, a problem of moderating behaviour and expressions of feelings, imaginative play and the desire to stand out, or present one's self in exceptional terms to others. Mediocrity may be defined as a process of moderating expressions until they fit within a narrowly defined range of normal expression or become non-exceptional. In class, making exceptions is taboo. Such a normal range prescribes within itself both excellence and indifference: one cannot make oneself an exception to the normal forms and ranges of assessment or examination. The classroom ideal of the model good child, the high flier, is an expression of the child who so fits with the expectations of others that he or she is thoroughly public property, the puppet of social expectations. They become the norm or criterion by which to judge, interpret and moderate the expressions of others. In the classroom, too much self-expression (which makes one an exception) can bring one into conflict with others. Where self-expression conflicts with classroom regulation, one crosses the boundary between what is normal (that which is non-exceptional or mediocre) and that which is 'too much'. Harry and Peter, for example, have built space ships from some plastic construction material and are following each other round and round the matted area making whooshing sounds engaged in their imaginative world:

T: 'Harry.'
Harry: 'Yeah.'
T: 'Peter . . . I think that's enough don't you? You're being a bit silly with those.'
Peter: 'Yeah, we're going, we're going somewhere.'

Here is a clash of interpretations, between 'being silly' and 'going somewhere'. Harry and Peter continued their game as the teacher's attention became distracted by other pupils. Classrooms, of course, are potentially dangerous places – all those hard and pointed surfaces. And too much rushing around increases the chance of accidents. In such an environment the teacher would be irresponsible not to calm and moderate any such activities. The classroom as a physical environment places limits upon the expression of individuality in ways which hinder not only learning and exploration of the imaginative and social environments but also of teaching. Teaching that is constrained always by needs to moderate, manage and make the behaviours of others non-exceptional becomes itself mediocre, that is, reduced to narrow ranges of behaviour. Aware of what she believed to be her control problem, the teacher when passing by me said 'Softly, softly, I think today. I've got enough to do . . .' And at the end of the day she commented: 'It's amazing how nice you can be first day and gradually you sort of (laughs) you sort of lick them into shape.' Licked into shape, their behaviour moderated, their autonomy reduced to playtime expressions, they hopefully become ideal pupils.

Licking children into shape is a gradual process involving being attentive to minutiae as well as the occasional crisis. Attention, in this class, was given to the process of socialisation; guiding the attention of the children to right ways of behaving. The teacher was continually conscious of creating a climate of praise (good boy/girl, that is beautiful/good/super) on the one hand as a means of reinforcement and on the other correcting behaviours which fell short of expectation:

> *girl*: 'Can I paint now?'
> *T*: 'Pardon?'
> *girl*: 'Can I paint please?'
> *T*: 'That's better. I like that magic word.'

All such as these can be called micro-manipulations – they are over in a few seconds; some, like raised eyebrows, can be over in parts of a second. There is a sense of the accumulation of such minutiae, a subliminal effect, which create a rhetorical climate or context in order to socialise the child towards becoming aware of and fulfilling more generalisable social expectations. The above micro-manipulation is directed towards an individual. Others are directed towards classes, or towards the construction of class-like behaviour and are deliberate attempts to reduce autonomy and thus make the autonomy of the self of mediocre importance:

> *T*: (claps) 'All children over here please on the carpet area ...
> Benny, Sylvia, *Jane*, come on you heard, didn't you? First time
> please. Show me your hands (pupils are to stop what they're
> doing and raise their hands palms towards the teacher) ... It
> means it's time to clear away ... So now I want you to put
> away the toys. (...) Jim, Sam and Billy, it would be nice if I
> saw you helping to clear away over here instead of just lolling
> about looking as if you were on holiday (pupils laugh).
> Wouldn't it? Yes, come on.'

Through gaining control of the children's movements (show me your hands) she reduces their autonomy and reinforces her command; extra attention is given to the three who are lolling about, they are made aware of the distinction between holiday (where you can do as you please) and work. A similar strategy of controlling physical behaviour is in evidence during the story period later. First, they are all sat in a certain area (the mat) and then, if any are not giving enough attention:

> *T*: 'Once upon a time there were two rows of happy little
> teeth. Billy – when I tell a story people sit very still and very
> quiet and they listen. They don't go la-la-la-la when
> somebody's talking. They use their eyes for watching me.'
> *pupil*: 'la-la-la-la-la'
> *T*: 'And I don't mind sitting here 'til it's time to go home.'

There is no room for a child to say 'I don't want to do this. I don't want to listen to you. I don't want to look at you. Goodbye.'

Moreover, the teacher cannot say, 'well, do as you wish'; she cannot respond to the boredom, irritation or initiatives of so many without her class disbanding. This limits her responses to a narrow range of strategies producing a mediocre rather than a creative educational environment for the individual pupils. What kind of community of selves does this aspire towards?

With individual relations one could be more responsive and provide more attention but 'Thank goodness for the one or two bright ones one can trust to get on while you are looking after the others.' By dividing the class, mentally, into those who can be trusted to 'get on' and those who cannot, actual class management problems are reduced. When problems arise they can be treated individually if the remainder of the class are 'getting on'. It is a community where the sense of 'we' is located in the aspirations of the teacher rather than in the actualities of the classroom. In the crowded classroom, however, 'getting on' frequently becomes problematic.

Two new boys were seen to be involved in trouble. One boy had thumped another because 'he banged my rocket':

> *T*: 'He banged your rocket, yes, but we don't do that to people do we? Mmm? Tell you when you can do that. You can do that when you see me going like that. Do you see me do it? No. So that means I don't really want to see you doing it.'

A little later she approached the other boy:

> *T*: 'Why did Tony get cross, mm? Did you bang his space ship?'
> *Tony*: 'No it was' (inaudible).
> *T*: 'Yes, but if you go too near people and bang on their desks they don't like it. You have to learn at school that to just keep away from people when people have made a model. And they're not going to get cross with you and you'll not get cross with them. All right? ... Have you got a brother at home?'
> *Tony*: 'Yeah, Joey and Mary, she bigger than me.'
> *T*: 'Is she? And what does she do to you if you go too near the things she's making? Does she get cross?'
> *Tony*: 'She don't get cross.'
> *T*: 'Well, she's very, very kind to you then isn't she?'
> *Tony*: 'No.'
> *T*: 'No.'
> *Tony*: 'She just kick me.'

T: 'Oh well, you see you don't want people kicking you at
school do you? So, you just keep away when people are
making models and you make your own. We don't want any,
any people getting cross, all right? And sad 'cos their models
get broken. All right, can you remember that one for me?'

Getting too near to people is almost inevitable whether at home or
in the classroom. It is a community where 'I' must be subject to
the 'Others' and in particular the problems of being in crowds.
With the first boy the teacher makes herself the model to be
followed. In the second instance, initially it appears that she em-
ploys a wrong strategy when she makes comparisons with home.
However, being kicked by big sister is used to show that 'getting
too near' is likely to call out a similar response from those in
school. It is a lesson to be learnt from being with others. Such
lessons, it would appear, are generalisable across contexts. In the
classroom, there are more people and therefore a greater chance of
'getting too near'.

In the crowded classroom such conflicts occur fairly regularly
but are typically soon over, even passing unnoticed by the teacher.
Sometimes pupils will bring their conflicts to the teacher for resolution, the teacher being the greater power by which to subdue the
other, when the child's own strength cannot right the wrong. In
these ways aggression and violence are brought under the surveillance and power of the teacher or within the bounds of manageable
classroom relationships. Thus a ladder of escalation is recognised
by which aggressive acts can be ordered. Both child and teacher
know what to do and have a reasonable expectation of success in
reducing or resolving aggression. The teacher may try to socialise
children into accepting some social rationale but in the end it is
power that counts. She resorts to it whenever she is in danger of
not getting her own way 'I don't mind sitting here 'til it's time to
go home'. She has the power to detain children against their will.
It is a generalisable power, all teachers have this power. And teachers like her, although, kind, quiet spoken, comforting, are *firm* in
making use of their power.

There is more than one level of meaning communicated by any
single act whether of firmness or of aggression. Juxtaposition of
such acts make a complex and potentially confusing, even destructive, web of possible meanings for adults as well as children. If we
could visualise the flow of communication (in terms of talking and
apparent listening relationships) as if it were water, it would flow
most often from adults to children; unsolicited communications

from children to adults are frequently blocked or ignored in class-rooms. Such communication becomes mediocre, lacking the reciprocity of interests, sensitivity to others, and openness through which a community of shared understandings, goals and needs may be built. Rather than participants of a dialogue children become the objects of concerns largely hidden from them. They are selves excommunicated from the community of adults. There is a public stage of adult action to which they are not privy, even when it concerns their own lives. No matter the kindness and the concern of the adults, children will make their own interpretations of this and act accordingly. Each instance experienced by a child is made intelligible to the child through the range of generalisable interpretations that may be made, on the one hand by the teacher, on the other by parents, friends, enemies and more importantly by the self in privacy. When there is a contest of such interpretations each prescribing alternative realities concerning self and other, the self may be placed under intense strain, may be torn, scarred, vandalised.

The vandalised self and its community

From the first day of schooling, however they or their family see themselves, children must now reckon with the ways teachers and fellow pupils see them. Experience is never mass produced, it is always individual, having a private face and a public face. Although in class one acts publicly, the experience for the individual is private. Every act whether in the face of others or in the privacy of imagination is a cultivation of experience. But each act is dialectical, acting upon and being transformed in the action by not only the present acts of others but by the images of previous acts - the cultural baggage which appears with moods, linguistic association, and habit. Teaching fettered by institutional organisation disregards these complexities and treats the class as if it could become homogeneous and all forms of communication could be given unambiguously thus restricting the range of alternative interpretations of any particular classroom act. Unless strategies are developed which can make space for the individuality of experience, individuals who cannot find adequate living space in the classroom will progressively feel alienated, hurt and misunderstood, their sense of individuality under attack, their needs, desires and interests devalued. For the most part, children and teachers manage to find sufficient strategies which recognise each other's individuality without class disruption or institutional breakdown. The dull routine is enlivened. However, in this section I want to focus upon those instances and individuals where institutional constraints so interfere with the process of education that it is correct to say the self experiences violation and hence the self becomes vandalised. *The Shorter Oxford English Dictionary* defines the vandal in this way: 'The conduct or spirit characteristic of the Vandals in respect of culture; ruthless destruction or spoiling of anything beautiful or venerable; in weakened sense, barbarous, ignorant, or inartistic treatment.' There is a sense in which we are all vandals towards each other, a sense in which we all share an insensitivity towards each other, and are ruthless towards the Other. The competitive pursuit of profit, honour, prestige, position means that all of us will experience sometime in our lives feelings of being trampled on, 'ripped off', second rate, uncared for, redundant, worthless. Some have these experiences more often and more intensely than others.

The inner life of a child is beautiful and venerable as it is, of itself. Such a position is in opposition to any dogma concerning Original Sin or the essential evil or filthiness of the life of the flesh. Whatever position is taken towards the individual nature of the child or of the adult the experience of being desecrated, torn, hurt, falling to bits, vandalised is still possible for the individual. The difference is that where one starts from a being as yet whole and unvandalised the other starts from the image of some primal act, the fall from grace, the original rebellious act of vandalism which desecrated paradise and condemned all generations to the disease, decay, pain and anguish of a life as punishment and atonement.

In the imagination of the first, utopia or at the very least if our technical understanding is inadequate, a more generalised social comfort is both possible and practical; in the second, there is only salvation if there is a God/Prophet/Leader/Father/Great Mother, hell on earth if not.

The child, physically and socially, is weaker than the adult, thus has less chance of seeing to it that his or her needs, desires, fancies are realised. Predominantly, the child is interpreted, treated and manipulated in the public sphere of action from the standpoint of the adult. The child is less likely to be successful in contesting the interpretations, acts and intentions of an adult. The violation through frustration of the child's impulses, actions and interpretations by the adult (even if acting in the 'best interests' of the child) is therefore that much more likely. Each individual, child or teacher, in class faces an anti-individual structure against which both must struggle if individuality is to be expressed and catered for in ways which contribute to or do not violate community and mutual respect. However, in any school some children are picked out as being unmanageable, too disruptive or too withdrawn to handle. They have *special* problems.

Some, like Charles, arrive even at First School, already with long case histories dragging at their heels: broken home, violent father. For him, is school a relief, or another weight? Or, as seems likely, a complex of both? He is not considered much trouble by his teachers – yet. He tends to test out the adults around him, and this could be interpreted as trouble. In particular, it places strain upon classroom management and that in itself contributes to the development of a troublesome image. An illustration can be seen in the way he treated me in the classroom. From the first day of meeting (his first day in school) he decided to sit near me. It was difficult to move around without him following me. Later I was told of his home life, the teacher saying that I would be seen as a father substitute. He was already viewed as a case whose problems in school would probably grow with time as he faced the less child-centred approaches typical of the later years of schooling. During my next meeting with him during the work period he immediately caught my hand, saying I was to help him. Despite very clear instructions being given by the teacher, Charles (in common with many other children) did not know what was supposed to be done. He could not read the simple instructions of the worksheet and even when I explained them to him he first took an interpretation, although quite logical, different from what I intended. How many other children made equally valid but different interpretations? Trying not to take a teacherly attitude, I frequently asked, why don't you go and ask the teacher to see if we're right? He resisted this for some time. He only went when he was assured by me that I thought his work was right. A teacher can never afford to give such individual attention to those who want it. Nor can all the needs and hopes of the child be fulfilled. On another occasion, when the class was taken for a day trip, Charles would be in no other group than mine. On the bus he insisted on sitting on my lap, would not be parted from his coat (despite it being a boiling hot day) nor from his plastic carrier bag (which he carried everywhere no matter how heavy it became). At the end of the day, he said simply 'I love you. I want you to be my daddy.'

The hopes a child may carry into school cannot all be satisfied, and some, the most basic (the desire for love and security), when not satisfied, can create a sense of hopelessness or brittleness; and the adult is left feeling inadequate, helpless, hurt. Another child, Billy, is considered the most aggressive in the class. His elder brother, I am told, is already in a special school due to his aggressively disruptive behaviour. So far, it is felt, the school is *containing* Billy and 'We'll contain him for as long as we can' – it is a school-created image, school as containment. The school was specially selected for Billy; it was felt by the authorities that a closer school was unsuitable and unlikely to manage him. Billy can be the centre of sudden flare-ups. Standing in a queue waiting to lead off to the dinner hall, there is a commotion, a group of boys push and tussle – 'Billy!' Always, so far, it is soon over. At the end of the day, Billy's mum comments on a previous day's problem to the teacher. 'I had a word with him and I don't think it's always his fault. But I have said he mustn't start anything.' After mum and Billy leave, the teacher rolls her eyes. A colleague comments that she was right in being firm with the mother. Billy must learn not to respond aggressively and mum must be schooled firmly to accept the teacher's interpretations of events. Most pupils can get away with aggression without being called aggressive, that is, without being labelled as having an aggressive personality, being maladjusted, emotionally disturbed. Billy cannot.

His teacher already has an image of him, one which fits a generalised type: 'He is easily led, one of life's little headaches. We'll have to watch him. However, he does have a nice side.' His behaviour is treated as having more serious consequences than others who also can be a problem and even more disruptive of classroom order.

Another in his class, Alan, is also a problem because he is always laughing, making comments, fidgeting, is frequently moved to sit near the teacher. He rarely works, but uses everything and everyone for play. Working on a cut-out chicken-shape with two other children, the colours are scribbled over the areas the other two are colouring, gradually the paper gets torn, a leg is ripped off, and ultimately the paper is screwed up into a ball then spread out again. Alan is helpless with laughter. The other two children fluctuate between laughter, anger and when they tell teacher, righteousness. Alan is told he is being silly and naughty. To the teacher 'Alan has a nice side. If someone's hurt he's usually the first to point it out to the teacher. However, he has a destructive side, usually with other people's property.' I remarked that when I observed him in the classroom he typically sat, body slanting away from the teacher, very rarely facing the teacher, frequently back to the teacher. She commented that Alan frequently had his back also to his parents whenever they are together. There is a sense in which he always seems to be in opposition, a sense symbolised by his body posture.

Sandra also typically sits back to the teacher. According to her teacher, she can be nasty to the others and they will then have nothing to do with her. Sandra 'is a deviant. When she first came to the school no one could get her to talk at all. When she first spoke to a teacher, the teacher did a double-take. That she is doing anything at all in the classroom is an improvement, so I'll praise it.' In a piece of written analysis I gave to the teacher for her comments I argued that some of the acts and interaction involving Sandra were potentially subversive of classroom order. 'She *is* subversive', the teacher replied strongly. It was a simple incident:

T: 'Right, let's see if you can count this morning. Hands shut. Hands open. Hands shut. Hands open. Shut. Now (...) count up to ten, one finger at a time.'

.)
.) (the count to ten is
.) repeated three times)
Sharon: 'Mrs White, Sandra wasn't putting her fingers up. She was only counting.'
T: 'She was only counting. Well, at least she was counting this morning, wasn't she? She didn't count yesterday. Right, perhaps Sandra can tell us what number this is ...'

It takes at least two to make a deviant. Because Sandra was not obeying a specific instruction, she became the object of the attention of another pupil. Sharon interpreted the teacher's instructions as being binding on all, hence Sandra becomes someone to bring to the attention of the teacher. On the public stage Sandra's behaviour was potentially subversive and so was Sharon's simple telling. Yet neither may have wanted to be so. Private intentions when placed on the public stage become open and vulnerable to a multiplicity of possible interpretations, each having their distinct historically determined frameworks.

In communications, personalities are formed; the kind of personality formed depends upon context and the kinds of communication self and other engage in; this personality has always two aspects (or faces) the person as interpreted by other, the person as experienced by self, that is, the public face and the private face. What kind of community of personalities is being formed in the communications of the teacher, Sandra and Sharon?

The teacher experienced a tension, a demand that she solve a particular problem which in itself is historically conditioned, identified for her by Sharon. The demand contained an implicit threat: 'what are you going to do about it?' The problem was experienced by the teacher as being potentially subversive and Sandra as being *really* deviant. Class control, however, was not the teacher's sole problem. The teacher wanted to relate to Sharon as an individual and coax her into responding to the educational demands being made. The teacher used her authority to recognise publicly an improvement in behaviour from the previous day and to provide Sandra with a further chance to receive public praise in a way which conforms to the task in hand. An atmosphere of tolerance appears to have been achieved: Sharon's vigilance has neither been rewarded not put down but recognised and employed to find some praise for Sandra and hence reinforcing the vigilance and the conformity to class behaviour. Such moves in the public domain of the classroom could be interpreted as a tactical game involving a power struggle concerning who has the right to define situations. The teacher must then display her power – she did so in a subtle manner which retained her influence on a definition of the situation conforming to the historically constructed range of definitions of what counts as good classroom practice and what counts as school deviance. Alternatively, it might be interpreted as showing the kind of pressure the group has to remind members, even leaders, of their duties towards maintaining group solidarity and conformity – otherwise they would lose the right to be leaders. In yet another interpretation, it can be employed to show how one person may facilitate another's self-development by providing a safe environment within which to take the first steps towards learning new things within the demands of the classroom. No doubt there are further perspectives concerning say, the social function of moulding responses in the reproduction of the social order; the subtle inhibition of individual autonomy. Each such perspective allows a partial glimpse of some of the dimensions of the whole, that network of meanings, desires and feelings which dialectically create the social dramas or images of everyday life.

Each individual has a public mask or persona created in the interaction of Self's intentions and Other's interpretations. Sharon becomes a 'tell tale', a role she frequently played. Sandra became a deviant. The teacher becomes a person who must continually prove her ability to control and maintain definitions of a situation. Social life becomes organised as a community of masks and orderly relations between masks, the definition of the mask only being partially in the power of the self through the self's actions in relation to others. To know the truth of a situation is to know the range of interpretations which have given rise to that situation. Where the public persona is experienced as not representing the private experience of the self, the situation is potentially or actually destructive: a violation of self; from such beginnings may be constituted a vandalised sense of relief.

It typically takes a while before a persona is labelled as *really* representing the self – either accepted as such by self or only by other (cf. Hargreaves, Hestor and Mellor 1975). Once stabilised, such a persona is hard to change. When moving from first school to middle school (or primary to secondary) the previous persona is frequently carried into the new school as an account in a case record or report. Even where a school deliberately ignores case histories (in order to give the new pupil a chance) the child is likely to respond in similar ways to similar circumstances and hence reproduce the same persona in the new school although others may deliberately take advantage of new schools to try out new personas or hope for a change in circumstances:

'Well, my last school I went to I got kicked out. Well I left
before I got kicked out of it. I came to here because the
teacher in my last school beat me up. He gave me concussion,
broken fingers, couple of lumps and bruises and that, so I tried
to sue him, and I couldn't, because of, I dunno, the LEA were
protecting him or something, so I couldn't get at him. So, I
came here and since I've been here nothing like that has
happened. The teachers here are good, eh, the lessons are
good. I like the way they – they don't have middle classes,
higher classes and lower classes here. That's, I think that's
better than my last school 'cos last school like everybody
would be looking down on the lowest classes, or whatever.'

Variations, it seems, in institutional arrangements facilitate variations in self-development and self-image for Harry. It is no doubt extremely rare that children move schools for such reasons. This boy, at the time of speaking, was thirteen. At his own admittance he was no angel and even now there is trouble which so far he is keeping at bay:

Harry: 'There's only one kid that I have trouble with. That is
in, eh, a couple of classes along the corridor from here – he
don't like me, he's bigger than me, so ...'
JFS: 'What does he do?'
Harry: 'Well, he just tries to start trouble with me. I just keep
out of his way.'
JFS: 'Fighting trouble or just ...'
Harry: 'Yeah. Fighting trouble and ... If he hits me I want to
kill him. I don't know what I'll do. I'll probably get suspended

again. I haven't been sent home or suspended here at any time yet.'

JFS: 'How do you reckon the teachers – well what do you think the teachers think about you here?'

Harry: 'I don't know I haven't got a clue. Most of 'm think I've got a majority towards trouble. They writ that down on my report. The rest of 'm think I'm very talkative in class and whatever.'

It is difficult, perhaps impossible, to bring about a complete transformation of self in a way which changes the Other's interpretation of Self. Harry alludes to many significant aspects of schooling: the experience of being looked down upon, teacher control of talk, the difficulty of overcoming professional silence and solidarity in cases of complaint, the power of teacher labelling, bullying, suspension. These are structural invariants of traditional forms of schooling to which Harry responds in ways typical for him. Harry's public interpretations may not agree with the pronounced interpretations of others (teachers, fellow pupils) but they are nevertheless plausible interpretations of his experience – interpretations by which he accounts for his life and which condition his public actions. As such they contribute to the drama of everyday life in a way which has consequences for teachers and policy makers. Most significant is his statement that he does not feel he knows what his teachers think of him except from indications on a recent school report for his parents. There is typically much discussion *about* pupils but little discussion *with* pupils. Adults find it easy to dismiss pupils' statements about their experience or feelings, as say childish, extravagant, deliberately controversial in order to wind up the interviewer or get even with the school. Of course it is all possible – but what does such a conception say about adult opinions of children? Is it not quite reasonable for Harry to say?

'I'm keeping myself to myself now with other teachers. I don't like any teacher touching me at all. I've got a phobia against teachers, so to say. I don't like teachers touching me or coming near me or pushing me or anything. I hate them now. (...)

When he, after he beat me up, I wanted to go up there with my baseball bat and kill him. I really did want to kill him. I mean I wanted to put him in a grave. I was so humiliated by him. He really got me upset. I've never heard of that being done before. A teacher beating up a kid, like I didn't know, I was just standing there, head down becase he was having a go at me and I just felt 'whack'. And then I felt this warm feeling in my head. And then I woke up on the floor. The teacher was looking down at me asking if I was all right. I just got up and walked home.'

That is a feeling which co-exists with his other statements that this is a 'good school. I like this one. I always wanted to come here but I got accepted for the other school, so I went there instead.' Yet, I took the whole second year off when I got done over by that teacher – and I wanted to come to school, I was looking forward to coming to school. And I've never done that before. I just wanted to come to school and then I came and now I want to go. Now I don't want to come at all. It's weird.' There are many currents of contradictory feelings.

The feeling of wanting to hit out can arise from causes apparently much smaller than Harry's experience. Tony, for example, has been suspended from various schools several times, been placed into a children's home, and finally sent to a special school. Why?

Tony: 'Well, the way I behaved and the way I dressed.'

JFS: 'What sort of things were you doing to . . .'

Tony: 'Well, the days I was there I got, that was at High School, I got suspended from, I was smoking everyday, got caught. Running away, I ran away quite a few times. I used to hit teachers and things like that.'

JFS: 'But, y'know, but what brought about the hitting of teachers?'

Tony: 'They just used to really piss me off. They was, they used to try to make you do work what you didn't know how to do and stuff like that, you know, and they used to complain about way I dressed and way I acted and they starting getting a bit heavy so I . . .'

JFS: 'Can you remember any, can you describe any particular incident, give me an example of . . .'

Tony: 'Well, there was one time, there was a kid there and he was sort of messing about and that and he started calling me a couple of names so I hit him. And the teacher came up to me and got everybody out. I didn't have a skinhead (appearance) then. And I just punched him and I got suspended for that. But that weren't me. That was the kid's own fault that I hit him and the teacher didn't realise. They still suspended me. I was suspended for three days that's all.'

It was all said matter-of-factly. It is the kind of anecdote which explains a particular present circumstance but in itself points towards more general structures. The move to the special school has removed him from these, removed him in such a way that teachers do not have to reflect upon or question their practices and institutional arrangements. Removed from the system, he cannot challenge the system.

Any public image is open to multiple interpretations, but not all interpretations are equally likely, nor are they necessarily consistent. Ortega Y Gasset (1957) called these 'presumptions or second-degree realities' which he distinguished from the 'radical reality' or one's genuine life, the life that is non-transferable, the life that in our alone-ness we are condemned to live (p. 46), and always condemned to choose (p. 58). We must make interpretations, suppositions, presumptions about the world of objects, the world of the Other – much of the world that we call ours and that we think we know is continually hidden from us. Self does not know what Other is thinking but must always reckon with what are presumed to be Other's opinions, knowledge, prejudice and ignorance of Self. We carry in our minds presumptive images of the whole. Images arouse feelings and reactions. Terry's image frequently arouses feelings of aggression, fear, even disgust – 'You're the sort my boss calls yobs. I'm only doing my job,' said the porter who wanted confirmation from someone in authority that Terry *really* was allowed into his somewhat sedate institution. Or, as one of his teachers said, 'Terry is the sort of lad that if you saw him approaching you in the street at night you'd cross over to the other side of the road to avoid.' Another teacher on first seeing Terry admitted he felt him to be 'antagonistic' and 'unlikeable'. However, as time went on 'I can really see that he has got some very nice traits in the end (...) he is one of those you can reach when you talk to him.' When placed into a context where *treatment* is to take place those who treat carry an image of themselves as trying to see behind the image others present. That there is an alternative image which is potentially realisable persuades them that treatment or change is possible. This change in the way an individual is interpreted may be more within the person who claims to be teaching or treating than the person taught or treated. Over time, in varying situations, as with anyone new dimensions are observed which may be interpreted as change. The initial presumptive images are 'filled out' or transformed through the evidence of experience. Another teacher in describing Terry compares him with Tony:

(Terry) enjoys getting against all authority. He really enjoys –
he swears a lot, a lot more than the others do and I have a

feeling it's not really Terry. Something is making him like this, whether it was because he was put into care, whether he was like this a bit and that's why he was put into care – I don't know where it started or when because I haven't heard really. I try to accept him as he is. I try to tell myself "here we have a nice large lad who is trying to find himself, feel his feet." He did hang after Tony. He had his hair cut like Tony. If Tony had a skinhead, he had a skinhead. He came with quite reasonably long rather nice hair but sort of fancied I suppose he'd like to look like Tony which he wouldn't do ever. He's not built like Tony and hasn't got the same shaped head as Tony – he hasn't got anything and it doesn't really suit him to have tight splodded jeans and skinhead or virtually a skinhead because he hasn't got the build for it (...) To be perfectly honest I'm still feeling my way with him. I don't really know how to get through to him because he doesn't want ... he wants to, appears to want to have this big macho sort of image. So he doesn't want any middle aged old lady or anyone in authority – and I happen to be both ... (...) But I have a feeling like I do with all these youngsters that it isn't really him, he has just built this aggressive anti-establishment business because of what's happened maybe in the last, I should think perhaps, ten years.'

For the teacher, Terry's image is not a straight copy of Tony's. As the teacher later points out, Tony is better looking and very much a leader. Both Terry and Tony have self-inflicted tattoos. But when Tony enters a room there is a change in atmosphere. He can inspire real fear and for good reason. The different images conjured up by each are important. Through the images, the teachers infer towards some 'deeper self', the hidden insides of their pupils. Thus:

'(Tony's) a very likeable chap. He's very nice. And I found that he can be very loyal too which is one of those personality traits which in previous places where he'd been people may not have discovered ...'

Tony's insides are up for grabs. They become the public property of social workers, teachers, probation officers, education welfare officers, researchers, journalists. ... His life can be read on file, his self, the drama of his biography inferred from the records. He is the object of the interpretations of professionals. When Tony was not more than two, his father went to prison. He was known as a 'hard case, a fighter' and mother was disowned by her family, 'they wouldn't speak to her or help her out'. By the time Tony was about four years old, mother and children had lived in 'a series of small damp houses and been moved around by the council. During that time Tony was found – I mean the earliest reports on file are things like "found two-and-a-half miles from home on his three-wheeler", sort of two years of age, no knickers on, no nothing by the police (...) His social worker uses the phrase, and it's on file "bad parenting", which is a terrible phrase. Also, at three-ish his younger brother hit him in the eye, apparently by accident (...) and he's only got something like ten per cent vision (in that eye). That is a much bigger thing in his life than he has ever admitted.' Like Charles and Billy, whose first days at school have already been discussed, Tony entered school already with a case history written by social workers. Nevertheless, when he speaks for himself he thinks there was a time in his life that was like a crossroads. He could have ended up as what he now calls a 'ponce'. He has his own images by which to explain himself:

> *Tony*: 'I reckon if I didn't go into trouble an' I was still at 'ome I'd be right ponce, right. No tattoos, nothin'. That's like when I first had my tattoos done (...) 'cos everyone else had 'em done. They say, "go on an' 'ave them done. You'll be one of the boys then." That's just how it goes on, y'know. Right, if I went in there for say, burglaries right, you would meet someone in there who's done this and shows you 'ow to do it an' then you go ahead an' do it, then you pass it on to someone else ... (...). If I 'adn't been in (the residential centre) an' you were speakin' to me now an' I'd never been in trouble or nuthin', I reckon I would have said the same (that is) I would have preferred to been myself (i.e., the 'ponce' self – JFS). But I'm myself now, so I may as well stick to it in a way. I ain't going to change. I tried to but I couldn't.'
>
> *JFS*: 'You've tried to?'
>
> *Tony*: 'Yeah, plenty times. It just didn't, don't work do it? If you sorta been used to, I dunno, fightin' for two years, you can't give it up just like that. I suppose you could but that's hard. Like smokin' I tried to give that up but can't.'

His fighting is now like a drug, he cannot give up its thrill, like the various drugs he has tried: glue for a year and a half but given up because it 'wasn't doing anything', then acid but that became 'scary' and now 'dope' (cannibis). Why?

> 'Like with LSD if you got, ... you'll get some of it last you about 8 or 9 hours, if you ain't got nuffin, if you're just bored

for 8 or 9 hours – that's why I used to take it 'cos it just pass
time away, just like that. I had to give that up 'cos it started
gettin' to me 'ead too much. I had a bad trip once. Just smoke
dope now that's about all I do (. . .). That's just, that's enjoying
y'self 'n' 'cos if you got about six or seven of you an' you're all
trippin' or somethin' that's a really great laugh, sort of seein'
things an' all that . . .'

He imagines his future as going on in much the same way, except
that:

Tony: 'Don't think I'll be alive in ten years time . . .'
JFS: 'Why's 'at?'
Tony: ''Cos I've been lucky the last couple of years. Nearly
got stabbed once, leg, got beat up loads of times. Got beat up
by several Pakkis the other night (. . .). Don't fancy me chances
much. That's why I want to do everyfing what I'm doin' while
I'm young. That's why I 'ave tattoos 'n' all that 'cos you might
as well enjoy yourself while you're young. Might not live to be
older. That's how I look at it anyway.'

A few weeks after saying this, Tony was convicted of inflicting
grievous bodily harm. In living to extremes he appears to be real-
ising a fantasy land of exploits with, perhaps, his version of the
heroic death.

Tony has an image of his life and of the kinds of community he
forms with others, a commonality of action, values, attitudes. He
likes to exploit images. He likes to change his haircut and his looks
occasionally, 'But everybody think just 'cos you've got a different
haircut, right, people take you as a different fing . . .' But there are
limits to manipulating images and one gets caught in the interpretations and pressures of others. In the group, he said, he felt powerless to go against what the group expected. He could never talk
in the way that he was talking to me in the privacy of the interview
or to one particular teacher he looked to for support. Tony cannot
act arbitrarily, nor in contradiction to the image expected of him.
He has to reckon with the views of others, particularly the others
he frequents either through choice or because he is thrown together
with them whether or not he likes it. For him, those with whom he
most frequents as mates, the other is thrill, a laugh and danger.

A very different person, Peter, from a well-off professional
family, arrived at the same special school as Tony and Terry. He
did not like the various schools he had been sent to, including a
private boarding school and ran away from them because:

'It was just mainly teachers and the people who are, sort of, trying to build up their image. I can't stand them. I can't stand schools 'cos of that, 'cos everyone's got an image, 'cos they've got to have an image to stay, sort of, above the (level) of the natural person. They've got to have a sort of hardened image of whatever. And that really makes me sick 'cos if you can't be your normal self . . .'

He tried to explain why he was the way he was. He talked of the pressures of schooling at a time when the individual is going through adolescence and 'you usually don't even know who you are':

'Well I didn't know who I was for ages (. . .) 'cos I didn't know whether I was part of the family or part of myself, or whatever, 'cos it all gets mixed up in this sort of mind. But that's all, I think that's what screwed-up people thinks when they go through lessons some of the time, and in bed, appearance and reality . . . 'cos you can't really tell who you are until you work it out. It's always difficult.'

Peter was and still is attracted to the drug-scene both as a form of fun and as a way of finding out who he is. Schooling, however, seems to have nothing to say to him, nothing worthwhile to offer. It does not address his concerns, the major being 'who am I?' – a topic of some educational significance. He has analysed school as a community of masks, images of hardness, people trying to be above others, trying not to be their natural selves. He sees himself as screwed-up, just one of many other screwed-up people who somehow have to sort themselves out. This question governs his attitude towards schooling and leads him into reflections on appearance and reality. Where at school has he found support for his concerns? To the schools he was compulsorily sent and to the people he found there, he was a permanent outsider and to him, they were a parade of masks. In such a context, who is he? Is he a part of others, mere extensions, or is there something else?

Laing (1976 edition) has written of the ways in which Self introjects the Other, in particular the 'family' so that a problem very much like Peter's occurs – is there an aspect of the self that is actually distinct from that of the family? To evict the family, the Other from the Self is not easy. And yet it can be argued is a necessary first step of freedom for the development of educative acts. The problem is to break out of a circle of confirmations set up by the Other by which to manipulate Self's self-image through the presentation of incontrovertable evidence of the nature of Self. Laing shows how this is done through the technique of mirroring.

> This is a conversation between a mother and her fourteen-year-old daughter.

> M (to fourteen-year-old daughter):   'You are evil.'
> D: 'No I'm not.'
> M: 'Yes, you are.'
> D: 'Uncle Jack doesn't think so.'
> M: 'He doesn't love you as I do. Only a mother really knows the truth about her daughter, and only one who loves you as I do will ever tell you the truth about yourself no matter what it is. If you don't believe me, just look at yourself in the mirror carefully and you will see that I'm telling the truth.'

> The daughter did, and saw that her mother was right after all, and realized how wrong she had been not to be grateful for having a mother who so loved her that she would tell her the truth about herself. Whatever it might be. (pp. 109–10)

Laing points out the invariance of the structure whether or not the words pretty or good, or ugly are substituted for the word evil. The structure may now be varied to include a content specific to schooling. Substitute in the words 'disruptive in school' for pretty. And instead of a mother let it be a teacher, a housemaster or a social worker; and let the argument run 'he doesn't have your best interests at heart as we do. Only a professional really knows the truth...'. Under such circumstances, what is appearance, what is reality, what of myself is me, what of myself is family/social worker/teacher? Looked at this way, Peter is attempting to break the mirror which traps him, enchants him through its reflections. However, escaping the entrancement of mirrors is not that easy.

When he arrived at the special school he was again an outsider – a soft, small, pretty, almost 1960s style hippy, rings dangling from his ear. He tried to buy friendship and acceptance from the bigger, harder, skinhead and punk style boys who thought him a poof, with cigarettes and dope (until he was stopped by his teachers). Here were new mirrors to entrance and entrap him, alternative mirrors presented by staff and pupils each with their rules for confirming the evidence presented.

Selves are experienced and interpreted within such situations, in action, in particular in the act of reckoning with others. That is to say, it is dramatic action, a drama of desires in conflictual contest or in co-operation to achieve what is wanted. And the social reality that is constructed for self is the product of these acts. This social facet of the self and the world of the self has led some to place the social above the individual in importance. Cooley (1956), for example, criticised Descartes' statement 'I think, therefore I am' as being eccentric, '"individualistic" in asserting the personal or "I" aspect to the exclusion of the social or "we" aspect, which is equally original with it' (p. 6). Like Mead (1934), a greater emphasis is given to the social over the individual. The 'we' aspect leads one to emphasise the consensual as underlying the formation of culture and the institutions of social life. However, social life is conflict ridden and this has led some to place greater emphasis on the relation Us–Them rather than We, particularly in social class analysis. For example, Marxists generally view social reality within capitalist societies as a class struggle. In their abhorrence of individualism (i.e. competitive individualism) the study of individuality is largely overlooked except where the individual is primarily a member of a class, a society, the product of social relations: 'Through the prevailing social consciousness, social relations give shape to the individual who is born and educated in a specific society. In this sense, social relations *create* the individual' (Schaff 1970: 66). And finally, Wrong (1961) has remarked upon the tendency of sociologists to construct an 'over-socialised' view of the individual. Nevertheless, inconvenient though it may be for the social sciences and for schooling, there is an aspect to being alive which is 'non-transferable', unsharable, opaque and truly alone. It is in this aloneness that the self must lick its wounds. Pain is unsharable. Again, for Cooley there is some 'whole' within which the individual finds existence where 'Mind is an organic whole made up of co-operating individualities, in somewhat the same way that the music of an orchestra is made up of divergent but related sounds' (p. 3). But what if this whole has the unity of a fight, a concentration upon wounding? The metaphor of the 'organic whole' then falls. Community, in an organic manner may be desirable but the pain of losing is nursed alone. Severed from any such whole an individual becomes little more than society's unwanted litter. Community then, rather than being organic, becomes merely a community of vandals, eroding its own ties, its own structural stability. Do such communities exist? For that we listen to the voices of those who have told us something of their lives in this chapter.

Chapter 5

Racism

Many teachers feel that questions of racism do not concern them either because they do not feel they are themselves racially prejudiced or because their school and community does not have a multi-racial population. For the liberally minded to be accused of racism or latent racism seems hurtful, particularly as the guilt seems distantly historical. Yet, it can be argued that contemporary social institutions and government are racist (Kapo 1981; CCCS 1982; *Race and Class*, Autumn 1983). Against this it could be argued that essentially society is fair but a few individuals act in a prejudiced manner and hence need re-educating. Henriques (1984: 63) has criticised the Scarman Report (1981) on the Brixton street disturbances for taking this attitude with regard to policing:

> The conservativism of the Report is typical of other attempts
> by the liberal establishment to reformulate policies to deal with
> the periodic crises in the regulation of the population. Their
> net effect is to leave power relations unchanged. In the case of
> racism, by directing attention to attitudes and to individuals it
> avoids questioning directly anything to do with the differences
> in power between whites and blacks. It is able to propose
> measures that seem feasible and reasonable from the point of
> view of the status quo while confirming what administrators
> regard as the mark of their political neutrality, namely that
> they do not impugn the legitimacy of the established social and
> power relations.

There is a case against schools in the matter of racial discrimination (Coard 1971; Jamdaigni, Phillips-Bell and Ward 1982). Moreover, children are born into a culture of racist myths, folktales, anecdotes – even literature and children's stories (Stinton 1979) – which feed their imaginations. And subject textbooks are not immune to perpetuating racist images (D. R. Wright 1984).

If it is no longer defensible simply to stand back and say, 'Well, it's only a few rotten apples in the school system, really the system is OK' then it is necessary to inquire more deeply into the practice of schooling, the inherent power relations which facilitate the emergence of a racist imagination and the acts which follow upon this. Against this, however, there is the demand that teachers should not introduce political bias, which means essentially that 'the system is OK and any criticism of it is anarchistic, trendy lefty, indoctrination and politically unacceptable'. The Thatcher government of the 1980s is particularly sensitive to political bias and what it sees as the undermining of traditional values by left-influenced doctrines and political stances. For example, it is concerned that the teaching of the social effects of innovations in physics and technology should not take place, the effects of peace studies being pursued in school, the effects of not teaching religious education and of not teaching the moral worth of the individualistic pursuit of profit. Recently, Sir Keith Joseph, Education Secretary, is looking into: 'Allegations of political bias levelled against Pimlico School by Lady Olga Maitland, chairman of Women and Families for Defence' (*The Times Educational Supplement* 17 August 1984). The evidence was provided by a nineteen-year-old ex-pupil of the school and member of the young conservatives who alleged left-wing indoctrination by teachers. Clearly, what schools do is under surveillance; schooling is of perennial political interest and as such is endemically political in all that schools do. The problem is not how to stop them being so but how to improve the quality of political debate within them.

Racism is one of the more sensitive political issues confronting schooling at the present time. Interpretations of, for example, West Indian failure at school are particularly sensitive. The *Times Educational Supplement* of 29 June 1984 carried a report on last-minute changes to the Swann report on ethnic minority children:

> A last-minute change to a draft of the report – believed to have been made by the committee chairman, Lord Swann – puts the blame for West Indian under-achievement mainly on home background and lifestyle. The large number of one-parent families are cited as an example.
>
> This is a distinctly different emphasis from an earlier draft, and indeed from an interim report of the committee under its then-chairman Mr Anthony Rampton, which placed the

blame for under-achievement more on racism than home background.

When it was published in 1985, criticisms focussed on the guide to the report which some considered as an attempt to play down the role of racism. People at school cannot avoid the politics of racism. There are three stances to consider: that of the racist, the individual as object of racism and the individual whose role places them in a position of mediation, therapy, education, that is, the teacher.

Racists

> *Joe:* 'What get me is right, come over here for one year, by the time they go back they've got Rolls Royces.'
> *Al:* 'Yeah.'
> *Joe:* 'That's right, i'n it?'
> *Al:* 'Pakkis are pimps, p equals pimp.'
> *Joe:* 'Their smile, clothes they wear.'
> *Al:* 'The way they talk.'
> *Joe:* 'Flower power. Flower power shirts, with a huge great collar out 'ere.'
> *Al:* 'It's just the clothes they wear, the smile and the way they talk.'
> *Joe:* (imitating accent) 'Fares please, thankyou fares.' (Laughing) 'Yes, the bus conductor he really grind on yer every time you got on all you hear is "fares please any more fares." '
> *Al:* 'No, it's just "fares please" and "thankyou fares" – that's the only two things, that's the only two – four – British words that he knows. "Fares please, thankyou fares." '

It is essential that in schools such attitudes are combated. However, in order to do so it is necessary to attempt to understand the social and personal functions that racism serves in the lives of racists. Al and Joe were nearly sixteen, considered maladjusted by teachers. The images they used, the opinions stated, are derived from folk-lore and these become substantiated through reference to their own life situations. There is a sense in which they feel under attack:

> *Al:* 'I think all the people that are on the dole that are white should really, should get a job before the people that are imported into this country and then I think that'd be a lot better and safer for the niggers. I think three quarters of the niggers that get beat up ... uh, I dunno, are for reasons to do

with people that are on the dole and have got nothing to do
and just take it out on black people.'

There is at least some apparent rationale for the prejudice but a
rationale open to challenge, particularly by Terry:

John: 'How many do you reckon there are over here? At a
guess.'
Al: 'Too many.'
Terry: 'Just fink about Oldtown, there ain't that many in
fucking Oldtown is there?'
Al: 'There's quite a few though.'
Terry: 'There's not about ten.'
Joe: 'No way, I know about a couple of hundred.'
Al: 'No way, there's more than that there's at least fifty down
the walk where I live.'
Bert: 'In Oldtown there's about 40 per cent coloured.'

This figure of 40 per cent was much disputed by Terry who believed
it to be less than 10 per cent, saying, 'Walk the streets and how
many niggers do you see and how many white do you see, you
don't hardly ever see a foreign person.' Despite his language, Terry
maintained he was anti-racist, indeed that he was a convert from
being a sympathiser with the National Front. Oldtown has no
black ethnic community, but does have some scattered black families.

In Schostak and Logan 1984 we tried to show that the racist
imagination of these boys was complex and contradictory. On the
general class of peoples 'Blacks' Bert, Joe and Al projected an
unreasoning and blanket hatred. Nevertheless, one of Al's best
mates was a West Indian, and Bert become attached to an Asian
student who frequently visited and helped out at their off-site
centre. However, their feelings for the individuals did not extend
to all, particularly others in their community:

... in (Bert's) local community he saw Asians as a threat. The
community is a decaying lower working class estate, inward
looking and defensive of its boundaries. The only local shop
has recently been bought by Asians. Bert keenly feels this as
further evidence of community erosion. His racism at once
creates the community and its enemy, strengthening the
community whilst also fearing its destruction. (p. 125)

When I asked 'suppose a black family moved in next door to you?'
Al immediately replied 'They'd get bricks through the window ...

I'd break the windows ... So they'd move.' It was clear in the discussion also that fundamental to the racist attitude was an image of what counts as a *real* person, and for these boys, a *real man*. The earlier description of Asians wearing 'flower power shirts' was an allusion to effeminacy, not just to being old fashioned (wearing 1960s style fashion and its association with Eastern-influenced hippy 'love and peace'). The manliness image, with its emphasis upon fighting, is given an added emphasis by Joe:

Joe: 'You get some horrible people, keep on scrapping away with other countries, what do we do? We just have a scrap with Argentina and that's the lot, innit? Finished in a year. An' you get somewhere like Asia they keep on fighting for bleedin' years, don't they?'
Terry: 'Not Asia. Israel, Israel, Lebanon.'
Al: 'We'd kill them. If the British army went to the Lebanon we'd finish them off within a week.'
Terry: 'Bollocks!'
Bert: 'I know but then Russia ...'
Terry: 'We wouldn't finish them all off, not all the factions. There's enough of 'em ...'
Joe: 'We would.'

In the racist minds of Al, Bert and Joe, there is the attractive superman image of the British soldier in contrast with the weaker image of the foreign soldier. Because Al, Bert and Joe are British, the glory of the soldier also reflects upon them, they too are superior as is proven so they think by the rapid success in the Falklands war. One has only to look to see that it is all true!

At this point in the discussion I wondered how these attitudes would influence their interpretations of the 1981 riots in Britain which occurred about two and a half years prior to this interview. I asked what they thought of those incidents:

Joe: 'Healthy. That's the pigs started that.'
Terry: 'Great. I'd love to be there.'
Joe: 'I thought the pigs started that off.'
Bert: 'I wouldn't have minded to have been there.'
Joe: 'They had every right to.'
JFS: 'Was it anything to do with ...?'
Terry: 'They's been treated bad by the pigs and so they had riots.'
Joe: 'I don't think it had nothing to do with the actual white public. I think that's pigs that started them.'

> *Terry:* 'No, there was a lot of white people there.'
> *Bert:* 'Yeah, but whites and the blacks were fighting there on the same side against the pigs.'
> *Joe:* 'Yeah, on the same side.'
> *Terry:* 'Exactly.'
> *Joe:* 'The pigs stirred shit up.'
> *Terry:* 'That's what they are though, aren't they?'

The accuracy of their memories is not at issue here but the images, which currently retain potency for them, are central. The common hatred of the police through the image of 'pigs' united them. Interpretations, it would seem, are dependent on context and the images specific to them. The police and the military have very distinct images. But this is not entirely the case. The fundamental characteristic of images is that they are multi-layered, equivocal, ambiguous. One cannot analyse them according to a logic requiring non-ambiguous structures, as in the case of mathematical or statistical inquiry. In logically dividing, separating and isolating the elements (as in the purification processes of chemicals) the alternative layers of meaning, the structural ambiguity, its ironic, schizoid or maze-like quality is hidden. Rather than a mirror on reality, the image is developing into a multi-faceted reflecting jewel. In everyday life there is as much a pursuit of variation as there is of typification; thus invariant structures are broken, fragmented, contextualised through the pursuit of variation, self-justification, power, interest; thus the novel and the situationally specific is formed. Human struggle is to transform the typical in the interests of the self, the gang, the community, the national identity as much as be transformed or transfigured by it.

The image for example, of manliness is played through many variations, its apparent unity justifying (not causing) all kinds of contradictory interpretations of social action. The image of 'hardness', which is often equated with manliness, can be appealed to by racists, the defenders of a liberal democracy identifying the qualities of good military personnel, gym teachers glorifying the qualities of their football team or, as in the case of a breakfast cereal a winning television advertising theme (images of the breakfast cereal are shown in the form of cartoon characters dressed as 'skinheads' exhibiting how 'hard' they are). Certainly, it is a powerful and prescriptive image not only for young people but generally for the nation – particularly with a prime minister glorying in her nickname as the 'iron lady' and employing the rhetoric of 'tough', 'stiff', 'dry', 'hardheaded' economic restraint and an

American president glorying in his younger tough-guy cinema image. Displays of hardness are therefore to be expected among young people and hardness becomes a criterion by which to judge the worthiness of others and the appropriateness of their beliefs and behaviour.

Learning about the Other is a vital part of the official and hidden curricula of schools and community life. Relations with the Other are reviewed in the history of wars (which typically passes as a history of Britain/USA/...) as well as in the aggressive fantasies which are the post-work relaxation diet of most children and adults. The Other as dangerous is the major organising principle of narrative, whether told at school or seen on television, whether called real or imagined. Racism is but a variant of the Other imagined as dangerous.

The underlying principle of social life which is taught in teacher–pupil relations is that of danger. In competitive education there is the pervasive danger of failure: failure to achieve according to one's teacher-defined potential; failure to fit in; failure to make playground friends. More generally, there is the danger of failing to be attractive to the opposite sex, failing to be manly, womanly, failing to be a success, to be desired, failing to have a future. In the competition for power there is the danger of being beaten up, losing face, being trampled on, losing possessions, territory and friends. Social institutions are structured for competitive struggle and defended on the assumption that what is not secured will be stolen, broken or otherwise abused. The philosophy and the practical structures of power premised on the supposition that the Other is dangerous provides a fertile environment for the growth of the racist imagination.

Conquest, rule and dominance create victims. But the racist imagination must not see victims; instead must be seen products of an inferior race, a race less than human, an inferiority which in itself justifies violence and the violation of rights and individuality in all its forms:

> 'No full-blooded Negro has ever been distinguished as a man of science, a poet, or an artist, and the fundamental equality claimed for him by ignorant philanthropists is belied by the whole history of the race throughout the historic period.'
> Political institutions were rudimentary among Negroes, they had no religion worthy of the name, they had never exploited the rich continent they occupied, so the theory went; they were strong but lacked brain-power, slaves to their own passions

and the natural slaves of other races. Children of Nature, the
Negroes apparently had no natural rights. (Bolt, 1971:209,
citing the *Encyclopedia Britannica XVII, 1884:318*)

Here is yet another variation on the mirroring strategy described
by Laing – just look and you'll see that it is true! At the heart of
this are the theories of Darwin and Spencer, the survival of the
fittest as the underlying principle of evolution and the justification
of one race's exploitation of another seemed justified by the experience of wars and class revolutions. As Harris (1968: 105-6)
comments:

> It would seem undeniable that the wedding between racism and
> the doctrine of struggle was in part an excrescence of this class
> and national warfare. Racism could be invoked to overcome
> the class and ethnic diversities of the modern nation. The
> fiction of common descent enshrined in the metaphor of
> fatherland and motherland, and applied indiscriminately to the
> overwhelmingly hybrid populations of Europe, improved the
> tone of civil and military organisation. The racial interpretation
> of nationhood imparted to the physical, cultural, and linguistic
> hodgepodges known as England, France, Germany, etc., a
> sense of community based on the illusion of a common origin
> and the mirage of a common destiny. In the mystique of
> racially inspired patriotism, nations made war with increased
> efficiency, while blunting the divisive effects of class antagonism
> at home. Romanticism in art and literature was an essential
> part of this mystique. National destinies, uncontrolled and
> uncontrollable, welling up from the racial past, were stridently
> proclaimed as the fulfillment of art and life. Racism also had
> its uses as a justification for class and caste hierarchies; it was a
> splendid explanation for both national and class privilege. It
> helped to maintain slavery and serfdom; it smoothed the way
> for the rape of Africa and the slaughter of the American
> Indian; it steeled the nerves of the Manchester captain of
> industry as they lowered wages, lengthened the working day,
> and hired more women and children.

Much of this rings uncomfortable bells in the new monetarism of
the 1980s. The old justificatory arguments are returning for unfet-
tered competition as being good for the citizenry. And, 'Any sof-
tening of its conditions in the name of Christian charity or political
sovereignty would inevitably decrease the well being of the citizenry. For the economic order was governed by immutable laws;

capitalism was a self-regulating machine whose mainspring was competition' (p. 106). The image of the race then was central to the development of British economic supremacy and vital for justifying economic disadvantage as between social classes and races. To understand today's institutions, the myths generated by racism are vital, particularly in trying to disentangle oneself from the implications of the self-confirming nature of the central doctrines of racism and their relationship to economic theory and practice. Thus, when teaching history, or the rise of industry, many would echo the advice of Sir Keith Joseph to teach the moral virtue of industry and the pursuit of profit and to teach pride in the common culture that has made Britain what it is. But in saying that, it is important, is it not, that children learn of the extent to which slave trading contributed to Britain's wealth, power and social development? Fryer (1984) considers that

> at the dawn of the factory system in Britain, the trade in black slaves directly nourished several important industries and boomed precisely those four provincial towns that, in the 1801 census, ranked immediately after London: Manchester, Liverpool, Birmingham and Bristol. . . . Funds accumulated from the triangular trade helped to finance James Watt's steam engine, the south Wales iron and coal industries, the south Yorkshire iron industry, the north Wales slate industry, the Liverpool and Manchester Railway, and the Great Western Railway. Rising British capitalism had a magic money machine, an endless chain with three links: sugar cultivation; manufacturing industry; and the slave trade. And the slave trade was the 'essential link'. The whole system 'was frankly regarded as resting on slavery'.

The honest pursuit of profit? And what are the implications for our 'common culture of shared values' when we come to consider say the 1981 Nationality Bill?

The place of the victim

Today it is progressively more difficult to point the accusing finger. Racism can hide behind an apparent liberal humanism. There is talk of freedom – all are free to compete, those who fail, fail only in honest competition, all have an equal chance of winning; or so it is claimed by the more enthusiastic white, middle-class and university-educated industrialists and politicians. There are not victims, therefore, but merely those who by virtue of their coming last in the race are to be found at the bottom of the socio-economic ladder, naturally incapable of climbing to the consumer paradise of free enterprise. They, poor souls, however, have nothing to fear because those who have made it have their best interests at heart and will provide them with the necessities (but not too many for fear of destroying the incentive we all know they haven't got) until the economic up-turn which is just around the corner, if only they'll be patient for another ten years, another lifetime. At least their great grandchildren will benefit!

Those who are black are more likely to be at the bottom than anyone else. The social logic which maintains such an obvious injustice is clearly a violation of any individual's hopes and ambitions to a happy, healthy and relatively secure economic base and sense of community from which to explore one's talents and contribute to the welfare, security and happiness of one's family, friends and neighbours. Instead of mutual support society presents the individual with his or her place in the hierarchy of victims, where one stratum exploits, controls and institutes defensive surveillance systems over the other. The Other is systematically treated as a potential threat to the mutually sustaining hierarchy of privilege and victimisation.

The victim of racism has a special function to play in the sustaining of a social order. The victim as a member of a clearly identified race focusses the political attention of the self-defined superior race, defining its fleshly boundaries, creating at once an embodiment of superiority and of inferiority. Self expands to US bounded by the flesh just like the self is bounded by the body; and the Other becomes THEM, they are all the same to US. We know their essence just as we know our own.

What does it feel like to be a victim of racism in a society which flaunts its rhetoric of liberal humanistic freedoms? Lucy (in Schostak 1983a:84–5) set the dilemma as it appears within apparent friendship:

> *Lucy:*   ... 'I'm black. I'm proud of it, right? But I know, it's a strain to be black. It is a strain. You could be proud of it or not proud of it. It's a strain. It's a damn strain because I mean, I could be talkin' to 'er (Lucy's white friend) an' that, at the end of the day she can say, "You fuckin' black bastard." She can say it but, you know what I mean, it can 'appen.'

At the back of the mind, eating away at a friendship, is the real plausibility of a lingering racism. The concrete existence of racism, its inevitable preservation by a social order which preserves all injustices (through its sanctioning and defence of inequality) sets the values of friendship, liberality, justice against the alternative set of practically enforced values condoning superiority, exploitation and inequality. This sets up an ironic structuring of experience, where professed values are systematically subverted by the values implicit in (and therefore reconstructable from) the results of social action. Such experiences led Paul, a black boy who had recently moved from a Northern city to a southern city, to say of his new school first. 'The school does a lot against racialism (...) You get into trouble for being racist'; and secondly:

'everyone's racist deep down ... (...) 'cos in the west-toilets, right, they have all these things on the wall. And they had one on my mate. Someone put on the wall, right, the name, that he's a "nigger"! All right? And I'm probably talking, I probably don't know this, but I'm probably talking to the person who wrote it. So I don't know, I don't know who writ it, so I could just be talking to them, and they could be talking to me. They must be badly two faced, mustn't they? If I found out who writ it I wouldn't talk to them.'

I interviewed virtually all the members of this boy's class, a class containing black British, Asians, Yugoslavians, an Afghan, a Pole and white British. Most stated that there was no racism (excluding the Polish boy and the boy from Afghanistan). However, two white British boys (on their second interview) expressed considerable racism. The campaign against racism had some success throughout the school, it would appear, but had the disadvantage of driving it under cover. It could not, therefore, entirely erase the suspicion of there being racist opinions.

Children, like adults, are critics of their situation, of the way others behave toward them. Like adults, they pick up the various stances towards others typical of society and hence are sensitive not only to overt statements but also to body language and innuendo as again is made clear in the many statements to be found by the people recorded in Jamdaigni, Philips-Bell and Ward (1982). Thus for example a West Indian pupil says:

'When you're white you receive more attention and more help to get to the top. In my junior school they were very prejudiced, not just the children, but most of the teachers, too. The teachers tried to hide this and were reasonable most of the time, but I was perceptive and noticed this in their glances and the way they talk to you.

101

There wasn't many other coloured children, and it was
common to be called a "black sambo". I used to fight with
white children when they called me that, but now I find I can
take no offence, as it's very immature. Although I find it quite
common to be walking along the road, a car will drive past
and somebody shouts out, "black sambo". It's not children
saying it, but an adult, and that's when it hurts deep down.

One particular incident I remember specifically, was when I
was in junior school, and we were discussing Jamaica.
Unexpectedly, the teacher asked me, 'cause I was the only
black person in the class, if the black people in Jamaica walked
barefooted. Well, of course, I was born in England, in the
same hospital as a white boy in my class. This boy said, "How
can she answer that? She's English; she was born in the same
hospital as me, in Marston Green." The teacher was perturbed,
and swiftly changed the subject, but it was an incident I've
never forgotten.'

Thus they are aliens in their own country as another pupil in the
same collection makes clear:

'It's like being a stranger in another world and even though we
was born here, the white people still say this is not our country
and we should go back to our own country.'

This conclusion was reinforced by the British Nationality Bill published in 1981. Such experiences when related to prospects for em-
ployment, housing conditions, relations with the police, lead to
resentment, frustration and anger in many – all factors contributing
to the 1981 street disturbances recognised in the Scarman Report,
factors recognised by many before that report. For example, Bishton and Homer (1978) edited a report on interviews with young
black men and women. One girl spoke of the time her boyfriend
was picked up by the police late one night and found the expensive
razor she had bought him for a birthday present:

. . . 'the next morning I saw him and the whole of his face was
full with bruises and he got marks all over his body, apparently
they beat him up because they didn't believe that the razor was
a birthday present, they kept insisting that maybe they stole it.
When he kept saying no it was a birthday present they kept
hitting him. It is things like this that brings the conclusion that
the police are racist. I pass people when they have been
stopped by the police, I mean, I have been in a car myself and
the police just stop us for no reason and they want to know all

kinds of irrelevant information, like who are the rest of people in the car beside the driver and where we are going.'

Being picked up on suspicion ('sus' laws) or stopped and searched ('sas') were major complaints in the riots of 1981. Landau (1981) showed that police treatment of young blacks was more severe than for whites. There was, according to Phillips (1981) a 'criminalisation' of blacks as they expected to be stopped, questioned, picked up, chased, held, beaten up. The image is strong and potent, the image of the black person as criminal: 'It's not "sus" that leads to hassle with the police, but the number of times that we're searched on the street – round here it's a crime to be black' (reported in Brogden 1981).

In an interview with Tom Logan (Schostak and Logan 1984) a black girl, Diana, adds another dimension to the experience of being within a society which expresses at once liberal and racist values. Anti-racism becomes a cause which can get between her and her personal relations with others:

'That's another thing that makes me sick about this school. It's supposed to be comprehensive and you've got all these hippy, no, all these rich high-class people coming and they act as though they're, well, they're not, they dress themselves down and everything, and they're not, they go on about "going on this march" and they go on at me because I'm black and say, "Oh, you should be going on this with us", and they're just "talking", and they're just going because it's the in-thing, and like all these left wingers in our school, you know, these girls, and that, that I'm supposed to go around with, fit in with – they're just doing it because they want to. They're just putting on an act and like some of the things they say, I mean they're telling me how a black person feels, right telling me, "Oh, you people have had things really bad", and everything. And some of the things they are feeling . . . it's just rubbish. I should know, first hand, right?

They're just telling me what I should do. Well, I don't like being told. I mean, I'm supposed to be in all these black groups too, and I just don't want to. I don't want to think in terms of colour . . . and then my parents say to me "Oh, you really think you're white", and I don't, and my black friends say the same. And the left wingers say, "Why don't you join with us in this?" and it's all really annoying. Like your true friends, I mean your mates, when I look around they aren't white, they aren't black, they're just in between.' (ibid.: 131)

There is a sense in which people can be caught out 'just talking' not being *really* engaged in the struggle. Diana is involved in a contest of interpretations, each trying to define her one way rather than another, each trying to subvert her own experience and interpretations. Sivanandan (1983) gave another variant on the theme in speaking of the vogue of multiculturalism:

> this was demonstrated clearly in a confrontation we recently had with a group of head-teachers who stumbled on the Institute in the course of their multicultural expedition – they know more about my culture than I do, or think they do! And this gives them a new arrogance, based no longer on feelings of superiority about their culture but on their superior knowledge of mine. One sahib even tried to talk Hindi to me – and I don't even know the language.

The experience is ironic in nature. Within such an historical context of racism dividing person from person mediation becomes at best an ambiguous exercise and at worst an active ingredient in inflaming racial tension.

The mediators

In situations of massive inequality the liberal mind wants a balanced assessment of his or her work of mediation. In schooling the teacher is not expected to express political views but to show all sides of an issue, particularly in the case of sensitive issues such as *peace*:

> 'I deplore attempts to preach one-sided disarmament to primary pupils ("Babes against the Bomb") under the guise of teaching them, as they must be taught, to be kind and considerate to others; or to offer older pupils only one of the many views about national defence' ... Teachers should not be asked, let alone obliged, to promote a certain view of the issue of peace and war, whether this takes the form of inviting consent to the present Government's defence policy as a practical duty or to the programme of the CND. (*Times Educational Supplement* 9 March 1984, reporting Sir Keith Joseph)

However, the teaching of the moral virtue of free enterprise and the pursuit of profit is seen as a fit and necessary role of the teacher (*TES* 26 March 1982) – an undoubtedly political issue which many would see as unsupportable bias, and a cause not only of wars but also of racial discrimination through the exploitation of nation by nation in the pursuit of profit. What then is the role of the educator – to obscure? To act as an apologist for whatever government is in power? Or to resource critical reflection?

Taking the long view, in comparing the 1880s with the 1980s, an improvement in educational provision and in the liberalisation of the classroom and the curriculum is largely undeniable. Taking the medium-term view, from 1944 to 1984, the position is less clear. Focussing upon the issue of race, this has been addressed in a variety of ways. The humanitarian intent of these were clear, but the implications frequently compounded the problem.

Over the last forty years there have been many movements aiming to increase opportunities for the most materially disadvantaged. Such movements have generally taken the stance that material deprivation also implies some degree of cultural or linguistic deprivation (cf. Friedman 1967; Houston 1969; Keddie 1971). Whole communities, races, nations have been defined in terms of their supposed emptiness (see for example, Bereiter and Engleman 1966; Dumont and Wax 1969; Kapo 1981; Husband 1982). They have been defined as people who lack rather than as people who have a cultural richness of experience which can enrich other cultures and provide standpoints for the understanding of humankind and the critique of social action by those who have material, legal and bureaucratic power over the lives of those they seek to control, manage, or rule. As such this is nothing short of a violence against their experience, culture, independence and intelligence.

The teacher is expected to be a transmitter of culture, a broker between the haves and the have-nots, the 'superior' and 'inferior' cultures. As a broker the effect is as much to keep apart as to bring together (Hunt and Hunt 1970). To the liberally minded, schooling was in some way to compensate for social and material disadvantage and programmes were established during the 1960s to pump 'culture' into the disadvantaged, such as *Head Start* in New York. These have received many criticisms, not least for the arrogance of the term 'compensatory education'.

In Britain, Carby (1982: 186) argues, the policies of the 1950s and 1960s aimed at assimilating immigrants made it possible to continue conceiving of black people as being deficient and moreover as laying:

the ideological basis for practices designed to protect the indigenous population. Hostility, for example, was not conceived as being perpetrated upon black communities in the form of racist attacks and racist street corner politics, nor was it seen that it was the black community who needed protection. Rather hostility was seen to be the result of whites' *justifiable* fear of the very presence of blacks.

Bernstein (1970), whose work itself appeared to lend support to notions of compensatory education, wrote an article entitled 'Education cannot compensate for society'. He stated plainly that he did not

> understand how we can talk about offering compensatory education to children who in the first place have not, as yet, been offered an adequate education environment. The Newsome Report on secondary schools showed that 79 per cent of all secondary modern schools in slum and problem areas were materially grossly inadequate, and that the holding power of these schools over the teachers was horrifyingly low.

His solution was:

> We need to distinguish between the principles and operations that teachers transmit and develop in the children, and the contexts they create in order to do this. We should start knowing that the social experience the child already possesses is valid and significant, and that this social experience should be reflected back to him if it is part of the texture of the learning experience we create. If we spent as much time thinking through the implications of this as we do thinking about the implications of Piaget's development sequences, then it would be possible for schools to become exciting and challenging environments for parents, the children themselves and teachers.

Is it now that society cannot compensate for school? The locus is shifted from the child to the school. The child's experience is to be treated as valid and reflected back to the child as such where appropriate. But this does not take us far. What can schools actually do? A child whose home had inadequate heating and lighting, who is under nourished, whose parents cannot find work because they are black – is school to reflect this back to the child? If it is, in what way is it to be reflected back?

In general British schools do not seriously take on board the experiences of the community as a part of their teaching function; relations with the community tend to be mediated through pastoral care – chasing up truants, behaviour problems, organising charity events, school trips, relaying pupil reports to parents on parents' evenings. In short, children are not typically provided with education in schools as a basis for social and personal choice and action within their own communities, confronting their own problems. Schooling is divorced from action, particularly political action. Education, since it requires a questioning stance towards experience, establishes the individual as the agent and mediator of his or her own experience and that experience inescapably involves personal and social action. Education is political in its consequences.

Teachers, as paid professionals, have a choice. They can either school the young people under their command, or they can contribute to the education of young people. I do not think they can do both without engaging in conflicts. Confronting racism is a major educational task. It requires innovation in curriculum, pedagogy, institutional organisation and a reassessment of teacher–pupil relations. These elements need to be mutually supportive. Thus, for example, if the principles on which teacher–pupil relations are formed are incompatible with the pedagogical principles adopted then, of course, the values implied in the one will subvert the values and intentions of the other. This then places both teacher and pupil in an absurd and untenable position.

In its broad form the curriculum (as a course for life), which is the focus of this book, faced by any individual is that of the Other-as-dangerous. The particular variant faced in this chapter is that of racism. What might such a curriculum look like? And what might its principles of pedagogy and organisational practice look like? These are questions requiring extensive thought and research and cannot be answered within this book. Some steps towards such developments are addressed in Stenhouse *et al.* (1982). The whole question of curriculum development in the effort to teach against racism is, however, made extremely complex due to the academic nature of racism in the school system. The attitudes of the teachers and the administrators can subvert any such effort. It is difficult to sustain the case that anti-racist policies fail or are ineffective because of the few rotten apples. Bristol (1984), for example, in recognising that about a quarter of the Local Education Authorities in England and Wales are adopting policy statements on racism or multicultural education, doubts the effectiveness of their strategies. He cites racial abuse in the staffroom as a factor and provides the example of a teacher from the *Multicultural Education Centre* set up by Avon county being racially abused in the staffroom of a primary school in front of the headmaster. He writes:

Four aspects of this case are particularly disturbing (apart from the fact it happened at all):

1 the teacher who uttered the abuse continues to teach children, many of whom are black
2 Avon initially sought to disclaim any responsibility for his action
3 the black teacher was given no support by senior education staff who claim to be opposed to racism (they argue that because of the disciplinary and legal proceedings they could not appear to be 'taking sides', until the case was settled)
4 it took eight months for the case to be settled – eight months of enormous personal strain for the black teacher – and the repercussions of the case continue still.

The institutional structure, presumably fuelled by the attitudes of the teachers and administrators, inhibits any sense that the legitimate MEC teacher was fully supported. Moreover, on a broader front, the Education Department advisors of Avon in 1982 prepared a paper called 'Multicultural Education in Avon'. This, writes Bristol, showed remarkable omissions. It wrote of 'The great commercial and industrial sea-port of Bristol, whose wealth was founded in the maritime traditions of our country ...' but never mentioned slavery. Moreover, it never mentioned the 1980 disturbances in the St Pauls district of Bristol. There is a desire not to remember.

This is not the only such incident. Each such incident is controversial and the facts disputed. But they happened and local black people feel incensed. Thus, for example, there is the case of Chris Perry, who was a supply teacher in a Bradford comprehensive school, objecting to the racist comments he heard from teachers in the staffroom. An article appeared on this in a national paper. He was then suspended from the school. Perry turned up at the school 'later that day when Mr Richard Knight, Bradford's director of education, and Mr Peter Gilmour, the then chairman of the education committee arrived at Wyke Manor for the opening of a community centre'. The article continues:

Seeing Mr Perry they told him to leave but he refused to do so despite repeated requests from Mr Knight.

When the police were called they advised Mr Knight and Mr Gilmour that under the law of trespass they were entitled to remove the defendant using the minimum of physical effort.

They finally carried Mr Perry into the car park where he lay

being requested by
ιter that day. (*Times*

parents for Mr Perry.
nittee has been organised
;m in their schools. The
en by a local headteacher,
which was published in the
'Honeyford's racist views
policy on race relations and
f the concept of "multi-cul-
turalism", but also grossly   arents' (Drummond Parents
Action Committee, Newsletter No. ι October 1984). Indeed, 'Out
of five hundred and thirty school pupils on the school register, two
hundred and fifty parents put their signature to a petition calling
for Honeyford's dismissal.' An example of a passage in the article
to which the parents object follows:

> 'Cultural enrichment' is an approved term for the West
> Indian's right to create an ear-splitting cacophony for most of
> the night to the detriment of his neighbour's sanity, or for the
> Nottinghill Festival whose success or failure is judged by the
> level of street crime which accompanies it.
>   The roots of black educational failure are, in reality, located
> in West Indian family structure and values, and the work of
> misguided radical teachers whose motives are basically
> political.

These, amongst others, are quoted in the newsletter.
    And finally, in a society where such racist attitudes abound and
have a high degree of institutional support, any broad advertising
campaign to combat racism may well 'boomerang'. Thus as Troyna
(1984) writes: 'the odds against a successful social advertising campaign for "racial harmony" are stacked even higher when one recognises that the racist attitudes of the audience are legitimated
and confirmed daily both in primary networks and by the mass
media.' He is writing of the Commission for Racial Equality's
'incursion into the sphere of social advertising' as 'one of the first
major attempts to promote "racial harmony" via advertising cam-
paigns'.
    J. Wright (1984), however, finds some hope in the political pressure
which black parents can bring to bear. Thus, 'In Brent, for example, parents secured from the LEA the assurance that their children

109

would not be referred to ESN units without their full consent.'
Black children referred to Educationally Sub-normal (Maladjusted)
– ESN(M) – units has been a concern for some time. ESN(M)
children form the largest group receiving treatment in special education schools or units; and black children are over-represented in
this group. Although the 1981 Education Act which came into
force in 1983 got rid of the separate categories of handicap, 'the
children previously categorised as ESN(M) remain in the units previously designated for them. And children continue to be assessed
and referred to these units in many Local Educational Authorities.'
Although there has been a change of names, there seems little
change in practice. The law is 'hedged with qualifications which in
practice will allow LEAs to continue to maintain separate off-site
units'.

In the light of these experiences teachers should recognise that
teaching has political consequences. Teaching is not outside of the
public domain of political action. Being involved wittingly or un-
wittingly in the institutional processes which reproduce discrimination is itself a political act with political consequences.

Chapter 6

Sex and sexism: public action and private parts

Western culture appears to be built upon principles of inequality. Of course, there have always been moves, or undercurrents, towards liberalism on the one hand and egalitarianism on the other, frequently suppressed, and scorned by the authorities who typically are the main beneficiaries of inequality. Racism, discussed in the previous chapter, is an obvious example of the denial of equality for commercial and political gain. Sexism is another. These forms of inequality frame policy making and hence make schooling ineradicably political. The position taken in this book is that the denial of equality is a violence against the individual who is a victim of discrimination or any other form of violation. Sexual violation will not here be couched exclusively in feminist terms. In this chapter it is proposed to develop what may be called a *sexual critique* of society and in particular of schooling, identifying the sexual basis of the images framing social life.

Freud, as is well known, saw civilisation in terms of the sublimation of sexuality and hence opened up the way for a sexual critique of society. Susan Isaacs (1930: 8), for example, attempted to translate Freudian understandings into school practice. She considered that:

> It is not what we are to ourselves and in our own intention
> that matters; but what the children make of us. Our real
> behaviour to them, and the actual conditions we create, are
> always *for them* set in the matrix of their own phantasies. And
> what they make of us in the years from two onwards is in large
> part a function of the already highly complex interplay of
> infantile love and hate impulses, and anxiety reactions towards
> these.

111

Freudian imagery itself focusses upon what it takes to be infantile sexuality and the role of the parents, particularly the father, in repressing or censoring the expression of sexuality or the uncivilised instinctual life of the child. The task for the psychoanalyst was to reduce such repressions to a comfortable minimum – adjustment to civilised norms, identities, roles – learning to live with the contradictions of social and personal life. For Freudians, the child must have a good father and mother model. The image of the family and of sexual relations that results is perhaps too much founded upon a narrow range of clinical experiences rather than everyday life.

In everyday terms, there is a clear image of what a man or a woman *ought* to be and hence what the relations between the sexes *ought* to be. But these images vary according to culture and their interpretations vary according to group and individual experience. Such images are important in understanding the sexual politics which influence the creation of identities and organise social reality according to gender. There have been several important attempts to identify the commonalities to all cultural variations and hence define some essence of maleness and femaleness. Like Freud they turned to the great explanatory myths of the world. Thus the great myths by which people have lived and continue to live speak of a male and a female principle (e.g. Campbell 1964). The male is typically taken to be the active and the female the passive principle. Abstract reason belongs to the male while feeling and intuition belong to the female. Yet, within the male archetype is not only the Apollonian (reason, order) but also the Dionysian (passion, destructiveness). And within the female is not only the irrational but also wisdom (Sophia) and destruction (Kali). Some, like Robert Graves (1959) have sought to set the female above the male, finding evidence in the great myths of the primordial supremacy of the female and the more recent usurpation of power by the male.

At the heart of the mythological images of male and female is an essential ambiguity of pointing towards the universal dilemmas of living. Being alive dialectically comprises life and death, creation and destruction, love and hate, courage and fear, desire and revulsion, having and losing ... dilemmas which confront both male and female. Jung saw at the centre of the psyche a double-structure, the duality of male and female, *anima* and *animus*. There is, he thought, in the life of the individual a kind of oscillation between the two principles. Thus, for example, reverie, wrote Bachelard (1969: 19–20) 'in its simplest and purest state belongs to the *anima*. Reverie without drama, without event of history gives us true repose, the repose of the feminine. There we gain gentleness of living. Gentleness, slowness, peace, such is the motto of reverie in *anima*.' The anima, the *cogito* of the reverie, is set in opposition to that of the thinker, the male principle, the active, dramatic principle which realises itself in narrative, event, incident. Each are the symbols of the kind of stances the sexuality of the body can take towards the worlds conjured in imagination or sensually experienced in confrontation with the world. While such descriptions as these are not real descriptions of flesh and blood individuals, they do condition one's thinking about what male and female *ought* to be as real living individuals. Why cannot the female be conceived as the active and the male as the passive principle? Why cannot individuals be left alone to explore their own natures without all these *Oughts* thrust upon them?

Feminism provides further impetus for a sexual critique of society, having implications for schooling. Sevenhuijsen and de Vries (1984: 15) see a new and an old feminism. The old feminism was anti-motherhood, marriage, heterosexuality – anti all the things the ancient images conditioned by paternalism said they should be. The authors, however, feel such a stance to be inadequate. In the new feminism they see a redefinition of motherhood which has important implications:

> If we look at society from the viewpoint of women with
> children there are many areas where feminist politics have still
> to be developed. The relationship between women and children
> is one. Society is extremely hostile to children. It is no accident
> that women and children are lumped together. Children are
> also oppressed by patriarchal attitudes. This shows itself in
> their total absence from public life. They are not tolerated in
> cafes, restaurants, public meetings. They cannot move away
> from their mothers, or they will be run over by a car. They
> cannot arrange their relations with other children and adults
> independently, because traffic and modern forms of living
> isolate people from one another. They are bound to their
> mothers and vice versa.
> We need a feminist view of the place and importance of
> children in the 'domestic sphere'.

Motherhood and children rather than fatherhood and children go together. Patriarchism is the common enemy.

The issue is, where do the children belong? They are not asked, of course. The squabble is over who belongs in the public and who belongs in the domestic or private realms? O'Brien (1981) writes:

Operating at the theoretical level, it is relatively easy to see the separation of the private and public as an abstract dialectical opposition of particular and universal, of individual and social, of the domestic and the biological, standing opposed to political and historical development. This is a commonplace sort of understanding, but male-stream thought has added the wrinkle that, as the biological is fixed and unchanging, development and change must take place in the public realm of politics, where man makes history.

Women and children are largely excluded from history (Walvin 1982; Deem 1980). The rights of adult women to participate at every level in society are being slowly won. Few take as seriously the rights of children to do the same (Holt 1974; Freeman 1983).

O'Brien considers that 'the separation of public and private realms is the material locus of generic struggle'. Women are associated with the private, the home, the centre of biological necessity and men are associated with the public, created under the freedom of rationality. Moreover

the separation of public and private in both the reproductive and productive spheres must have a political component. Paterfamilias, to preserve his freedom, requires family law, fraternal co-operation and ideological legitimization. He also, then as now, retained the option of brutality to enforce his domestic power. Far from being a paradigm of political power or the social precondition of public renown, patriarchy and the doctrine of potency are the products of political power, the creations of a brotherhood of fathers acting collectively to implement their definitions of manhood in social and ideological forms (pp. 103–4).

School, as a childrearing institution, is relegated to the private realm; politicians appear united in the belief that school should not be a political stage. In practice schooling is highly political. It is created as a deliberate act of intervention in the lives of the nation's children and that intervention is backed up through the force of law. School therefore, is ambivalent; it is an instrument by which the public realm invades or intervenes in the private realm of the individual. Nevertheless, school is, in a sense, unreal when compared to *the real world*. The real world is the world of the public stage of action. In the first instance, boy and girl are required to accept that they live within that unreal stage, that they are consigned to the world of the private where political activity is deemed inappropriate. In the second instance, boys are culturally directed towards the hope that they may act upon the public stage when childhood and schooling are left behind; girls are culturally directed to the private sphere of the home, of motherhood. The facts of educational and occupational discrimination support this. In the third instance, there is what may be called *the liberal trick* or the smokescreen of utilitarian individualism; O'Brien (1981) explains:

> revolutionary liberalism in its early enthusiasms thought it had
> solved (the public v. private domain) problems by the happy
> discovery that the individual and private interest coincided
> neatly with collective and public interest, and the articulation
> of this harmony of interests was the important ideological task
> of Adam Smith and his followers. It is a comforting doctrine
> for entrepreneurs, who to this day insist that their individual
> pursuit of profit is, happily, the best thing that can happen to
> society: what is good for General Motors being good for
> America, and then presumably what is good for America being
> good for the world at large. The failure of this radical
> utilitarianism to reflect the realities of lived lives was already
> apparent in the early years of the nineteenth century, and
> paved the way for the new political ideologies of socialism.
> (p. 97)

This third level justifies both the separation of public and private and also holds out the tantalising possibility of individual political action if it is expressed in a way to which the system can respond. The system, of course, has a safety-net; it is not the system that fails but the individual who fails if the opportunity cannot be realised.

Schooling, if analysed in terms of this 'genderic struggle' between private and public, becomes a complex battleground. In the first instance, both boy and girl are brought within a system of legal and professional care which separates them both from the domestic sphere and the real world of public affairs. Substitute parents are trained and hired, who, rather than being agents of the real parents, are agents of the 'public interest', executors of the law relating to education, experts who can be relied upon to intervene in the private lives of children for the public good. At the level of genderic differentiation, the public realities of male power and the cultural images of male jobs and female jobs erode any structural support school organisation and teacher practice may give to equality in subject choice. But sexism undeniably pervades the curriculum of schooling reinforcing the invisibility of women and, just as ironically, that of children. Where in the teaching of history, for example, is the historical importance of women or of children? In particular, Spender (1982: 4–5) points out:

> It is simply not possible for a fifteen-year-old girl, tired of hearing about men's wars in the nineteenth century, to confront the teacher with three possible alternative histories on the nineteenth century, viewed from the perspective of women, and to request that these books be included on the course. Even if such a fifteen-year-old did suspect that women had made just as much history as men but that men had chosen not to enter it in their records, even if she did suspect that men's records would look very different if women, and not just men, were to comment on them, where could she find a collection of books to make her point?

This directs attention towards a key educational issue, how can a child, in this case a girl, challenge a prevailing interpretation of the world or normative order? And, is it not the responsibility of teachers to resource such questioning and challenging so that the child may grow in his or her education? However, in classroom practice and pupil interpretation of the curriculum, the prevailing order is further reinforced. Measor (1984: 95–6), for example, described the different reactions of boys and girls to the science curriculum. Girls expressed squeamishness, disgust, fear, at experiments or dissections, boys expressed excitement:

> the activities in science contravened conventional views of what 'proper' girls should do, and therefore the girls resisted doing them. The pupils were reading sex-related characteristics into activities and things, and responding to them as a result. This response goes to make their sex-based identity clear to those round them. My suggestion is that the girls actively used aspects of the school to construct their identity, in this case their feminine identity. They are not therefore simply responding passively to school in terms of gender stereotypes. Science lessons provided an arena for the acting out of feminine susceptibilities in a public setting. They were a kind of backdrop against which signals could be displayed about feminine identity.

To teachers, girls are seen to be submissive and this submissiveness is seen to be a factor in their relatively greater achievement, although boys have 'much more imagination' and have 'real ability' (Clarricoates, in Deem, 1980: 29, 33). Unsurprisingly, girls become 'faceless' in the classroom (Stanworth 1981: 47). Research has shown the differential treatment given to boys and girls by teachers. It starts very early as shown in the research, for example of Rudduck and May (1983), so clear that the message has been received at ministerial level. The *Times Educational Supplement* (18 November 1983) reported Sir Keith Joseph as being 'disquieted' that girls were failing to reach their potential in maths and science.

The complaint is that while school provides opportunities open to both boys and girls for the individual pursuit of educational profit, in, say, the currency of examination qualifications, teachers (together with community expectations) inhibit this. Could it be that currently school could not operate any other way? School, as previously argued, is not viewed as a political arena, that is, an arena in which individuals act politically on a world historical stage – it is part of the private and not the public sphere. In short, such liberalism fails by any trick of the imagination to unite the public and private spheres in the pursuit of private educational profit as an asset for the future competitive struggle in the market place for equal job opportunity, just as it fails in terms of social class and in race.

Private face, public action

The formation of identity in school is, unsurprisingly, gender based. The division between public and private sphere also splits identity into what may be called private face and public action. Hollway (1984) identified the dilemma that private and public presented her as follows:

> ... 'man' and 'person' have been synonymous in western, patriarchal thought, as is evidenced by the use of the terms 'man', 'mankind' and 'he/him' as universals. As women we can strive to be 'people' and 'women'. However, because 'person' actually consist of all the attributes which are meant to be characteristic of men, there is an underlying contradiction. I think I managed this contradiction by being (or trying to be) as good as men in the public world, and even competitive in my relationships with men. At the same time, by virtue of maintaining a heterosexual relationship, I preserved my feminine identity.

The heterosexual relationship in the private domain preserved for her a feminine identity, while wanting to compete with men and

117

hence taking on a 'male' personality in the public domain. Alternatively we have seen that such an ambivalence in school may be resolved by rejecting 'male' subjects (Measor 1984). In this section, the focus will be on the construction of identity in ambivalent situations and the kinds of resolution an individual may attempt.

School, as earlier stated, has an ambivalent status. At one level, it is part of the private domain reserved for childbearing. At another level, as an institution for mass child management, it is a public and political arena. Again, at the level of child meets adult, child meets child and boy meets girl, it is a public stage for the public presentation of personality and gender identity. But in comparison with the real world, whether of home or the high street, school is a world apart, unreal, irrelevant to future action in the real world. These levels combine, like onion rings, to create the complex context to the private face of the individual, that vulnerable centre, opaque to the eyes of others, yet which invites probings and projections of all kinds from the Other who is suspicious of all that is private. The private then becomes a topic for public discourse and becomes an arena for political action when the Other becomes internalised as a censor, a superego controlling or influencing or in a sense, scripting, behaviour. For self the other becomes dangerous to the extent that the other can control or determine detrimentally the public definition of self. Both male and female are vulnerable to such detrimental public definitions. In chapter 4, during the discussion of the vandalised self, public image was shown to have multiple interpretations and consequences for the individual's sense of self and community. For the individual there is a desire to express one's self, to explore the possibilities which imagination devises and partake of the opportunities which others are seen to enjoy. Against this, the individual is vulnerable to Other in many ways. The desired-Other can be particularly powerful in defining one's self and can set up a variety of contradictory demands. Such a desired-Other is particularly dangerous and can exert a pressure toward conformity.

In particular, women have to resolve a number of powerful images constructed by men as the desired-Others in their lives – particularly deviance-images. As Davies (1979: 61) points out, 'girls in school seem to have to counter certain imputations of deviance and immorality which are applied only to the sex.' She continues:

> One girl tells me repeatedly one day how a male teacher had told her, 'You'm nothing but common.' Another two recount an episode:

'... called 'er a prostitute'.
"E says, by the way you're going on, you'll have to get
married before you're sixteen. I went mad, I did.'

The Deputy Headmistress herself tells me of another member
of staff who called a girl a slut. The examples of this kind of
stigma are numerous. Boys do not seem to have slurs cast on
their sexual morality in this way; thus it may be that girls
suffer a particular category of insult, are reacting to slights
specifically on their feminine identity.

Moreover, 'A top stream girl commented on not being allowed to
do child care: "They think if you're clever you're not going to go
out an' get married and have children, but if you're thick you are."
And of course the labels "thick" and "female" are not just additive
but interactive' (p. 62). Being female and 'thick' therefore consigns
the individual to the domestic realm of motherhood, whereas being
clever presumably widens opportunity or at least delays the
moment of domesticity.

Boys seem to enter the public stage with a better press than girls;
teachers tend to be more positive towards boys than girls. Boys are
open, girls are nasty behind your back; boys are active, girls are
passive – the cultural archetypes are systematically reproduced,
public and private self-image is controlled through various forms
of sexual imagery. Thus, while there is no real male counterpart to
the abusive term 'slut' and no real female counterpart to the use of
the male terms 'dog' and 'stud', such sexual imagery forms the
material through which self-images and images of others are
created. The point is that these are not exceptional images; they are
the images of everyday conversation and through their common-
placeness exert a powerful pressure which reduces the individual's
confidence to act spontaneously, individually.

The man, so the image goes, has to be strong in all his public
actions; to cry is to reveal weakness, to be girlish. There are a
variety of cultural forms for the public demonstration of male
hardness in relation to female softness: retaining the power of
decision-making in the public sphere; distancing the male from the
female through protective acts of politeness or shielding from un-
pleasantness; making aggressive demands or being aggressively dis-
missive; violent acts of molestation or rape. There are two poles to
the forms of demonstration: the one distances the woman from
public action and hence reduces her, the other assaults her and
hence reduces her; in both cases she is victim of male acts of
superiority. Both violate.

119

There is a sense in which it is assumed to be natural for men to diminish women by concerted distancing or aggression. In the example of Darren (Schostak 1983b: 92) women were by definition soft, they were incapable of controlling the boys who were 'messers'. Women teachers should, he felt, only be given to the 'brainy' ones who would not 'mess'. In such a perspective girls were fair game, to be dominated, stolen from, molested. Darren was a gang leader having close contacts with the community's adult underworld. He had already been convicted of robbing a post office and at the time was under a curfew order after having been picked up during one of the 1981 riots. Darren was in the fifth year. His brother, Joe, in the first year, was learning fast. He had several times been seen by teachers molesting girls. In one instance, he had been seen pushing a girl over, standing on her fingers, then running off with her bag. Such incidents were relatively common throughout the school. The public identity of 'trouble' develops. To be troublesome is to generate notoriety, to be known amongst one's peers, to stand out. One becomes an *outstanding* representative of the ideal image, the image desired by the desired-Other (in Darren's and Joe's case, their mates).

Private experience, however, can undermine the public image and become a challenge to identity. For Darren, such a moment was when he realised he was not going to get the job that he wanted. 'Tears came to my eyes,' he said. The hard man image broke. For Tony (see chapter 4) it came when he was 'in his best interests' placed in a residential centre. He took on the image of hard man, he tattooed it into his skin. Later, he told me about his life of fighting which he attributed to these experiences. He defined for me his public face and revealed something of his private face.

He had changed his image a number of times,'just because you got a different haircut people take you as a different thing'. More importantly, he realised that with different choices made in the past he could have been a very different person. He does not want his brother to go through what he has been through, 'it's the only thing I'd never want to see, see me brother put away or something like that, 'cos he wouldn't be able to I fink to be able to 'andle it. He's only just fifteen, he's got tattoo an' that. No different. All his mates have.' And, the conversation turned to Prince Andrew:

> 'I reckon if he, if he had say my parents for a mum and dad, reckon he'd be a different person 'cos it's just that his mum and dad make him dress like that and all that stuff. I bet that

some of them take drugs or something like that, it's obvious
innit, 'cos they've got the money for it . . .'
J.F.S.:   'So, all doing the same things but . . .'
Tony: 'Everyone's the same, everyone'll dress different and
that but they're roughly the same underneath, but different
ways. Everyone's different but they're the same, they're the
same in one way.'

Underneath the different public images he believes there is a private
'sameness'. For him, what is the same was made clear in discussing
the necessity of law and order. He spontaneously identified as one
of his pet hates people who believed in anarchy, a term made
popular by those who called themselves 'punks':

'I'm always arguing with anarchists 'cos they say "Oh, we
don't want the law an' that." But if there weren't no law you'd
probably get pratts walkin' in an' blowing you to bits with
shotguns an' all that. I would. I'd go out an' beat people up I
didn't like . . .'

Unless there are people to stop you doing things then 'Look at the
time the law are having now keepin' everyone in control. Can you
imagine what it's be like without them?' Central to his image of
self and of the Other is that both self and Other are essentially
dangerous unless controlled by an even more dangerous Other, the
police (who essentially, he hates). Thus, underneath it all, despite
the differences in public image, he and Prince Andrew are the same:
a variant of the mirroring strategy – just look in the mirror and
you'll see it's true. But there is another level to Tony, more private
still, a level he does not express in the public domain of the gang.
Although fighting is essential to his public image of hardness, he
has a developed sense of fairness which in turn conflicts sometimes
with his public image:

'Like if I'm in a group, if someone starts a fight I'll make sure
it's one on to one. But the other night two Yanks walked down
the road and, I don't know, one of them said something or
something and there was about twenty of us. They all run up
the road an' one of them started fighting with them. The rest
were all for joining in on the other one, but I say 'leave it, it's
one to one'. And they stop fighting, and I said to him 'cos this
little Yank he was a right cocky one and I say to him I say 'it
ain't worth the hassle 'cos look there's fifty of us, an' you only
going to get your mate an' yourself beat up so why don't you
leave it.' And that was just it. I like to see a fair fight. (. . . So)

121

> I don't like to see loads of people on to one person. Some of
> my mates will listen to me, the others'll just bundle in. But I
> won't. (... However, he later said) If you were with all your
> mates, say there's seven of you and there's seven other geysers
> and you all start fighting, you ain't going to stand there and
> watch your mates fighting without joining in, are you?'
> (... later)
>
> *J.F.S.:* 'Well you obviously make up your own mind about
> things, but I mean when you're in a group do you find it hard
> to sort of not do what other people do?'
> *Tony:* 'Yeah, yeah, that is hard.'
> *J.F.S.:* 'Can you describe what's hard about it?'
> *Tony:* 'If all your mates want to do something you can't
> really say "Oh, no I don't want to do it," can you? 'Cos
> they're all going to start calling me a cunt an' all that aren't
> they?'

The public image with the gang dominates his sense of self. For
Tony in the public world of the male-defined drama of hardness,
trouble and 'law 'n' order' there is virtually no one to talk with, no
one with whom he can present and explore his private sense of self.
One day, he had taken LSD and was having a 'bad trip'. He spent
the night searching for the one person in his life with whom he felt
he could talk and get help, the teacher at his off-site unit. He never
found him. There is a complex interaction of public and private
domains. In the classroom the private domain of individuals like
Tony becomes concealed and overlooked. There is no time for
talking. Sensitive to the public stage of the gang, Tony therefore
had no safe space within it, in which to explore and find support
for his private values, experience, problems. Nevertheless, there was
an alternative domestic realm defined in relation to his public world
of hardness – the world of women. The relation can be described
through the example of Carol, who also saw herself as hard.

She had been suspended from her school for beating up a teacher
and had finally arrived in the same off-site unit as Tony. While on
the one hand being hard, she also wanted to cultivate a caring
image. Thus at school:

> 'I had about two days a week at school, most of the time I was
> nipping out. When I did go I used to beat up Mr Haynes and
> Mr Stones. 'Cos they keep tryin' to pull my hair. I used to
> swear at 'm. Just didn't like it there. The teachers didn't like
> me and I didn't like them. We just didn't get on. (...) (The
> Headteacher) reckoned that was me, Terry, Sharon, Jill and

Heather, he reckoned we were the five worst in the school and
he wanted us out. He's only got Terry there now. He expelled
all of us really for no reason, really. 'Cos he didn't know about
me hittin' Mr Haynes or nothin 'cos he didn't used to grass me
up. That was for swearin' at Miss Sykes.'
J.F.S.: 'What sort of things made you swear at them?'
Carol: 'I don't know, I just, eh, come up to you and they
start going like this, poking you, an' think they can pull your
hair and everything, really treat you horribly. I think I just
couldn't handle it so I used to ... 'cos I got a very bad temper
once I lose it, I used to keep losing my temper with them.'

She would like to work at a place like the off-site unit. She feels
she would be good at it because:

'I helped a lot here. I helped Terry.'
J.F.S.: 'In what way?'
Carol: 'He used to take glue. I stopped him from doing that
didn't I?'
Sheila: 'And Brian.'
Carol: 'Brian. I really did help Brian (telephone rings ...) til
um, (a teacher did something) and that made him lose his
temper and that just threw him. ... They always come and talk
to me. All the boys come and talk to me 'cos they know I
don't say nothing. But Terry, he was really bad, he was really
into glue when I first come here and I stopped him from doing
that. He don't touch glue now ...'

She did not talk of the girls coming to her for help. She repeated
several times during the interview that the boys could talk to her.
With her she thought they could reveal something of their private
pain: 'I'm always helping other people an' everyfing, y' know, help
me forget about mine.' Her own problems did not include drugs:

'(It) put me off seeing how stupid they reacted afterwards 'cos I
was in a room with a load of 'm, there was one who thought
he was Spiderman. He was trying to climb up the wall. Chrissy
chasing the pavement stones and everything, and I thought,
"well, if that's the sort of thing that do to you I don't want
that". I just packed it in. I've only done it once – won't do it
anymore. It just get you though, you just act like an idiot
don't you? They reckon they do it 'cos they've got problems.
As soon as you come out of that your problems are still gonna
be there. They aren't going to go away. Same's drink really, y'
know.'

She 'just kept away from all the people that done it and I didn't do it no more' - a solution Tony could not manage. She manipulated her public stage in order to control her own behaviour at least to some extent. However, her own deeper problems were not that easy to manage. She could never forget her background, as she called it: 'Everybody here's got a background. Everybody's got a background here, that's why they're here.' Her problem is her temper: 'I want to stop it if I could but I can't see how I can':

> 'people out there that can turn round, you know, (and say) "control your temper" and things like that 'cos (...) I've only been like this about three years ago, since we left my dad I've been like this'.
> *J.F.S.:* 'Since leaving your dad?'
> *Carol:* 'Yeah, think me dad made me like it. 'Cos I lived with me dad. He beat me up an' everything. Just turned me vicious to everybody then because of what he *done* to me. I can't stop myself being' (inaudible due to outside noises).

She is aware, in outline, of the cause of her emotional problems. The problems are defined according to the effects they have on others. Temper is directed towards others and is in itself meaningless without reference to others. Temper becomes intensely meaningful to her in relation to the *vicious-Other* who in turn reproduces himself in her as the *vicious-self*. She contrasts this with her relationship to the teacher at the off-site unit. There is a sense in which he does nothing. For example, another strategy (other than 'caring' - listening to their problems) by which she defines her relationship with boys is through 'winding up'. She is an expert in winding-up (an example of this in a complex interaction with 'caring' will be analysed in the next chapter); it is a way in which she constructs her own sexual identity and manipulates male responses to her and to others in often a cruel manner - something few teachers she has met understood:

> 'It's like here (boys and girls) are all really treated the same, aren't we? Like, if the boys don't get on they get told but you find - like (the teacher) always know if we been winding up the boys. He don't turn round and blame the boys. We wind up the boys and we are the ones that are getting into trouble. That is different in a normal school. They always prefer to tell the boys off, most of the time. They reckon it's always the boy who swipes the girl who always tend to turn round and try and blame the boy. We do here, don't we? We never get away with

it because (the teacher) know we are lying. He never really
punish you or anything do he? He – you know, say it is really
bad but no one do anything about it, really. And you get some
stupid boys that go and do the pool table in and the seats an'
that – which I think is a bit stupid – because if it weren't for
(the teacher) we wouldn't be nowhere now, would we? We'd
hang about the streets and that.'

Winding-up is a strategy which can be used to reproduce in others
viciousness, vindictiveness, and foolishness. The teacher is fooled
by misconstruing the cause and nature of the interaction, and the
boys become vicious towards one another, they fight or try and get
their own back on the girls. The teachers get involved and also
become wound-up in the process of attempting to re-assert authority in a situation where they have been deceived into acting inappropriately. On the public stage each actor attempts to retrieve
something of their role-defined identity. Carol, however, identifies
the importance of the private domain as a way of winding-down
and allowing the sexes to be 'treated the same'. It is, of course,
not an instant solution, nor is it a complete solution. A critique
of her own sexual identity has not begun, nor even of the sexual
identity of others, nor of the sexually defined power relations
each hold toward the other. The world is still divided into what
boys do and what girls do. There is, however, a start towards wanting 'fairness', even with regard to subject choice in school. In her
experience:

'(here) we're allowed to do everything like. In a normal school,
if I had a motorbike – that motorbike thing we're having 'ere,
training yer how to ride a motorbike an' that. If that was in a
normal school the girls wouldn't be able to do that. You know,
like (the teacher here), if we want to, I don't know – like
football and things like that, when I went to (my other school)
to play football we weren't allowed to play it, 'cos they
reckoned that was a boy's game, things like that and we liked
playing, messin' about with footballs and that and we weren't
allowed to do that because we were girls. (. . .) in schools you
get mechanics work and things like that. You can do in
mechanics studies and they've got engines and everything and
they won't even let you do that, will they? Like boys they like
to go in and do cooking, school needlework. At school the
only thing you are allowed to do what the boys do is
metalwork and woodwork. But they really funny about letting
you go and do that . . . machines. (. . .) I loved woodwork and

metalwork I did. I loved it. (...) (But) they put me in cooking and needlework and that's how I started off skiving because I didn't like it. I couldn't handle it. I didn't like it. (...) And the cookery teacher hated me and the woodwork teacher didn't mind me. I never had to do nothing so I didn't mind. I used to just go round and help my mates and that.'

She wanted the opportunity to do those things that for some reason gave her a sense of satisfaction. The public stage of subject choice gave further opportunity for the drama of 'care' and 'hate', 'handling' a situation and losing control of it.

For many young people the demands made upon them to construct a suitable sexual identity are contradictory. Images of manhood and womanhood are caricatured everywhere in the ideal images of advertising, film and comic book; the caricatures to be taken as realistic and desirable goals. The public image of sexual maturity – the image of how to be the desired-Other – conflicts with private experiences, the vulnerable-self. The crowd at once torments, tyrannises and provides a self-denying support. To Carol, the boys are always fighting, always spoiling things, always destroying things, just showing off, but 'Get some of them, when they are on their own, they are all right really, once they get with their friends they just change and they think that's great to go and beat up fings (...) 'cos they feel stupid in front of their friends and that.' It's an open secret. Like Tony said, 'If all your mates want to do something you can't really say "Oh, no I don't want to do it," can you? 'Cos they're all going to start callin' me a cunt an' all that aren't they?' Tony belongs to the world of the gang, an all-male world, where virtue is defined in terms of hardness, fighting, having a laugh. Carol's world is defined in reference to it at two distinct levels: the public and the private. At the public level she winds up the boys, makes them caricatures of their ideal of manly hardness, as she becomes a caricature of the temptress winding men around her little finger. At the private level she winds them down, allows them to tell her their problems, mothers them. She is compelled into a role, the female role of caring. However, she is a catalyst also. For some of the boys she has created the conditions for their re-assessment of their public presentation of self. Terry, for example, changed quite dramatically during his stay at the off-site unit, not in appearance, but in his attitude towards others. Carol was convinced she had had a major role in bringing about this transformation. Terry attributed it to 'thinking'. He did some private thinking whilst out fishing, a passion of his. His changed attitude on race was discussed during the previous chapter (see also Schostak and Logan 1984). He moreover reduced his dependency on glue sniffing and eventually eliminated it (as did another boy in the group) and became significantly less aggressive yet more assertive of his changed views in the group. He had begun a systematic critique of values he had held unquestioningly, values represented in the ideal image of manly violence represented for him initially by Tony, the person he emulated in dress, hair style and behaviour during his early days at the centre. Tony himself finally left the centre. For a laugh he had chased and beaten-up a black boy, crushing him into unconsciousness, hospitalising him. For some weeks it was possible the charge might be manslaughter. But the boy recovered. Tony served his time, became a model prisoner – the world he had entered was too hard for him to handle. But there the story for us must end. Tony is still working on his problems, working through what kind of self he wants to be in relation to the kind of self his public demands.

The integration of public and private

The separation of the private and the public, the vulnerable and the hard, is at times brutally enforced, physically, psychologically. The public stage of the gang is as much at odds with the private sphere as is the ambivalent realm of schooling. Ling (1984) cited the headmaster who wrote that he had counselled a boy 'to avoid bringing his feelings into school'. School, like gang, is not about private feelings; that is a domestic matter. Private feelings are a threat to public order, whether of gang or of school. The world for self is genitally organised, not the children's but the parents':

> In genital organisation we identify with the penis; but the penis we are is not our own, but daddy's; or at least, in it we and the father are one. In genital organisation body and soul are haunted, possessed, by the ghost of father; coitus is performed in a dream, by the ghost. (Brown 1966: 57–8)

Carol and Tony, as many others, had brutal fathers (compare also Debbie in Schostak 1983b). Historically we all have brutal fathers – childhood is a nightmare from which we are only just awakening (de Mause 1974). Politically the public sphere dominates the private sphere, penetrating it, rendering it passive, subordinating it to a servicing function. Mothers, teachers, those who care, service the needs of the state, the male order, whether conceived as patriarchy or fraternity. Schooling usurps the power of the patriarch to control the experiences of the sons and daughters, separates both home and patriarch from the citizens of the state. In *locus parentis* schooling returns to children an alienated domestic sphere, a false family which at another level is set against the rebellion of youth against the 'fathers' which would set into motion the old cycle which first gave birth to fraternal organisation, the state. 'To know the reality of politics', says Brown (p. 15), 'we have to believe the myth, to believe what we were told as children. Roman history is the story of the brothers Romulus and Remus, the sons of the she-wolf; leaders of gangs of juvenile delinquents ...' Revolution is born in youthful energy and critique (Heer 1974). The forms of the genital organisation of the political are: matriarchy, patriarchy, fraternity and the sisterhood. There seems to be an historical order here, the later a rebellion against the first, each defining a moment in the genital organisation of the social, defining the boundaries between the private and the public, the passive and the active, the subordinate and the dominant.

Everyday life becomes a complex interplay between these different stances, these distinct genital orderings of the social as between private and public. At any point the individual can be rendered absurd; a deft move from one standpoint to another will accomplish it – parental authority can be set against youthful rebellion, brotherhood against sisterhood; each winding the other up in a continual shifting of ground, no reconstruction towards a stable set of values is possible. These are the marks of a destructive irony which pervades social life, where multiple and mutually exclusive public values and private values together undercut whatever securities and cetainties they separately proclaim.

Unless there is some firm value which can anchor the self, both self and Other become dangerous, mutually destructive in games of 'hardness', winding-up – games which both girls and boys play in their different ways. The play is a laugh, it is also deadly and frequently experienced as 'my problem', a function of 'background'. It is, of course, a myth that girls must not be hard, not violent. They fight. But boys are supported in their hardness by the equation of hardness with manliness (proclaimed in adverts to join the army, proclaimed in hero-worship of the military, proclaimed in film after film, proclaimed in sport). Girls, although as likely to experience hardness and take on hardness as a strategy for reducing public vulnerability, are not supported by the ideal visions of femininity proclaimed throughout the media and in the folklore of everyday life. Their courses therefore differ. Boys take the public career, girls the domestic. The problems, however, are unlikely to be resolved, but rather reproduced in their children in the way that both Tony and Carol carry images of their fathers and reproduce in themselves the violence of their fathers (cf. Renvoize 1979; Pizzey 1982). The most violent institution in society after the police and the military is the family:

> With the exception of the police and the military, the family is perhaps the most violent social group, and the home the most violent social setting, in our society. A person is more likely to be hit or killed in his or her home by another family member than anywhere else or by anyone else. Nearly one out of every four murder victims in the United States is a family member. Similarly, in Africa, Great Britain, and Denmark the greatest proportion of murders are intrafamilial. (Gelles and Straus 1979)

And what of school? From the point of view of the young people such as Tony and Carol school is a violent place, it reinforces them in their images of hardness and getting what you want through force regardless of the wishes of the other.

Constructing an alternative vision of the self, a self established upon firm values, is not easy. It is possible especially if it finds the support of others. Fuller (1984) writes of some black girls who, being black and female, 'are in a doubly subordinate position within the social formation' but they had a positive acceptance of themselves as both black and female. This positive acceptance appears to be crucial:

> their positive identity as black but knowledge of racial discrimination in Britain, their positive identity as female but belief that both in Britain and the Caribbean women were often accorded less than their due status – meant that the girls were angry at the foreclosing of options available to them as blacks and as women.

As a result

> Their consequent anger and frustration, unlike that of their black male peers, was not turned against themselves or translated into an automatic general dislike of whites or the opposite sex. Rather their feelings and understandings gave particular meanings to achievement through the acquisition of educational qualifications.

However,

> their sense of self-worth did not derive from the acquisition of
> academic qualifications nor, in the future, from obtaining a
> 'good' job; rather their pursuit of these ends was given
> meaning by their existing knowledge of their own worth and
> their understanding that this was often denied.

Such attitudes made the girls more independent than others in that
they had 'adopted a programme of "going it alone" in which those
aspects of schooling to do with acquiring qualifications had an
important part.'

From a standpoint of certainty of self-worth it becomes possible
both to 'go it alone' and to challenge and resist the powers of
others. That certainty may be reinforced through sub-cultural images of self. The integration of public and private spheres comes
about when self can on the basis of private experience of self transform the cultural environment as given toward the desired; the
private becomes a basis for political action, the transformation of
self and others' views of self through action.

Chapter 7

Violence and the construction of reality

The process of schooling (not education) occurs not solely within the confines of school buildings, but wherever one person seeks to instruct another in right conduct and ensure (via surveillance and sanctions) compliance. What is being schooled is the individual's vision of reality. This vision of reality is developed through the cultural symbols of society – people are schooled in expert opinion, that is, any opinion which counts as *the real and commonsensical view of the world which only mad people would dispute.* Schooling sets the boundaries to the kinds of questions and challenges that individuals can direct towards this *real world.* Such schooling is in strict opposition to education.

Education requires as its first principle unconditional freedom to question and to challenge and to celebrate life. Education leads towards a sense of individuality as schooling leads towards socialisation in group-defined identities: the one violates the principles of the other. As Ortega y Gasset has pointed out, one's knowledge of the world is not built up through direct experience of it alone but through one's acceptance of others' conceptions of the world. The reality thus conceived is presumptive rather than directly experienced or immediately known; it exists more in one's imagination of it as conceived and proclaimed by trusted-others than in one's sensual, concrete grasp of it. The world, then, is largely vicarious, constructed out of presumptive images of it conceived not by self but by others, historical others whose names may long be forgotten. The reality that is said to be known by any individual is as much imagined as real, as much myth as empirical as in the sexual or racial myths already explored. A dialectic arises between the experienced and the presumed. Experience can be schooled through the images of presumed realities. A presumed reality identifies for the individual the stances that he or she can *realistically* take towards the world. And these stances essentially reproduce the presumptive realities embraced as real. In the case of the violent imagination the dialectic in simple form can be described in this way:

> For an act to be considered as violent it must be interpreted and/or experienced as such by *at least one* of the participators. At an existential level – in the gut, the bones, the heart – one feels torn, raped, violated. There is a pain which perhaps cannot be articulated. However, the images of those involved in the felt sense of violation, their acts, their words, their postures, remain. Such images may stay personal, never finding expression in communication to others. Perhaps the imagination plays with the images at night, in dreams. If communication becomes possible, images become shared. They may be shared in conversation as anecdotes or may come to serve an almost mythic purpose. This matrix of violent images, anecdotes, folk tales, myths, forms a context within which any future act is interpreted as being violent and becomes communicable to others. (Schostak 1983b: 168)

The matrix of violent images is dialectically shaped through presumptive images conceived through the processes of myth, folklore and gossip in interaction with any immediate experiences of violation. Thus the circularity of image colouring experience and experience being raw material for imagination maintains a sense of historical reality which is dialectically produced. It is like lifting one's self up by one's bootstraps – the self creates itself and its explanations of the world out of the images conceived in some presumptive reality and finds confirmations in that presumptive world. Breaking out of this circularity is not easy and may even prove to be impossible for many. To be thus schooled is to be schooled into a circular track. It is the circularity of peering into mirrors which are positioned to reflect the self in an infinite series, each reflection reflecting its own image. To challenge the safe circularity of image and experience in a way which breaks the infinite mirroring leads to feelings of great anxiety as can be seen in the experiments of Garfinkel (1967). The comforting taken-for-grantedness of the world for some unsuspecting victims can be violently ripped apart by acts which, on the surface at least, seem quite innocuous. For example, a student would return home and act as a stranger, treating parents or wife as host. Such acts caused deep emotional rifts which were not easy to repair.

The schooled self is a comfort to itself; the questioned self is anxious, defensive, touchy; the one who questions, places the self into doubt, is offensive to the schooled self. For example, a teacher concerned to create an environment of self-directed learning in her classroom rarely used instructional techniques, would continually question and throw pupils back upon their own resources. For many, this style of classroom management where the teacher became a resource to the pupil rather than a controller worked well. Others felt de-skilled, lost and spent their time messing about. During one lesson the children were working at their own pace, and the teacher walked around asking if they needed any help. She carried a tape recorder because she was interested in action research as a means of improving her own practice. As she approached one table of boys, Ginger suddenly said:

Ginger: 'Quiet everybody on this table ... I think we'd better get on. We're gonna be taped.'
Teacher: 'It's a bit late getting on though isn't it?'
Joe: 'But I did start.'
Teacher: 'No point just going all silent just because I'm standing here.'

Rather than tell them off she wanted them to realise that just because she was near by there was no need for a sudden pretence to work or even show interest in work. Why, she frequently asked me, did pupils project attitudes upon her that she didn't have? For these boys the teacher was supposed to tell them what to do and make them do it. She, however, wanted to break down such attitudes in order to pave the way for what she saw as *real* learning, self-motivated learning, learning for the enjoyment of it. This attitude however, breached their taken-for-granted expectations as to how a teacher should behave and how pupils should behave. She was not reflecting back to them their image of a teacher and a pupil. The boys entered into a caricature of working. At random a boy began to make plays upon the words used in his textbook. The teacher responds to a comment by one of the boys and asks:

Teacher: 'Joe, what did you say then?'
Joe: 'Can we read in our heads?' (he had actually been saying 'Candid camera, isn't it?' He felt the lesson was a joke)
Teacher: 'I've no objection.'
Joe: 'Ah good.' (said superciliously)
Teacher: (continuing) 'I never had. I've said you could choose how you went about your learning ...'

133

> *Joe*: 'Well we'd rather not learn ...'
> *Teacher*: '... in your own way.'
> *Joe*: '... being on a tape.'

The interaction is strained. The boys become giggly while maintaining an exaggerated air of politeness until Ginger says:

> *Ginger*: 'The tape-recorder, can you do it round 'ere?'
> (giggles)
> *Teacher*: 'I'm sorry, what did you say?'
> *Ginger*: 'Nothing.' (giggles)
> *Teacher*: 'Uh, did you say something that bothers you to
> have to repeat. Do you feel ashamed?'
> *Ginger*: 'No.'
> *Joe*: 'No you can hear that on the tape.' (loudly, scoffingly)

Due to the manner in which the boys are behaving the teacher thinks that Ginger had said something derogatory whereas in fact it had been quite trivial. In fact, Ginger has forgotten what he did say. However, the attitude each is taking towards the other escalate or wind-up the emotions of each. Both sides feel highly threatened but in different ways. The context has become one of mutual suspicion and barely disguised hostility until one of the boys says:

> *Dave*: 'Miss, can we move?'
> *Teacher*: 'David, you know the procedures I set up in the
> classroom. You don't need to ask me.'
> *Joe*: 'They don't want to move. That was a hint for
> something else I think.'
> *Dave*: 'No it wasn't.'
> *Joe*: 'I don't want to be on tape that'll be ...'
> *Teacher*: 'I'm simply recording your learning experience at the
> moment. That's all.'
> *Ginger*: 'Oh, um, l. ...' (reads questions from his textbook)
> (a girl attracts the teacher's attention)
> *June*: 'Um, you know the results of the test what they
> done ...?'
> *Alan*: 'Horlicks, Horlicks.'

The teacher continually tries to clarify her attitude towards classroom management, the procedures she wants to establish – that the pupils have a high degree of autonomy concerning seating arrangements, work pace, task choice and the extent to which the teacher is used as a resource for the learning aims of the pupil. Out of habit David asks permission, indicating that he expects the typical teacher–pupil authority relationship to be in force. The teacher, however, reasserts the opposite. Joe reads a meaning into David's request which David denies. Joe appears to assume that in the context of suspicion being generated in the various exchanges, that David intends an alternative meaning, a meaning hostile to the teacher, a meaning which reinforces and reproduces the expected distance between teacher and pupil. The teacher again tries to make her intention clear, 'I'm simply recording your learning experience', employing terminology probably alien to the pupils. Ginger immediately responds by taking on a caricatured and quite hollow posture of the pupil busily engaged in apparent learning. At this point June, a girl who is highly supportive of the teacher, asks a question. The response from another of the boys on the table is 'Horlicks, Horlicks' with the emphasis upon 'licks', 'licks' (although no doubt the homonymic alternative 'whore' is not missed) the term employed to all pupils who appear to be 'sucking up', 'creeping', 'crawling' to the teacher. Thus, again pupil identities are at stake, as through name-calling the boys reassert their view of the expected relations between pupils and teachers. There is a clear 'genital ordering' (see previous chapter) to the drama; the boys have a view of classroom life that seeks to reproduce desired male identities (being 'one of the lads', 'having a laugh') which are threatened by any teacher style which returns to the individual the responsibility for his or her own learning. In such a situation there can no longer be 'creeps' who 'lick' the teacher in order to obtain teacher praise and favours – there is only the pupil engaged in his or her own learning requesting help from the teacher at his or her own pace. That is why the boys must maintain and project an attitude of suspicion and hostility quite at variance with the teacher's expressed intentions. Throughout the incident the boys maintain their sexual identities through sexual puns (e.g. one boy is going to America; a boy says 'Southern Yank' and another replies 'I thought you were going to say something else then' i.e., wank). Finally, the high point of suspicion arrives:

Joe: (loudly, getting close to tape-recorder)'No, I just want to make a point. The 'ead is taping this just to get us into trouble.'

Dave: 'Trying to find out what we've learnt, is that why you're taping us? You see, I ain't been in for too long. So, I don't know nothin' practically. I only been to ...'

Joe: 'Whenever we go to see (the head of department) we'll be in trouble won't we?'

> *Ginger*: 'Like we did when we had to go and see him last time.'
> *Dave*: 'Well, I didn't I only been to three lessons.'
> *Joe*: 'Yeah, I know 'cos the rest you bunked off Dave.'
> *Dave*: 'Don't tell everyone (laughs). No, I didn't because ...'

The taping, according to Joe, can only mean one thing, that it is to be used as proof for the headteacher to get them into trouble. Since the conventions of the classroom have been broken, this can be the only conventional explanation. This leads to Dave presenting his excuse which is immediately revealed as truancy by Joe. The fraternity is tied by and equal only in its guilt; individualistic moves to escape blame are not supported.

Pupils are frequently a conservative force against any move to innovate in the classroom (MacDonald 1970; Hull and Rudduck 1981; Hull 1984). For an innovation to be successful, a teacher must make allies of the pupils. The schooled expectations of the pupils were challenged by what was perceived as the inappropriate stance taken by the teacher. The presumed reality behind the tape recording confirmed the pupils in their suspicious attitude towards the teacher. It was a circularity which they could not see through. The teacher herself felt very anxious and hurt by the episode. She found that pupils needed time to relearn what classroom learning could be under different circumstances and that any change in the taken-for-granted rules of the classroom would lead to emotional stress, frequently releasing hostile feelings towards teachers. The underlying experience is that of violation, a violence against intended and presumed realities. In order to analyse this process in some depth an incident in which Carol (who was discussed in the previous chapter) will be discussed next.

Carol's day

The incidents involve Carol and two teachers, Harry and Mary, at an off-site unit for pupils that conventional schools felt unable to deal with. The teacher in charge at the centre, Barry, is away ill that day. Carol, it may be recalled, is a self-acknowledged expert at 'winding-up'. The process begins this day with Carol objecting to the work demands being made by Harry. Moreover, Harry is not pleased to have Carol in the centre. He made it clear to me that he was apprehensive about her having turned up. He tells her that 'two or three things' she has already done have made him feel

upset. It is clear that even at the start of the day, Harry's appre-
hension has had its effect. Also, Carol is not pleased at the absence
of Barry and this has affected her mood and her responses to the
two teachers. A divide quickly establishes itself between the teachers and the pupils, with Carol as the focus of attention. The group
of girls around Carol talk while two or three boys are getting on
with some reading. Mary asks if the group of girls are reading. One
curtly replies 'Yes! Yes! Yes!' Carol accuses Mary of giving people
a headache or a tummy ache. Mary replies:

Mary: 'Why do you say that to me 'cos I've spoken about
one sentence to you that's all. Do you have to be, do you have
to .... Look if you don't want to come here ...'
Carol: 'I don't like it when Barry's not here. That's what I
don't like 'cos you two take airs an' fink you're it.'

(During this one boy, Terry, whistles the theme tune of the
Laurel and Hardy pictures)

Mary: 'Well because we do take over when Barry's not here.'
Carol: 'I reckon you'd chuck me, ask Barry if you could
chuck me out for just being like this. 'Cos you can't. (....)
You got Brian chucked out because you didn't like him but
you're not going to get me chucked out.'
Mary: 'I did not chuck him out. I asked him to go home and
I was to talk to him and that was years and years ago.'
Carol: 'Why's that *years and years ago*?' (parroting Mary's
voice)

It will be useful to move towards a formal analysis of this. Barry
is a central character in the drama and influences the course of
events and their interpretation *because of* his absence – he was not
there to present any alternative explanations. Therefore, his
absence facilitated the clash of presumed realities played out between Mary and Carol. Barry, in this case, as is Brian (but for
different reasons), is the desired-Other. Mary and Harry are negatively defined in relation to the desired-Other. Brian, for Carol,
becomes also an object of care. It has been argued previously that
Carol uses care as a way of defining an adequate gender identity
for herself in relation to the boys. Each member of the drama as
it is unfolding has reasons for feeling violated. Mary justifies the
action against Brian:

Mary: '... because it's lies, that's his problem dear, that he
lies.'

> *Carol*: 'Yeah, an' everybody treats 'im as though 'e was mental an' 'e's not mental 'e never spook at me 'cos I never used to nag 'im.'

Carol's voice falls in tone and there seems to be an emotional lull. Brian would flare up violently and became too much for the centre to handle. Mary and Carol are challenging each other's version of the truth. It is important that Brian is absent, again because he cannot present his own story. Therefore there is no final arbiter of the truth, even if Mary could be persuaded to accept the words of one she considers a liar. Carol identifies her own experience with Brian, emphasising the importance of not nagging him. In these exchanges Carol and Mary are working upon each other's self-images; the one tries to transform the other through the medium of contests concerning the true intentions of another, one who is a desired-Other for Carol, but a dangerous-Other for Mary. Carol placed the problem with Mary's teaching strategy (nagging) whereas Mary placed the problem within Brian's nature (lying).

After a period of relatively quiet work the contest begins again. Yet again a trivial issue initiates it. An argument develops over the placing of name cards on work trays. Carol feels the practice is childish. Mary replies that Barry had insisted on it. Carol notices that no name card exists for Brian and sharply points this out. Mary calmly replies that there is a blank card and tray if he should return. Carol returns to the attack:

> *Carol*: 'If you'd your way, Mary, you wouldn't 'ave me back.'
> *Mary*: 'You can't put, you can't say what I would think because you don't *know* what I think.'
> *Carol*: 'We know quite well what you thought of Brian.'
> *Mary*: (overriding Carol) 'You don't, you have no idea . . .'
> *Carol*: 'You think the same, the same of Brian what you think of us now.'
> *Terry*: 'Yeah.'
> *Mary*: 'You have no idea what I think because I haven't told you what I think. You can't say it out of the top of your head.'

At this point Carol has brought about a tactical victory. She has now generalised the issue from 'this is how you think of me and Brian' to 'this is how you think of us – all the pupils'. She has tactically transformed the situation into one of Us v. Them. Mary brings a temporary halt to the process by pointing out that Carol cannot reach within Mary's head and *know* what she is thinking. That is, what is known, what is being contested, is in fact a presumed knowledge; the reality of the intention cannot be tested or proven.

Attention drifts either to work or, in the case of the girls, to a conversation about a particular boy's style of dress. The next stage of the drama occurs when Harry becomes concerned about the obvious lack of work:

Harry: 'Carol, I think I'm getting serious about this. *Nothing* is happening here.'
Carol: '*STOP*' (then it becomes inaudible)
Harry: 'All out of here. All out of here. Either you do that or you do something.'
Carol: '*I was reading!!!*'
Harry: 'Carol, since you came in here this morning every thing was upset.'
(some giggling)
Carol: 'Don't make me laugh. I've been readin'. I can show you what I've read. I read to there, right up to there. So don't start on me. Start on the people ain't done nothing.'
Harry: 'Right, then shut your mouth.'
Carol: 'Try to shut me then.' (grumpy cadence)
Harry: 'And do it quietly.'
Sally: 'Ho dear.' (affected tiredness)
Harry: 'Otherwise my girl we'll have you out of here.'
Sally: 'Eh?'
Carol: 'Got rid of Tony, you got rid of Brian, and now you're trying to get rid of me.'

Carol begins to define others as more deserving of blame, 'start on the people ain't done nothing' – a theme she returns to later. At times the shouting is shrill. Emotions are at this point being wound tautly. Carol again accuses Harry and Mary of wanting to get rid of her and those boys she cared for. Mary rejoins the battle but her air of calm is shattered and her voice is on edge:

Mary: 'What do you mean got rid of Tony? Now will you talk sensible. He's *inside!*'
Carol: 'I *know* he is.'
Mary: 'Well, how did we get rid of him?'
Carol: 'I s'pose you ... No one used to help him' (...)

Tony, at that time, awaited trial for a brutal assault of which he was later convicted. Tony, as Carol put it in her interview, had a background, a background of problems (described in the previous chapter). Carol's accusation is very clear and very hurtful. Tony has been scarred by life and returns those scars to others through his perpetual fighting. He is a vandal and is vandalised. And Mary, it is implied, has contributed to Tony's problems not through what she has done, but through what she has neglected to do. Mary, who affects a mothering attitude to all the pupils, is upset:

Mary: 'Oh God, we used to cuddle him and talk to 'im for hours on end. You've only been here about four weeks, since Whitsun dear.'
Sally: 'Yeah, because she's been in 'ospital.'
Mary: 'Well, it's not our fault. It's not her fault.'

It may at this point be usefully mentioned that Carol in her interviews had said that in thinking of another's problems she could lose her own. She had been in hospital for an abortion. The ambiguity in whether or not it was 'her fault' became the topic of ribald joking amongst the girls. Cuddling and talking for hours are ultimately not enough. Carol clearly points to the major issue, the problems of Tony and by implication of all the pupils had failed to be adequately addressed and resolved in some realistic manner. Tony's tragedy was one that could have been avoided if only ... if only what? The solution seems as if it ought to be within reach but it is not. Neither Mary nor Harry have fully realised this. They appear to offer a solution which is essentially inadequate to the problems requiring solution. They have to deal with a whole 'background' as Carol understands it, a biography which has been exploited, torn, abused. Against this background the acts of help offered by teachers stand out as either hollow, shabby or irrelevant at worst, well meaning but futile at best. And, of course, both sides feel hurt. Carol again turns to her fear of being chucked out – abandoned, like Tony and Brian. Abandonment, being chucked out, is a potent image. All of them have had a background of abandonment, being chucked out, and in return, of running away, becoming absent. One might call these 'framing images', they pattern all experiences by being the background against which all future experiences are seen, interpreted, shaped.

The off-site unit carries the implicit promise that they have arrived at a place which will not abandon them, a place to which they can choose to come. It appears this promise is being contested. As Terry says to Carol, 'We don't chuck anyone out.' The sense of 'ownership' here does not reside in the teachers alone. Yet, both Terry and Brian have gone, appearing to prove the contrary:

Sally: 'Chucking Carol out?'
Mary: 'Nooo.'
Jane: 'Yes you are.'
Mary: (turning to Terry) 'Terry and I know what . . .'
Carol: 'Terry can't stick you! (. . .) It's the way you treat us lot . . .'

Carol goes round the group saying each would not be there if Mary had her way. She leaves one girl out who strongly objects to being left out: 'What about me?' 'Yeah, nor you wouldn't. She wouldn't be 'ere.' Carol has successfully mobilised everyone's feelings against the teachers. Terry becomes very protective of the girls. He is a big, heavy boy and could clearly become aggressive. Carol reaches shrieking pitch several times.

The teachers, however, offer no physical challenge. Instead the battle remains over interpretations and Mary makes a tactical move to regain control over the definition of the situation:

Mary: 'The other three girls and Terry know very well what it's (normally) like.'
Carol: (quietly) 'I'm not taking any notice.'. . .
Mary: (soothingly calm) 'You know how we are normally. And you *know* that today is different. Oh, all right then, it's not, it's not the normal, and it's not how we want it.'
Carol: 'It's that at (her previous school) every time I came to school, they all played up and I got blamed for it.'

Mary appears to have made a successful bid to change the direction of the drama by appealing to what is *Known*. By making the day abnormal, blame is shifted from the teachers. Carol appears to reinforce the shift by attempting to shift blame from herself by appealing to her experience of the previous school. Mary has tried to transform the other pupils into allies. Carol takes an individualistic strategy and by implication shifts blame for 'playing up' to others. Harry does not let her get away with this move: 'You are the one who starts it. You are the one who spoils things.' Harry returns again and again to this theme. Carol tries to close off from the attack: 'I'm ignorin' yuh, I can't 'andle this in me mind.' Carol begins to be worn down under a relentless pressure from Harry: 'I will keep on day after day, hour after hour until *you* change it.'

Carol has been ejected from mainstream schooling because of her tendency to wind-up situations until they result in some form of physical violence. Clearly, in a class of thirty she would be totally disruptive of normal classroom order. Such a protracted interaction between one pupil and the teacher could not take place. The classroom teacher would be under pressure to manage the class rather than deal with the emotional problem of one child. There is a clear line which must not be passed or else the child is counted as 'too much', 'unhandleable', 'disturbed', 'maladjusted'. Moreover, there is a distinction between what may be called *normal violence* and *deviant violence*. The 'dividing line' is an image projected to pertain between the normal and the abnormal. Carol continually crosses that divide.

In the commentary on Carol's day attention has frequently been drawn to the double structure of values, alternative interpretations of reality, of what is presumed and what is intended. In chapter 4 the vandalised self was described as developing through a process which destroys its own basis for stability. The more Carol and her teachers struggle for stability, the more instability is created; each asserts values and interpretations which subvert or eat into those of the other. Moreover, there is a 'normal violence' which legitimately and uncontroversially may be applied to such as Carol to make them do, or keep them where the other wants them to be; in more than one sense Carol's freedom can be aborted in the interests of some presumed or desired stability. It is vital to understand the processes by which the image of stability is created and situations in which it works to undermine its own stability leading to a sense of existential violation.

Normality and its destabilisation

In the mathematical discipline of topology – rubber geometry as it is often known – a structure is investigated by systematically varying its structural properties until a dividing line is crossed whereby one thing becomes another. It is an analysis of environments, localities, spaces described mathematically. In topology a football and a rugby ball are the same thing; in the social world of sport, they display different properties and are employed in different contexts, employing different rules. In examining anything it is important to see the range of variations it can undergo in specific contexts without losing its essential identity. It is equally important to analyse the processes and circumstances under which an object becomes so varied, so stretched out of shape, that it becomes something else, something quite different. This is the essential process of phenomenological analysis as conceived by Husserl (e.g. Husserl 1970) and called *eidetic variation*. It is the essential method of scientific work (Levin 1968–69; Tragesser 1977). It is also the process through which social forms change into other forms; the break-through from one form to another may be experienced either as a violation or as a release. When do normal variations become so distended as to become counted as abnormal?

Recently I made a study of a housemaster's day, recorded by notes and tape recorded using a radio microphone (1984). It was part of a larger study. In this the distinction between a *character* and a *deviant* was made which would be helpful here. The following is based upon that study. The housemaster in a large comprehensive school, George, talks to me during a lesson about a pupil, Joe:

> 'He's a character that one, a case of eggs him (. . .). Quite good at acting. He was sent to me yesterday for swearing in the classroom. He does that the whole time (laughs). Usually, when I go in there (indicating his office) when the phone calls, I'll hear him "You fuckin' bastard", you know, to somebody. It's normal. And that's what, he always does as well (Joe is rocking in his chair), he always rocks in his chair, never has a clue he's doing it. Joe!' (Joe sits forward in his chair)

There is an ironic tension (that is, two sets of competing values, norms) between George's understanding that Joe is acting normally but that is threatening to teachers who want to create an alternative normality and cannot handle Joe's form of normality in the classroom. The task is to reassert the teacher's definition of the normal. A character appears to achieve a certain autonomy or notoriety without being too threatening, maintaining a basic friendliness, a willingness, at least under certain circumstances to toe the line, or toe sufficient lines. Such a character is Paul. Paul lived in a children's home and the person in charge rang George up to find out how Paul was doing at school. George answers with a tone that is informal, knowledgeable, edged with a kind of pessimistic realism concerning Paul's feelings about school:

> 'I've talked to Paul about it, I mean basically he's never had any great incentive to go to school but I mean, it's even less now, it's sort of Mickey Mouse now. So, we can't really be too uh hard and harsh or surprised to be honest.
>
> (. . .) The history is, once he learnt to read and write, you know, which he could hardly do when he came here in the second year – once he'd cracked that, I mean, that was it as far as he was concerned, his schooling was over, you know. I mean, if we look at it academically, it was total and abysmal

failure, you know, but, uh, in fact, he's not developed too
badly. Given the right sort of company then, you know,
reasonable opportunity ... Oh, I'm convinced Paul can make it
'cos he's no mug, you know. I don't think he's the sort who
would easily get into crime. I think he does, uh think about
that, that side, I mean he's prepared to uh ... do some certain
things but there's a limit you know ... (listens to caller). Yeah,
Yeah. He argues the point a lot now doesn't he but you see, I
mean, he's got to assert himself and well, while he reacts badly
sometimes you give him long enough, he comes round doesn't
he? He doesn't hold grudges for very long (...). Yeah, I know
what he's like, he argues an' he does, he does get up your nose
a little bit when he's like that. He can be very uh stick his heels
an' very stubborn ... it doesn't last though does it, you know,
'cos basically he isn't a bad lad at all. He's qui', he wants to be
liked and uh popular rather than disliked. So, uh that's a good
point ...'

The description of Paul is broadly defined in terms of his responses
to control, academic demands and social relationships. There is a
tension between class demands and individual wants. It seems Paul
exhibits what might be called a degree of controlled autonomy. On
the one hand, his characteristic of standing up against teachers and
adults generally brings him into conflict. On the other, this very
characteristic allows him to keep his distance from 'bad company'.
Paul knows the limit and always 'comes round in the end'.

Clearly, Paul stretches the pattern of what is normal for a pupil
to be, very close to the limit. However, he falls back from crossing
the line from characterhood, or the normal or tolerable range of
deviance or autonomy to the abnormal range. Sally, for example,
has crossed the line. Lilly, George's assistant, talks of her:

Lilly: 'I'll get them both down (Sally and her sister) and tell
them that I've spoken to (the social worker) today and told
them to please tell her attendance has improved.'
George: 'Yeah.'
Lilly: 'But uh, one more bunking an' that's it I'm afraid. It's
fair enough isn't it?'
George: 'Of course it is. Well, I mean, I've warned Sally,
didn't I?'
Lilly: 'Yes.'
George: 'You know, I said I'll, you know, this time I'll wear
it but if you do it again then you just ...'
Lilly: 'Said, "I can't give a toss."'

George: 'Deliberately and openly going against ...'
Lilly: 'Yeah, since July her attendance is appalling.'

The process of bending rules, giving another chance, suddenly comes to an end in the reported statement 'I can't give a toss'. With that Sally crossed the line. The mark between the 'character' and the 'abnormal deviant' is the deliberate oppositional stance which leads to the open attitude of 'I can't give a toss'. Where Paul took an oppositional stance he could always redeem himself, at least in the eyes of his housemaster; Sally has gone beyond that.

In the case of the character, Paul, and the 'abnormal deviant', Sally, the interacting sets of values remained stable within the context of the housemaster's understanding and the relationship each pupil had towards him. There is a normal deviance which can be coped with within the structure of the school and a form of deviance which could not. In contexts where such decisions could be made the alternative sets of values could remain distinct and stable. Two connected incidents will now be analysed which display an inherent instability in the values of the teachers themselves. First, a number of kids are hanging around the office doorway, babbling. Lilly asks one of the girls, June, if Sally's sister Alice is in. She is not. A conversation starts concerning a girl Mary, who is being picked on. June is accused of upsetting Mary:

Lilly: 'You know her uncle died the other day.'
June: (mentioning glue sniffing in connection with Mary) 'I don't sniff it (but) I smelt it yesterday (...) We smelt it yesterday, didn't we? Can still smell it on her breath.'
Lilly: 'OK June thanks but you know, next time she tells you anything come and tell Mr Black or I but don't, try not to pick on her at the moment, she is a bit sensitive, OK?'

Their intentions were good. They wanted to stop Mary from glue sniffing but in the process were picking on her and upsetting her, a process previously described in terms of the vandalised self, her self picked to pieces. Lilly's response is to accept the good intentions while requesting greater sensitivity and understanding of Mary's private experiences. Shortly, the second incident occurred. A teacher from Mary's class suddenly burst into the office talking about a girl who walked out of his class:

Teacher: 'Well, she just uh suddenly disappeared (from the class).'
Lilly: 'Where?'
Teacher: 'Out the room and then the 'turkey' girls (laughs),

4C: "'ere! Aren't you goin' to do anythin' about 'er! Look, you
don't care do you?" (laughs)'
(Lilly and George laugh)
Teacher: '"Um, yeah, go up stairs, go on" (still imitating the
voices of the girls)'
Lilly: 'You mean your favourite class, 4C?'
Teacher: '"Look at 'im, just stands there, just lets 'em cry."
So she said that, they'd all been saying that she's been sniffing
glue. But she just said it for a laugh ...'
George: 'Do you think, Jane she would?'
Lilly: 'I don't know she, wouldn't think she'd smoke but she
smokes.'
George: 'Ah, smokin's a bit ...'
Teacher: 'They reckon Alice had ...'
George: 'Oh, I can believe that yeah. I can believe that 'cos
she knocks around with older girls and that, you know.'

There is a clear tension displayed between the values of the pupils
and those of the teacher which is preserved in his caricature of the
'turkey girls'. Compare the two incidents, both concerning members of the same group of girls. There is clearly something very
unpleasant happening to some of the girls which makes others of
the girls feel concerned, concerned enough to 'pick on' their friends
in some misguided hope of making them see sense. There is a great
deal of pain and anguish being experienced. The girls accuse the
teacher of gross insensitivity, 'just stands there, just lets 'em cry'.
And his caricature certainly expresses a tone of verbal sadism, a
cutting into the souls of the girls. Neither George nor Lilly makes
known any special circumstances, as Lilly did in the previous incident, which the teacher should be taking into account; nor do they
remonstrate with him to be more sensitive and stop 'picking on'
the girls. Obviously, this incident has a history of bad relationships,
'You mean your favourite class, 4C?' Past and future observations
revealed that to be so.

Both George and Lilly are sensitive teachers who care about the
children they meet, even the roughest and the hardest of them and
particlarly the ones whose lives are blighted, vandalised by the
brutality of their homes, the restrictions of their fortunes, the tragedy of their lives. And in this school, there were many such as
these (George at one point gave a conservative estimate, as he
called it, that about a third of his House of 350 pupils had serious
social problems to confront that he knew about). Yet, in the company of a teacher who does not hold such values, indeed, is the

antithesis of everything they try to do, there is no attempt to challenge those views. They become accomplices to the satire. The values of the school are to protect teachers, to close ranks (as George himself put it) around the weak teacher, the brutal teacher, in the face of accusations from pupils or the wider community. The situation that results is unstable, leaving the pupils confused at best, revengeful at worst. The humane and sensitive values are eaten away by the coarse and incompetent actions of another. This was not an isolated incident, an aberration in the system. Nor is it unique only to one school. Such instabilities are pervasive throughout schooling. They are of the essence of schooling where people are compelled, coerced, inhibited all in the name of freedom, democracy, education. The violation is not so much in the obvious and relatively infrequent brutalities, or more frequent normal punishments (detentions, canings, slappings, pokings, shouting-downs) but in the more pervasive control nature of the school:

Sheila: 'Sir, what time is it?'
George: 'It's about five minutes before you can go.'
Sheila: 'God! (whispered)'
George: 'Before you can be released. (Sheila says something) Pardon?'
Sheila: 'It's a cage – we get released.'
George: 'That's a bit like it, isn't it, do you feel like that? Do you feel like that sometimes?'
Sheila plus friend: 'Yeah.'
George: 'That's life though, isn't it? I mean, if you start work it's the same idea, isn't it?'
Sheila: 'I know.'
George: 'You can't just come and go as you please, you know.'
Sheila: (laughing) 'Um, you can at school.'
George: 'You got to be there say at half-past-eight in the morning. You can't run away before half-past-five, you get, you get three-quarters of an hour for your dinner and ...'
Sheila: (laughing) 'My brother does ...'
George: 'Where does he work though, what does he do? (He works on a YOP scheme) Ah, but that's not work though is it?'
Sheila: 'No.'
George: 'It's not real work that. There's no way you could do that working for a real employer.'

There is an everydayness to the conversation. It can be heard in offices, department stores, factories – everywhere. It happened in a school – I have heard it many hundreds of times in classrooms, staffrooms and in interviews. Caged. And then, in an area of massive unemployment being prepared for work when there is no real work – only the unreal work of YOP (Youth Opportunities Programme) or YTS (Youth Training Scheme). What is there that is *real* for them to do, in an area where the only reality is that they can do nothing? There are many such areas of hyper-unemployment in the 1980s, as research carried out by CES Ltd called it, where besides the inner city slums there are about two million people living on 'forgotten estates' facing more than three times the national average unemployment (*Guardian* 24 October 1984, John Carvel reported):

> Mr Keith Waller is headmaster of a primary school on the Brambles Farm estate in East Middlesbrough. Male unemployment in this north-east section of East Middlesbrough is officially recorded at 47 per cent and Mr Waller says that on Brambles Farm it tops 60 per cent. 'That causes insecurity on this estate and a problem of role reversal. The men won't take on the domestic routine. So the mothers are expected to go out to do low-status jobs and then come back and look after all the domestic chores. This causes insecurity and stress in the home.
>
> 'Children are allowed to make a lot of decisions. They choose when they go to bed, what they wear, what TV to watch. They arrive at school tired and demanding the right to make their own decisions. This imposes tremendous stress on the teachers. On average we have one breakdown a year among the staff.'
>
> Mr Waller reports that the biggest problems are vandalism, burglaries, and teenage glue sniffing. 'Two of our school windows are smashed every day of the year, and we have a standing order with the glazier for 15 windows a week.'
>
> There used to be a police station on the estate, but it was closed and the beat bobby withdrawn. There is no doctor on the estate. The vicar left a year ago and has not yet been replaced. 'The people are confined to the estate and confined to their homes.'

George's school is in a comparable area. And there are many such areas, where 80–90 per cent of one's neighbours are unemployed (cf. Fiddy 1983). In such an area where does the real power lie, what real power do individuals have to wrest from fortune a few favours?

Intelligence, image and power

Youth should and must have its designs on the future – for when else is there the chance? I have previously defined intelligence in terms of the power to transform the given towards the desired (Schostak 1984). Intelligence, in its widest sense, is related to knowledge or information and hence to power. Set over and against the given is the infinite range of possibility seen in the eye of the imagination. The future is on the one hand infinite in its possibilities but finite in its probabilities. It takes intelligence to wrest from a presumed future sufficient freedom to create desired futures. In order to effect change there must be an honest and sustained reflection on the present; there can be no other starting place than the present, for all that is given to work with is in the present. Deception, however, is pervasive, if by deception one means the deliberate concealment of truths (Schostak 1983b: 151–9; 1983c). In the creation of a public image, the private image is concealed. Chapter 6 revealed the extent to which such deception is employed, particularly in the construction of identity within patriarchal and fraternal social organisation. Similarly, there are private and public futures; presumptive futures to be demonstrated on the public stage; and feared futures to be concealed from view, banished from mind.

Schools have a public, are accountable and must present some acceptable image. Few schools will admit they are failing; most will polish up their image for the press. Schools in the hardest-pressed areas must of necessity fail, the social problems are too great for them to handle. Suspensions from school for many areas, even areas where there is no major economic problem, are rising. There has been a massive increase in the number of off-site units, 140 per cent in five years, providing approximately 7000 places (Ling and Davies 1984). Even so, the problem of schools being unwilling to take children back into their classrooms and off-site units being full is growing. However, the failure tends to reflect upon the child rather than upon the school. Too often there is an abnegation of responsibility in the desire to present an image of coping, albeit in adversity.

George, the housemaster, provided an example. He asked me to read an article written by the headteacher of the rival school:

'That's a terrible article that. As a matter of fact he's a very
nice guy. You wouldn't guess so from that. Much more human
than uh this fellow (i.e., his own headteacher!) but I mean uh

149

most of that I mean is an absolute ... (...) It's a load of crap.
John, I mean I went over there the Friday before half term
(nearly two weeks previously) (...) because I was being ... This
block here at the back was under sort of siege. It was being
bombarded by half bricks and hunks of wood and sticks (...)
the staff cars were being bloody hit with these stones. I went
out and uh they all started moving away towards their own
school. I thought, "Sod this, I'm going to tell somebody (...)."
So, I walked up to the school, I dodged three half bricks on
the way. One just, just missed me head, you know and hit a
squad of their staff cars. The verbal abuse was just (...)
unbelievable from kids about this high (probably second and
third years). Went into the school there. Went to the office and
there's a woman sat in there used to work here. I said, "Is
there somebody I can speak to about these lads?" (...) She
said, "I don't think there's anybody about to tell," which is
about two minutes before their afternoon school starts. I said,
"You're joking, aren't you?" She said, "No, it's like this every
lunch time. They all clear off out." (...) A minute later she
said, "Oh, the head of lower school is coming down." And he
finally arrived. By which time the bell had gone and all these
lads had gone inside for their registration. (...) I told him and
he said he'd not heard anything and wandered off. And this
woman I was speaking to was coming out and going for her
lunch time. And she said, "Do you know we've had a phone
call every lunch hour from the people in the flats or the
caretakers about the lads behind the flats, you see." Running
bloody riot.'

In his view the duty of the pastoral staff, and particularly head and
deputy head, is to provide a system of surveillance outside classroom hours which serves as a community service: 'to me that's
a community job because you're thinking about your neighbours
and the neighbourhood, you're thinking about the wider issues
and the good order of your lads....' The previous summer during
the street disturbances (as the 1981 Scarman report called them)
the pastoral system of his school acted as a forward warning system
for the police, able to provide street-wise information through its
community-wide contacts as to the likely occurrence and where-
abouts of disturbances. Two or three riots involving up to 250
people did occur locally. However, fights involving that number of
young people were not untypical. As George went on to say, if one
brings young people from different territories and places them to-

gether, each territory has its gangs thus there will be trouble. Years
ago, he continued, there had been an agreement between the two
schools to stagger the end of the school day by ten minutes in
order to avoid the riots, an agreement now seriously eroded, he
felt.

There was a serious rift between private and public image; maintained, in fact, by both schools. George's school merely had a more
efficient surveillance and control system. By concealing the problems there can be no wider public awareness and demand for
solution. Action instead is directed to the politics of suppression;
if the energies of the young are sufficiently suppressed then there
is no problem with which to worry the public.

In 1981 the media became fully aware that there was a problem.
Of course, it is now once again suppressed (even though riots still
occur). Then the fantasies of youth violence exploded onto television and, instead of watching Starsky and Hutch, the young
watched themselves:

Larry: (...) 'I was born (in Birmingham). I lived there. And
there was riots in Brixton. There was riots down there as well.
My sister, she got arrested. Well, not exactly arrested but they
just took her in the van and told her - 'cos they tell you they
want to clear the area and she didn't go, so they just
reprimanded her. And there was - I could see out of my
window - there was some big place on fire, and these people
who probably tried to bomb the place or whatever.'
J.F.S.: 'Do you reckon it might happen again?'
Larry: 'It will happen again I reckon. I think it definitely will
happen again 'cos there's hardly any jobs or whatever, and
everyone's getting bolder by the day, so one day it's just gonna
explode and fink "Oh let's go an' start riotin'"'.
  (...) '... the last riots in Brixton were started because the
police arrested this geezer, beat him up, left him on the
pavement and his head was bleeding or something like that. He
was really bleeding badly and this geezer just walked over to
the car and started beating it up, pushed the car over and you
know, and then more police came here and one just joined in,
started fighting. It just carried on and on.'

Larry is speaking two years after the riots. The images (it does not
matter for present purposes if they are true) are clear and powerful
and the causes those typically stated, unemployment, boredom and
so on. The riots can be seen as an exercise of power - that is, from
the point of view of the rioters. From that point of view a riot

becomes an intelligent act, an act which can contribute towards the transformation of the given toward the desired. A riot is a public act, gangs of delinquents on the rampage, politics is juvenile delinquency as Brown (1966) calls it. It transforms the environment and may contribute to a transformation for the better. Michael Heseltine, the environment secretary, was given responsibility to inject resources into the inner cities following the riots. But the changes are slow, too slow and negligible in the face of the massive problems. Perhaps more widespread riots will occur.

Violent processes involve the systematic transformation of self, other and environment. These transformations may be achieved through physical means or through the manipulation of consciousness or ways of seeing, the manipulation of public or private images. Where physical violence such as rioting acts outwards to transform reality, drugs act inwards to transform reality. Where rioting lays waste to the environment, drugs can be used to lay waste to the self. Similarly, in a study of anorexia, Ross (1984) argued that both drug abuse and anorexia satisfy a pre-existing need, fill a gap, as it were in the self-system. But this is not the full story:

> *Peter*: 'I take drugs but I don't glue sniff. It's pointless. It's a quick way to die. (...) I smoke lots of dope (...) I used to take acid and speed but I've given it up now ... (...) I had a bad time with an acid trip, I was sort of taken apart and I think it all built up inside me. I had lots of aggressions an' it sort of went wrong ... and I just gave it up and said I'm not going to take it any more (...) (on the bad trip) I was just sort of angry, really angry, and I could sort of feel it. It sort of overcame me and I smashed up something in my bedroom and I went outside and sort of walked about for ages, not knowing sort of what I was doing (...) at least dope's got some sort of 'ology, some sort of leaf or whatever it is and I like it. It's sort of a good way to relax and get on with people (...) I sort of believe in the beliefs about it and all this. (...) All the meditations ...'

The drug is creating for him a cultural environment, a private peace and relaxation which he wants, transforming the inner and outer environment to the desired. He has worked through the harder, more debilitating drugs to one which he feels he can handle.

For some drugs open up new realms of exploration. Some boys talked about their experiences of glue sniffing, the 'buzz', the hallucinations. One boy, in particular, gave a detailed analysis of his experiences. He managed to maintain a sense of knowing reality throughout the hallucinations, 'you are not really out of your head, you know what you are doing.' And more particularly: 'As long as you got something in your head saying, no, none of this is true, then you are all right. That's the main thing, see that's all right. Because then you can make hallucinations out of it, that's what I sometimes do. If not, they sometimes come to you.' He had learnt how to get the kind of hallucinations he wanted:

'If you can imagine things, use your imagination, if you can imagine things you know, you can guess how that happen and if you are on glue and you think how that happen you see it happen. Just things like that. But you see then I give people hallucinations, you see, not give them say, give them hallucinations, but you tell them how to keep thinking of it, trying to draw it out of them. And they come out and they say "Oh yeah". 'Cos my mate didn't believe me, but you know, I can help you have hallucinations ...'

The education of hallucinations! A drawing out, was how he described the process. It was important to him to manage the distinction between reality and hallucination and even maintain a sense of reality during the hallucination in order to keep a feeling of control and sanity. In his gang he was like the shaman.

For some time drugs and, in particular, glue-inspired hallucinations were the only realm in his life that he could call successful, a private realm that could be made public only within his gang. He had re-discovered skills associated with shamanic practices – the skilful inducement and manipulation of hallucinations. When he talked, he talked with real excitement. Looking at his transcript, it is difficult to believe that this was a person who rarely talked with great fluency and at length on anything. The transcript is full of pages of uninterrupted script, more like a teacher's script talking about the task of teaching. However, it is important not to romanticise this. He knew the harm that glue was doing to him and could graphically describe it:

'... soon as your body has had enough, when you are high on that, you see hallucinations trying to put the wind up you to stop, for some reason. So there are things, like, I get this thing every time I sniff, this thing keep trying to eat my ... that felt as if there were maggots tryin' to eat my nose. And that just got every time I picked my bag up, that was in there, that same thing on my nose, you know, that was slowly eating my nose away, you know that was really horrible.'

And, of course there is trouble with girls:

'... you sort of fall out with girls when you are glue sniffing. You smell of glue and (...) things like that, and then one day I met some bird I really liked and then I give up on glue all the time because I was with her and then as soon as I ... well, she chucked me or whatever I got really upset. I went straight back to taking glue, but mainly, like sort of now, I have given up because I am going about with girls again. That's the main thing.'

This boy wants to be more successful socially. Glue is clearly both an escape and a support, providing him with experiences he would not normally have. He has weaned himself away from glue, not solely through meeting girls and wanting to be attractive to them (and more important, finding out that he is desirable to them) but also through the agency of a softer drug he calls dope (*cannabis*). It is for him a more social drug:

'... well, on dope, yeah, you talk more (...) you know, you talk sensible and learn who your mates are and all that you know. I can go round my mates' bedrooms and we just sit there talking about things. You just sort of talk about things like nicking an' that. Say, "Why don't you nick," and you just come straight out and say (inaudible) and my mate say "You ought to do a burglary," burglary being nicking and he say I can do one. "I help you out." And you start talking about that.'

He had no belief that he would ever get a job at the time of these interviews and discussions. One day his teacher saw him looking very sad and decided to ask him what was the matter. Reluctantly he spoke, tears falling, he believed there was no future for him. What was there that was real for him to hold on to in his life, his community? What real decisions could be make about his life? What real power did he have to affect anything? He had no sense of being able to determine his future in the way that he wanted. This powerlessness was at the heart of his own violent imagination which became expressed in the private domain of glue sniffing.

At this point, it is necessary to gather together the themes of the book in order to present a summary account of the violent imagination, its genesis and its articulation in experience. What is it that is common to the variations illustrated by the many individuals who have voiced their experience in this book? The central question is, what is the relation between the violent imagination and the presumed and intended realities as experienced by individuals? A teacher asked a young man of sixteen why he hated social workers. His answer 'They stole my fuckin' life. They stole my fuckin' future.' His was a life of violence and of hopelessness. And he is not alone. In the tower blocks of Birkenhead, like many other places, the lives, the futures, of the young have been stolen. Two boys casually talked to each other. One said he never watched the news, it was too depressing. Yes, said the other, that's why I get stoned on drugs. There is no future. If this seems a bizarre and eccentric attitude, one may refer to the Avon Peace Education Project survey as reported in the *Sunday Times* (21 October 1984):

> Large numbers of children feel helpless about the possibility of nuclear war (. . .) Of 561 comprehensive school children questioned, 91% think they would not survive a nuclear holocaust, 30% think a nuclear war is likely to happen in their lifetime and 21% think one could happen at any moment.

Implications – a summary

This book has tried to marry description and analysis in order to ground theory construction in the voices of those who are the subjects of the study. Thus the theory is dialectically related to the experience as expressed by the individuals concerned. Some have called this, or processes like it, grounded theory (Glaser and Strauss 1967). What does the theory look like in summary?

Self enters a pre-existing world, a world which is not arbitrary but which is capable of modification. Most of what self comes to know about the world is told to self by others who also have been told by others. Self goes through various social phases where others treat self in particular ways. Certain others have the power to label and project identities upon the self: gender identity, racial identity, social class identity, religious identity. Such a projected self may carry with it either a history of privilege or of violation. Thus the other becomes conceived in terms of the one who provides security in the face of danger or the one who threatens danger. The dangerous-Other is a major theme of the violent imagination.

The self may be cast in the role by others as a dangerous-Other. To be born with a particular skin colour, to live on a particular housing estate, to pray in a particular church – these are sufficient for some to be cast in such a role. Entering then into mass people management institutions such as schools, one arrives with a history projected by others and presumed to be true, presumed to be real.

When Self tries to transform the given state of affairs into some desired objective the Other can either help or at least not stand in the way, or hinder. There are many forms of the Other that Self meets in such projects: the Other as individual, the Other as group, the Other as institution, the Other as impersonal or unspecified They, the Other as deity or demon. The forms of violation which Self experiences with Other vary from physical brutality to subtle psychological discriminations which reduce the power of the individual to explore talents and fulfil desires and needs. Self may either accept or reject the presumptive realities projected by Other. If for Self, life is necessarily a life of suffering (as for example in some versions of Christianity) and humanity is by nature consumed with corruption and sinfulness then Self may accept the violence of the Other as a necessary and *just* means of creating and maintaining social order, and hence of benefit to individuals. Alternatively, the violence of the Other may become legitimised through the process of emulation – everyone behaves like this, therefore it must be right to behave like this; or, the ideal-Other behaves like this (e.g. various cinema and TV heroes shown during children's hour or early family time entertainment) therefore I will behave like this and you *ought* to behave like this and if you don't then that is a violation of reason. Violence then divides into justifiable and unjustifiable violence or normal and abnormal violence.

Normal violence is broadly uncontroversial. For example, comic book violence, and family TV and cinema violence is largely uncontroversial and rarely counted or seen as being violent. Thus children are able to reproduce within their fantasy lives images of uncontroversial violence – the bombings, the machine gunnings, the fights, the car chases that end in crashes, all part of a story of justifiable retribution which adults consider to be harmless family entertainment. On the public scene the distinction between normal and abnormal violence is still drawn, but where to draw the lines of the distinction may be more controversial. Thus, for example, in the miners' dispute during 1984 there were many scenes of violence and brutality. There were also many arguments justifying the violence. The struggle was over how to represent the Other in the minds of the public. To the miner the police were using abnormal force and were largely to blame for the violence; to the police and the Conservative government the miners were bully boys, vandals, delinquents. To the miners facing the possible desolation of their communities, the government and the coalboard were the vandals and the police their means of bringing this about.

The issue within the context of the violent imagination is not violence as such but the distinction between justifiable and non-justifiable (and hence punishable) violence. The first lesson of schooling is to present legitimate impersonal force to the child in the image of the teacher controlling the classroom, manipulating scarce resources and opportunities. The classroom can be analysed as a political economy where each individual is supposed to have equal opportunity but only a few get the rewards.

Self and Other face the problem of defining legitimate and illegitimate violence. The situation is made more complex by the existence of alternative presumptive realities. From Self's point of view the presumed nature of the world is not identical to the point of view of Other. When this occurs acts made against each other become justified by alternative values, hence perpetual use of force against each other may be perpetually justified through the alternative value and belief systems. The situation never then achieves resolution until there is the annihilation of one of the parties. Self and Other attempt to transform the reality of the other or annihilate the other.

In the private realm of the self, or the domestic sphere of the Self and the family (or lover) other layers of complexity arise. First, there is the issue of the demarcation between private and public and their interrelations; and secondly, there is the problem of the private face being in discord with the public face of the Self. What is private to the individual and what can legitimately be invaded by the Other and brought to public attention?

Schooling is involved in the development of personality. Is personality private or public? Is knowledge private or public? Is education private or public? These are not easy questions to answer, particularly as the answers will not remain stable from context to context. Knowledge is on the one hand private because it is the Self that knows; yet, it is also public because the Self can act through knowledge on the public domain to transform the public towards the desires of the private. Schooling itself is a public act directed towards the private Self to transform the Self in accordance with the aims of the public. Education founded upon the principle of unconditional freedom to question, criticise, challenge and celebrate is the private act of the individual directed unconditionally outward into the public sphere. The privacy of the individual is highly political, not least because in that privacy the seeds of challenge and revolt may stir. Similarly, schooling as the stage for the

157

public cultivation of the private individual is highly political. In such circumstances the private and the public are, potentially at least, mutual violations of the other.

When the private face and public face of the Self conflict, the values of the one eat into the values of the other, subverting any sense of stability. The Self moves in any direction that offers a feeling of stability – losing one's self in the crowd or the gang, in hallucinations, in political ideologies – anywhere which gives back to the Self some power to transform the given sense of instability towards a sense of stability. The task is to look for something that makes sense.

Another level of complexity is reached when Self observes the public and private variations on Other's beliefs and actions; and vice versa. The potential for alternative ranges of explanations and interpretations of social interaction are thereby increased. Social life is thus not an unambiguous reality describable with the exactitude of mathematical definitions. It is essentially ambiguous, provisional, presumptive. Conflicts necessarily occur if an authoritative-Other intends to school Self in certain versions of social reality; the violation of alternative interpretations becomes inevitable. If education through discourse is denied, then alternative forms of challenge become attractive and even inevitable.

The violent imagination is a product of the relations between Self and Other in a world which pre-exists them as individuals and of which they hold predominantly only a presumptive knowledge. The violent imagination consists of the images of violation produced through direct experience and through folklore, myth, story and the exploitation of image through the media. Violence is essential to maintenance of public order in a society where opportunities. and resources are distributed without regard to need or at best scant regard for need. Such violence becomes considered normal violence. It is uncontroversial. There are of course disputes arising between what is to be counted as normal and abnormal violence in some incidents, but as a principle normal violence is accepted by all. It is necessary to have a military and a police force. It is necessary that schooling is backed by the power of the police, for example. However, disputes arise over specific expressions of that power. Normal violence is used to meet and control abnormal uses of violence. However, in the violent imagination the image of the legitimate use of force can become indistinguishable from its illegitimate use. Killing someone is killing someone. The use of power to get one's way is the use of power to get one's way. Violence is violence. The values of normal violence become confused with alternative values and construct ironic structures, where one set of values eats into other sets of values. These may structure both Self and Other in terms of their private and public faces. In such circumstances the task of growing up becomes a process of working through a shifting maze where both entrance and exit are blurred and continually transformed into dead-ends. The work of violence is to transform Self, Other and the relations between Self and Other in some desired form regardless of the needs and desires of the one being acted upon. The form of the violation may be brutally simple or extremely subtle. The form of the justification of violation equally may be simple or subtle. Poverty may be excused, for example as the result of a system of private property that ultimately is in the best interests of the poor. Punishments may be given in the best interests of the punished. Rebellion or resistance against social injustice may be forcibly put down in the interests of wider public order. Citizens have to realise that it is in their best interests that military and police power exist. The violent imagination must be schooled to accept a version of normal violence which is required for the continued functioning of the state. The stage of political struggle is the imagination itself, the ways in which Self and Other imagine each other and the world into which they are born and work and play. What the young think of the world and know of the world is thus of vital importance. They must learn the lessons of the violent imagination.

Chapter 8

Lessons of violence

A teacher may say, 'You must learn to sit still', or 'You must learn to do as you are told'. These are, perhaps, not thought of as part of the ordinary curriculum taught in lessons, but are nevertheless lessons. These are lessons just as much as are lessons in algebra. A child who sits bored for an hour or so because 'you must learn to sit still' is learning that in certain situations his or her wants are subject to the will of another. It is a violation of one's freedom to move, to leave boring situations. It is a lesson in strength and weakness. Such lessons are not, of course, restricted to school, yet any place where such lessons occur may be called a school. The processes of schooling minds and bodies into conformity with the will-to-power of another can occur anywhere. Thus, it is necessary to have a broad definition of schools and schooling. A school is anywhere where two or more meet to dispute, contest, examine, reflect upon some object or objects in order to construct or present some reading, interpretation or lesson concerning life and the world. Such a definition embraces both education and schooling as these terms are employed in this book. Each leads to distinct forms of curriculum wherein each violates the principles of the other. Responsibility for instituting education largely remains with the Self whereas schooling resides with the Other. In this sense, one may refer to Self-elected schools and Other-elected schools; the latter being imposed upon Self unless Self resists in some way. In a similar way, the curriculum of each divides into Self-elected and Other-elected curricula. One of the original meanings of the term 'curriculum' is racing-chariot! The image conjured up is of one who drives a course through life with as much skill and daring as possible, keeping a grip on the reins of his or her fate. Taking this interpretation of the image, the self-elected curriculum is one where

Self chooses a course of action which drives towards the fulfilment of interests, needs, desires or the solution of problems. Alterna tively, there is the image of being driven, passively in the care of some expert (or overpowering fool) towards a goal not of the Self's choosing. Self may trust the Other who acts 'in self's best interests'; Other, indeed, may intend to hand over the reins when Self can be trusted 'to make the right decisions'. Thus the feeling of being driven may be pleasant or unpleasant depending on the kinds of pleasures or pains experienced: it may be a course of privilege or of disadvantage. Equally, the self-elected course may be one of pain and anxiety or of ecstasy. These, of course, are ideal types, extreme positions. An actual lived-course is likely to be a dialectic, an interplay of the extreme positions. It would be rather tedious to ask 'why' of every trivial act. It is useful to take for granted that much of social life will proceed routinely. Nevertheless, there are times when one must stop and challenge this routine, or aspects of it, and question what it means for one's life, one's sense of validity, of purpose. One can ascertain the extent to which one is being compulsorily schooled through the limits placed upon one's free- dom to question and the limits placed upon freedoms of movement and expression.

A curriculum of violence begins in experienced acts of violation, whether these are violations of routine norms or violations of one's right to question. The Other, as one who imposes norms or resists norms, or questions and subverts, becomes dangerous to the one who experiences violation. Self, in response, may become danger- ous in order to fight back or become the powerful one. The vandalised-self and the dangerous-Other may become entwined as private face and public face as self pursues a course of action, at times leading, at times led – driven by forces too strong to resist.

The individual grows up in a world of obvious inequalities, in- equalities maintained through the power of the law. This estab- lishes for the individual a pre-existing course which may be rejected or embraced, but through which the individual is driven unless acts of resistance transform the course. Both success and failure in such acts of transformation are themselves lessons. For example, the feeling of being driven is hard to overcome, particularly if the compulsion appears to come from within:

Carol: 'I just, everybody keep saying to me, try and control your temper. But I just can't. And once I, someone do something to me I just fly and that's it. I never go for my mum though. I always tend to go for the ornaments, windows, you know, stupid things like that. That's because I got in a mood. I got a really bad temper. Got my dad's temper, so my mum reckon ... (...) I can't help it. And I don't even ... sometimes I sit there and if I'm in a bad mood and someone will say – even me friends when I'm at home – say anything to me, I turn round and fly at them. I don't even realise that I've done it. Just turn round and shout at them, threatening to smack them down an' everything like that. I don't even realise I've done it. Then I'm all right to them. The next minute I'm nasty. The next minute I'm all right. (...) I want to stop it if I could but I can't see how I can. So that people out, so that people out there that can turn round, you know, "control your temper" and things like that 'cos (inaudible) so ... I've only been like this about three years ago, since we left my dad I've been like this.'

She presents an image of the mood being quite arbitrary, as the result of some inner, uncontrollable compulsion. She has learnt the lesson presented to her by her family that she is like her dad ... 'look in the mirror and you'll see that I am right'. Every outburst and every failure to control the outburst proves the mother's judgment. She placed the change in her character at the time of leaving her father, a violent man, it may be recalled. There is an implication that some alternative course might have been possible if.... Such crisis points create a sense of 'no turning back'.

For Tony (chapter 4) there was a point where he could have made one decision rather than another. However, others made a decision for him 'in his best interests' which set him along a course he felt he could not resist. Indeed, the course began to provide him with certain satisfactions – drugs, fighting, financing a life-style of thrill seeking – and provide him with an identity. And there were the teachers who provided him with the lessons he required to develop his skills. He became a willing pupil. However, it would be misleading to think that Tony had been drawn into' some subculture of deviance or of violence. The images and interpretations of these common to his way of thinking cannot be parcelled off as being distinct from the wider culture which informs the ways of thinking and being of the rest of us. The images of manliness and hardness are everywhere. He engaged in a curriculum of violence attempting to live the life which others watch on TV. One of the heroes of the group of boys at the off-site centre with him was Mr T, a fictional character in the TV series the A-Team, good family entertainment, where millions of dolls and other toys based on the series were being promoted. The *Sunday Times Magazine* ran a feature on Mr T, which made little secret of his violent youth, a hard man who sought hard vengeance on those who crossed him. The reality had become fiction. The fantasy becomes reality – all good family entertainment. The violence shown in most children's and teenagers' TV entertainment is largely uncontroversial, hardly noticeable. The argument may run, it is only cartoon-like violence, nobody *really* gets hurt and only people who are not normal, who are in some way sick, would take it seriously. That is one possible interpretation of such entertainment. But co-present with this interpretation are alternative interpretations. These are images of *real men*; people who play these are adored, earn fantastic sums of money and have exciting lives. They present a way of how to become exciting. And, of course, when I act like these I'm only 'having a laugh', it is not *real*. This is a technique which allows anyone to shift ground almost imperceptively. The image remains the same, one merely shifts through the various interpretations it carries with it. Thus, one can engage in violence without it ever being defined as *real*:

> *Tony*: (talking about a teacher he particularly admired at the off-site centre) 'There's only one thing he don't like in there, that's bullying. But he, right, just because you muck about, to say, there's a little kid in there, say, we muck about wiv 'im, push him around a bit just mucking about. (The teacher) always looking at it as bullying, but we don't, even the kid who we push around don't. We're just having a laugh. But that's how he saw. That get up the arse a bit but you mess about a bit three or four times with different people, he says, "You're bullying", he usually send you 'ome. An' that really piss you off that do 'cos you know you weren't muckin' about.'

There is a conflict here between two distinct interpretations as to what counts as *normal violence*, or 'only messin' around'. Tony added, 'Fair enough, you've done something wrong, an' you know you 'ave it's all right. But if you were just messin' about wiv 'im 'e always look at it as bullying.' Frequently, the contests extended to the teacher himself, with Tony taunting him toward some sort of violent act. 'Only messin'' takes on an ironic edge, it is double-edged. Tony tried to teach the lesson that 'it is only messin'' means that when he is pushing someone around (teacher or pupil) it is not for *real*. The teacher tried to teach the lesson that aggression has a very much lower threshold than Tony would admit. The interplay between the two left feelings of dissatisfaction in both. An escalation occurred where it became more and more difficult to keep Tony in the centre.

Every lesson, like any other symbolic course of acts, has multiple interpretations depending upon the viewpoint taken. These interpretations may interlace to produce layers of ironic meanings which, through acts of deconstruction and reconstruction, produce readings which reinforce the opposite of the actor's surface intent (as in the case of Tony). For example, the teacher who wants a pupil to learn a hard fact of life may use his or her authority to compel the pupil to take punishment in order to make the pupil learn that disobedience (or whatever) does not pay. Instead, an alternative reading is that the one with the big stick always wins and can enforce his or her will upon another. It may be recalled that Tony was very supportive of law and order (the big stick version). Force demonstrates that force is necessary. It does not present alternative non-coercive forms of building and maintaining community relations. Hence, it reproduces itself in the demand for the necessary external force to curb inner drives. In turn, the violent individual (like Tony) could fairly claim, following this logic, that his or her outbursts are a result of the failure of the Other to assert sufficient control. The necessity of such force becomes an uncontroversial fact, a lesson learnt in every such encounter. In such lessons, the individual learns about the Self, the Other and the course of life. These three act dialectically to produce each other. It will be convenient however to focus on each in turn.

The Self

The Self can be either victim or perpetrator of violence. In each case Self learns the limits which are imposed on the imagination to conceive realisable transformations of the environment. In its explorations of the world, the Self may be said to bump into certain resistances to the whims of the imagination (cf. Tragesser 1977). Each such resistance can be said to provide the possibility of a lesson, a lesson in limitations to the imaginative control or manipulation of the world. Each lesson, however, is open to alternative ranges of readings or interpretations. Individuals become schooled in the readings supported by one group rather than another. Resisting the readings promulgated by one's own group or some group having power over the course of one's life may be grounds for expulsion or re-education (detention, isolation, punishment and/ or readjustment of the maladjusted). Self as victim may learn lessons of avoidance; Self as violator may learn lessons of carrying out actions of normal violence and getting away with deviant acts.

In each case the kinds of lessons learnt are not arbitrary nor are they the product of isolated situations, or the whimsical inventions of individuals and hence so unique or particular as to prevent generalisation. It is tempting to talk of such a self as being the product of membership of some sub-culture or culture cut off from the mainstream culture or other cultures (see Cohen 1955 on the one hand and Miller 1958, on the other). The forms of modern cultural communication make this an absurdity. We are all members of a communication network, we all take part in the production of meanings and their interpretation and in the conflicts of meanings that arise. The task of abstract analysis is to start from the ways people use images in their lives and contribute to the identification of the ranges of meanings which make instances both recognisable and significant in the lives of individuals. The method appropriate to this is *eidetic variation*, the imaginative variation of phenomena in order to reveal their generalisable properties or qualities (i.e. those qualities common to the variations on a theme). Metaphorically, the individual is wrapped in ever more general contextual meanings which it is the task of analysis to identify.

For example, in chapter 4 when the reception class children said goodbye to their mummies and daddies, each goodbye was a unique act, but they were wrapped in the historical contexts which compelled these acts. In imagination, one may recall other kinds of goodbyes. What is common between them? And what separates these acts in the reception class from all others? What is common to all such reception-class acts of saying goodbye for the first time in school? The acts of goodbye were not voluntary, were not cheerful (saying goodbye to some despised-Other, would no doubt be cheerful).

At its most general, its most universal, there was a lesson in compulsion, in the strange force which sent their parents away and left them with strangers called teachers. Their own wants were now to be subject to the attentions, goals and demands of some impersonal force personally represented by the teacher. This is not to say that the experience of school cannot be for them enjoyable and profitable; nor is it to say that the teacher is thereby some ogre. It is to point to an important interpretation provided by taking into account the context of compulsion which initiates and frames the acts of parents leaving their children in school.

Alternative contexts are also implicit. Schools are considered important, so important that valuable resources are freely provided for the education of children. However, these alternative interpretations and their implicit value and belief systems co-exist, providing for the possibility of conflict and subversion. In the lesson of the benevolent gift of free education is also the lesson of compulsion which disregards the immediate wants of the child in favour of the designs of the adult, and more particularly of *Them* who compel even the adults known to the child. One lesson is: through power one can manipulate others in disregard of their immediate wants and experiences. Other lessons concern the appropriate contexts for the exercise of such power.

What then are the variations on the theme of the exercise of power over others that a growing child will meet? In chapter 3 childrearing practices were discussed. Clearly, at home the child experiences one or more of the variety of childrearing practices available to the parent. Only the helping mode of childrearing takes seriously any ideology of treating the child as having the right to contribute fully to his or her own self-development in a manner that fits within broad democratic ideals. The others in varying degrees violate the autonomy and freedom of the child to make decisions. The family, then, is an alternative source of variation on the theme of the exercise of power. Further variation can be found in the history and current practice concerning the relations between people of different races, different sexes, different social classes, different positions at work. The lessons of power are deep within the institutions and culture of society. Take away coercive power and the majority of institutions would cease to function or be so transformed as to be unrecognisable. The only question which most would consider practical or realistic would focus not upon the eradication of coercive power but upon agreements as to what should count as the uncontroversial use of it. The task becomes to place limits on the legitimate use of coercion. It is then a question of justice under the law.

Having accepted coercion as a necessary social principle, this opens the way to discussion of its legitimate use. For the individual this is a matter of interpretation. There is much evidence in the voices of the young that they feel many of the aspects of their lives to be unfair. Indeed, there is much evidence that unfairness, or inequality, is considered natural, right, just, by the most powerful people of society. And coercion through property rights both reproduces these forms of injustice and supports them. Of course, 'justice' is being used in two different but interacting ways here. There is a conception of natural justice – the inalienable rights of the individual *qua* individual – and the justice as it has come to be interpreted in the courts of law. The two do not necessarily match. However, justification of the latter is typically by appeal to the former. Hence it is right to judge the practical effects of the latter by some discussion of the former. An ironic effect is constructed. A teacher may have the legal right to punish a child but this may be interpreted as unfair under the child's conception of fairness, a fairness he or she may well find supported in some more general conception of natural justice.

The lesson under such circumstances being presented to the child is that legitimate coercion can be used to support a violation of natural justice. There is a gradual subtraction, as it were, of the features of what counts as the legitimate limits to the use of coercive power as the child experiences the variations on its practical use. If the child's experiences have been, for example, particularly brutal, then the final lesson may well be 'force is legitimate under all circumstances – but don't get caught'.

The playground where child meets child away from the supervision of more powerful Others is yet another source for practical variation on the theme of power. It is there that the child can practise the power game as it has been presented in other contexts and see what happens. Because the adult cannot see what happens, there is, for the adult, the problem of proof. The lesson is learnt that what happens outside of the vision of the powerful-Other is difficult to prove. Thus the child can uphold an account which completely exonerates him or her from blame. The teacher then takes on the role of interrogator and the child learns the skills of creating plausible accounts of events and maintaining them in public under duress (Schostak 1983c). In these interactions a vision of Self, both in its private and public faces, is created in relation to the experience of violation. The vision may be of one too hard to crack or of one too easily broken.

The Other

Since the public face of the Self cannot be discussed without reference to the Other, the powerful-Other has already received attention. In this section the focus will be on the transformation of the Other to dangerous-Other. Chapter 2 discussed one broadly accepted view of the person as essentially dangerous, a seething cauldron of passions which if not kept in check by some more powerful force would inevitably wreak destruction on the world. The conception of the dangerous-Other as representative of all people thus constitutes the need for some powerful-Other (God, Monarch, State) who will be the ultimate force creating order and obedience. Chapter 6 found this view strongly held by Tony. It was particularly associated with a male view of the world and had implications for females in terms of power relations, gender identities and roles.

Even if any one particular individual does not hold that people are naturally violent, it is a stance which must be reckoned with because social life is premissed upon this principle of inherent disorder arising without external or internal coercive influences – the police, the military, political organisation, hierarchical power structures of any kind. It is thus a stance which influences behaviour and interpretations. Indeed, so pervasive is the stance that many have considered some notion of the dangerous-Other to be essential for the development of social order: it is a theme found in the writings of Hobbes and Freud.

In chapter 3 it was shown how schooling emerged as a response to fears concerning the lower classes who became the dangerous-Others requiring to learn their station in life and later requiring to be moulded to make the 'right' decisions in political life. A right of interference in the lives of others has been asserted.

This, however, is a long way from asserting the right to interfere in any way and under any circumstances. There is, therefore, a limitation on interference and beyond that it becomes abnormal interference. However, individuals on the receiving end of unwanted but legal or socially acceptable interference are placed in a position of being violated, yet if they do anything about it they risk becoming deviants. In particular, there are offences which only children can commit: truancy, underage drinking/smoking/driving/sex. In addition, setting up home and earning a living – all quite reasonable adult activities – are denied to children. Schools frequently introduce further rules seen by most if not all pupils as trivial: compulsory uniform, written permission to go to the toilet, rules concerning talking and moving about school buildings and grounds. Some rules can be supported for safety reasons; others presuppose an inherent irresponsibility in children and leave many children feeling insulted and/or resentful for their teachers or fellow pupils.

This provides a context within which children learn about themselves and about the Other. Certainly, the experiences of individuals vary; certainly, some attitudes are more prevalent than others and some institutions more gentle and more democratic than others. However, the contexts of coercion in its various forms exist and cannot seriously be denied. Each exists as possible variations having a common or invariant or family core of structural features and qualities. The dispute arises over whether act v′ is the same as act v″. For example, when a teacher strikes a pupil because that pupil has disobeyed a school rule or norm is that the same thing as one pupil striking another because of the disobedience of some gang rule or norm? Clearly, both are *the same thing* considered only in their bare abstract form as punishment for the violation of some group-defined norm or rule. Teachers, however, have greater social authority than gang members and hence would want to argue their case differently; theirs is legal punishment. But this does not get very far if placed within the context of 'might makes right'. It can be reformulated to be applicable to any situation where one has the power to enforce a punishment as being legal. Thus, the gang leader who punishes and can enforce that punishment as right is doing the same sort of things as a teacher who punishes.

The situation, however, can be further varied by taking into account notions of natural justice, religious commandments and hence distinctions between the two can be drawn. But the distinctions are not necessarily stable and may take on ironic relations. The values asserted by the teacher in defence of the punishment may be deconstructed to reveal identities with other more brutal and arbitrary forms of punishment and the alternative interpretations of the act of punishment reconstructed in place of the teacher's explanations – at least in the mind of the person on the receiving end, or members of the audience to that punishment.

Individuals such as Carol, in chapter 6, who have experiences of a wide range of violent acts, have many examples to call upon in order to draw out the essential sameness of one person's act of violation and another's. Experiences, of course, vary. Many are lucky enough never to have had brutal parents or to have been brutalised by others. Hence their interpretations of what counts as acts of violation will differ. An object, whether physical or mental, is built up through the variation of perspective on it. At any one moment a certain profile of, say, a house is present to consciousness. The other possible profiles are said to be in appresentation to it. Thus, appresented with the perceived profile of the front of the house as its back, its top, its insides. There is a sense of the whole house. Further variations in perspective may reveal that the house does not have a back or a top but is in fact a film prop made to look like a solid house. In a similar manner, an act may be labelled violent by an observer but further investigation reveals it to be part of a game or fictional drama. This theory of appresentation was developed by Husserl and employed by Schutz and Ortega y Gasset amongst others in their sociological interpretations of Husserl's phenomenology.

Experiences of phenomena *defined as the same thing by one or more persons* are held appresentationally with any current experience of it. This allows any individual to claim that he or she *knows* what is at the back of any expressed intention by another just as one may claim to know that walking around a house will reveal its back profiles, and entering the door will reveal its insides. In any social situation more than one interpretation may be made, indeed, any social situation will hold in appresentation all interpretations which can be said *by someone* to be possible, probable, plausible or *the real* interpretation. A good example of the kind of conflict this might generate can be seen in 'Carol's day' in chapter 7. The task confronting any individual is to drive a course through these shifting levels of meaning which can create a sense of stability, purposefulness.

The course of life

The course of a life can be said to be comprised of a number of lessons or readings which together fill out or make substantial any particular experience. The reading of any particular experience is conditioned by those other experiences held appresentationally. This provides a sense of continuity to experience, a sense of direction to the course of life, a sense of being in the driver's seat or of being driven regardless of one's desires, needs, interests. Experiences become schooled, moulded, fashioned in two ways: when a present experience is uncritically or unquestioningly judged by self to be a variant profile of previous experiences; and when some other manipulates experiences covertly for an individual in order to predispose one sort of judgment rather than another. A curriculum of violence can be constituted in both these ways. An example of the first was when in chapter 4 it was shown how Billy, just five years old, cannot get away with aggressive behaviours like other pupils without being labelled maladjusted; an example of the second is the intent of child-centred, or progressive, forms of schooling in the tradition of Rousseau as described in chapter 3.

Throughout the course of one's life any event is open to multiple interpretations and re-interpretations at later times. That is to say, there is no definitive statement which exhausts the meaning of any one particular event or experience. This may lead either to a sense of instability or to a sense of progressive understanding of the whole of one's life course, depending upon the kinds of feelings generated and whether re-interpretations integrate previous understandings or tear them apart leaving nothing in their place. In the case of Harry in chapter 4, the self had been scarred by the act of the teacher who knocked him unconscious. This experience undermined his later meetings with teachers at his new school, a school which he liked, leaving him anxious and distrustful of all teachers. Or, as Carol put it, people like her have 'backgrounds' (chapter 7). These backgrounds predispose the continuing development of a curriculum of violence, a moulding of present experience in the light of previous experience of violations. Individuals like Tony (chapters 6 and 7) recognise crisis points in their lives when, had they not occurred, they might have become very different people with different career prospects; but having passed that point they say they choose to stay as they have become. The curriculum of violence at that point becomes self-elected. It may be an uncritical self-election or one which is the result of systematic critical reflection on experience. Tony gave many reasons for his decision which indicated a considerable degree of critical self-awareness.

Tony's views, and those like him, have been schooled through experience of a violent curriculum. This curriculum found expression not only in the violence of parents and gang members but was also reinforced through wider cultural images involving manliness, racism and the rights of the state to control or interfere in the lives of citizens whether in compulsory state schooling or in the enforcing of care orders. Each source has provided reasons or motives for the course of Tony's life, not causes. It would be a mistake to suppose, for example, compulsory schooling *caused* Tony to behave in the way he did. There is no simple cause and effect relationship upon which to build theories and test hypotheses. There are, however, the multiplicity of meanings, interpretations, images, values, beliefs, accounts and explanations of experience which provide reasons for behaving one way rather than another. Thus, this is a study of meanings which can become reasons, rather than events that can become causes. By being capable of questioning the acts and interpretations of others the individual stands outside of the mechanics of cause and effect and educes reasons for considering the world to be essentially this rather than that. It is this that differentiates the study of social acts from physical acts: the potential for freedom, the potential to question.

Education for freedom

The relationship between education and schooling has so far been analysed as one of opposition. This opposition will now be related to the life of the individual. In the life of the individual many social analysts have emphasised some distinction between the social aspect of the self and the natural, or creative, or instinctual aspect of the self. For Freud there was the distinction between the unconscious and the conscious; for existentialists there is the distinction between reason and passion; for phenomenologists the distinction between the world of the taken for granted and the world which arises through the free act of questioning. These, at one level at least, can be seen as variations on the theme of necessity and freedom. The self is not the product of one alone but is constituted out of the interaction, or dialectical interplay of both.

It is perhaps unreasonable to question every small act of life. Without some degree of unquestioned regularity or order social life could hardly take place on a scale as complex and massive as most modern societies. Even in a family it would be difficult to have to renegotiate every trivial act of social life. To have a realm of uncontroversial acts and with it an uncontroversial public self facilitates the smooth running of social interaction. This constitutes a non-problematic social or public self. It is not hard to see the parallelism between schooling and the development of such an unproblematic self.

Much of the discussion in this book, however, has been to identify the negative aspects of schooling in the promotion of experiences of violation rather than social ease. At the point where acts of schooling become a burden or a violation or inhibit creativity and reassessments, that is where there is the need to question, to challenge and to assert an alternative view. In the life of the individual there is likely to be an oscillation between attitudes of schooling and attitudes of education. Similarly, Burridge (1979), in his analysis of the individual, saw an oscillation between the 'person' (the uncritical social self) and 'individuality' (the stance whereby one sets into question prevailing social orders).

In Mead's analysis of the relationship between the 'I' (the creative unpredictable innovative aspect of the self) and the 'me' (the conservative aspect of the self which reproduces the social status quo) innovation arises mainly in answer to a problem or due to an act of spontaneity from the 'I' when the guard of the 'me' is down. Broadly, the 'I' is kept in check by the 'me'; innovations persist only when meeting approval by the 'me', which in turn is but an internalisation of the 'generalised other', the others whose approval self wants or whose power self fears. In this schema the.major function of the 'me' appears to be that of schooling and being schooled. The acts of the 'I' can be interpreted from this standpoint as a violation of predictable order.

Social arrangements tend to take on a fixity, a sense of being inert. Sartre (1976) has analysed how social arrangements entered into freely then act back on the individuals, restricting their freedom. The more impersonal such arrangements become the more difficult it is to break free of them, to challenge and question them. The social arrangements that prevail are mostly those which pre-date the birth of any individual and may or may not be appropriate to the life of that individual. The ideology of democracy asserts the right of any individual to take part in the decision-making which affects his or her life. The practice is very different. Decisions are made 'in the best interests of' a public which may or may not have voted for the decision-maker. It is difficult to think how in largely authoritarian institutions such as state (and public) schools individuals can be prepared to encourage the development of democratic ideals in their lives. Yet the ideology of democratic forms of freedom is proclaimed without much attempt to induct the young into the major forms of decision-making that affect their lives at school.

Chapter 3, in describing the predominant forms of childrearing practice, identified the dominant ideologies behind these - patriarchy, the creation of citizens, the belief in the natural evil of the child, the belief in the infinite plasticity of the child, and so on. In a world which is a madhouse of warring factions and paranoid fears that the other side is building up a greater holocaust potential than one's own, adults are presumed to know best and expert adults presumed to know best of all. Children, so the dominant ideology goes, are incapable of knowing what is in their own best interests without the interference of an adult.

In schooling the role of the teacher can be defined in terms of interference or intervention in the lives of others. However, rather than discussing the role of the teacher, it is more useful to discuss the context within which teaching might occur. In this way education becomes a relation between persons who are reflecting upon some experience, one of whom may be an adult the other a child – each may question the other and each may show the other their own point of view, neither need necessarily take on an institutional role as teacher or pupil. Since both allow each other the right to question and to challenge and to proclaim their view, both can feel that the one is taking the other seriously. Thus the contradiction of private questioning but public acceptance or submission does not arise. The task for both is to show reasons for their views.

Clearly, there would need to be a radical change in the underlying principles upon which schools are run if this kind of fluid teaching association were to take place. It can be objected that such fluidity is utopian and hence cannot be taken seriously in situations of scarce resources and the mass management of young people; that it would require a complete turn around in the views of society. This, of course, would be true if the ideal of perpetual questioning and challenging were to be implemented. However, taking the model of the individual expressed by Burridge, it seems quite reasonable to suppose that most people would not either want or need to question and challenge all the time, but would want to suspend critical stances in order to carry out or learn the more routine aspects of living; nevertheless, they would want to reserve the right to be able to say, 'hey, wait a moment, I question the validity of that' or, 'hold on, I want to make my views heard here because I feel they are not being taken seriously and so I want to be given the chance to reveal my reasons'. The question, in practical terms, then reduces to 'How may schools be organised to fulfil both the needs for schooling and the needs for education in ways which do not violate, or at least reduce, the possibilities of violatory experiences?'

At school some pupils are labelled deviant, maladjusted, troublesome. For many of those pupils it is their circumstances rather than their inherent nature that is troublesome. If this were not so then one would be driven to the position of accepting some notion of inherent evil, the child that is born evil. For example, Tony in chapters 6 and 7 was shown to be troublesome, violent and also as an individual whose self can be said to be vandalised. Certainly, there is some appeal in labelling one such as Tony inherently evil. One senior teacher at an off-site residential unit admitted believing that he could find no other explanation for the behaviour of some of his charges than saying that they were inherently evil. Indeed, the judge at Tony's trial likened his behaviour to that of the Hitler Youth in the 1930s – a byword for evil.

In her book Midgley (1984) identifies evil as a purely negative phenomenon, anti-life, while also recognising that destruction may also have positive aims (as in the destruction of evil). In this definition Tony was not evil, although certain of his actions might be called evil, as should also some of the acts committed against him during his early life have been called evil. In chapter 7 it was argued that many people like Tony have no opportunity to talk with others about their private pain. Schooling does not provide an appropriate context, although there is no reason against schools giving time and resources to the education (drawing out) of such problems within suitable contexts. It was at his off-site unit that for the first time he met an adult to whom he could, within an educational setting, begin to talk about his experiences. For him, however, it proved to be too little, too late.

Tony may be called an extreme case. However, the problem exists for us all. As Midgley reminds us:

> As Jung has pointed out, every solid object has its shadow-side. The shadowy parts of the mind are an essential part of its form. To deny one's shadow is to lose solidity, to become something of a phantom. Self-deception about it may increase our confidence, but it surely threatens our wholeness. (p. 12)

The self and the self's relation to the world is a proper subject and provides directions for the content of education. In schooling as conceived by traditional authoritarian approaches (see chapter 3) the self is not a proper subject except as a member of a class which subsumes the self's identity and individuality within a competitive struggle for achievement as measured by unquestioned group norms. The evil-Other is seen as the un-schooled self, the self that will not submit to the greater good as defined by the leader. In schooling as conceived in the progressive tradition, the child is centre stage, but as a being to be moulded, to be protected from some influences but subjected covertly to others. There is a notion of the evil Other from whom the child is to be shielded; for Rousseau this was society itself. In libertarian approaches, again the child is centre stage and the evil-Other is characterised as anyone who sets themselves up in authority over the child. Two forms of libertarianism emerge, one is founded upon the classical economic model of the rugged individual pursuing *his* (typically as opposed to her) most profitable course, a curriculum of struggle, winning and losing where the other is always a danger (for with the Other one faces the danger of losing). The alternative libertarianism defines relations with the other more fully in terms of some notion of 'wholeness', balance or harmony with others (very much in the ecological sense) emphasising the interdependency of all with all in a relation of mutual self-aid.

Education for freedom seems closest to the libertarian traditions. However, education which claims the right to question and to challenge cannot as such identify itself with any one particular political orthodoxy or tradition else it falls into schooling. Education as such is a violation of the principles of unquestioned authority. In the history of ideas the subversive powers of education are all too visible. Children at school on certain occasions are likely to exercise their rights of criticism, challenge and resistance to being controlled. Perhaps to some extent their questionings are a matter of re-inventing the wheel and very tiresome to adults. Certainly, when members of a mass suddenly question the wisdom and the legal rights of adults it is all very inconvenient and, at worst, can be frightening. Yet, it is the argument of this book, and there is evidence of the case studies to support this, that school contributes to the problems it wants to solve. While schools remain unwilling to examine the consequences of compulsion, of undemocratic modes of teaching, school organisation and curriculum development, their unexamined contribution to the development of a violent imagination, and the formation of the identity of the dangerous-Other to be punished by law will persist.

Last rights

> The rules of the riot game were perhaps first elaborated in
> England, where the urban mob was for about a century and a
> half a weapon of some value in political struggle within a
> stable system. Montesquieu, Rousseau and de Lolme
> commented at the time on the curious character of English
> elections; other contemporary observers (above all Hogarth
> and Dickens) pictured more vividly the part of the English
> mob in sustaining English liberty. Indeed, more recent
> observers have described the great period of Whig ascendency
> as one of oligarchy tempered by riot; as in the remark about
> nineteenth-century Russia, 'Every country has its constitution;
> ours is absolutism moderated by assassination.' (Mackenzie
> 1975: 150-1)

There is a positive value to violence as well as a negative. After all,
violence may be employed to overthrow despotism, to win a degree
of freedom. The 1981 riots, for example, on the one hand may
seem an expression of mindlessness, of thuggery; on the other, they
may seem the expression of an anger and a demand to be heard –
oligarchy tempered by riot. Taken out of context, violence, like any
other act, always seems meaningless, bizarre. However, no act is
without its history. Violence from one point of view may be conceived as a game, from another, an expression of primitive destructiveness, from yet another the scream of a damaged life, or the
desire to transform reality towards the desired. And so on.

Similarly, classroom absolutism may be conceived as being tempered by disruption, having a laugh, rebellion. Such an analogy
may not be welcome. It may even seem absurd, the result, perhaps,
of an absurd ideology which presupposes the right of any indivi-

dual to be consulted and offered choice in any decision affecting his or her life; and secondly, presupposes that to learn democratic and non-violatory ways of behaviour one must live within a conducive environment:

It is children, and only children, in our society who lack adequate legal protection from violence.

Violence, as Mrs Thatcher and her colleagues are only too ready to tell us in other contemporary contexts, breeds violence. And so, as the Association of Education Psychologists spelled out in a submission a few years ago: 'There is evidence that children imitate the actions of their elders, and that the methods of childrearing depending heavily on punishments of a physically aggressive kind produce children who themselves behave in a physically violent fashion. Children who are beaten tend in their turn, to beat and to bully.' (Peter Newell, *The Times Educational Supplement*, 30 November 1984)

Beating, however, is only one of the more obvious forms of violence. Moreover, it has to be interpreted before one can know its personal and social significance. One favoured interpretation is, 'I received a good beating when I was a child and it never did me any harm.' Another is:

My father gave me such a beating when I was little that I was black and blue from the beating. All the time he was an alcoholic and he beats us all the time. My mother married when she was fifteen years old. There are fourteen children. (Konopka 1966: 51)

And:

I don't understand adults. The adults say they never got into trouble, that they never had any problems. How is that possible? I don't believe them. They lie. . . . Why do they act so perfect? I think they just try to push us into the ground and make us feel like nothing. (p. 57)

These are the words of girls whose lives can truly be said to have been vandalised. Within the context of such lives a good beating is evil.

Such lives are lived within a wider context conceived out of the interactions of all. The kind of economic and political structure maintained as a benefit to the powerful affects all lives. The morality of such decisions is to be judged by the ways in which it supports or damages lives. In a system conceived to support and increase inequality, it can only be expected that at the financial level it makes sense to increase the wealth of the rich at the expense of the poor. According to *Hansard* (4 April 1984 cols 542-4W) since the tax year of 1978-79 £4.17 billion have been given away due to tax changes of which the top 1 per cent in the income group got 44 per cent and the bottom 25 per cent got 3 per cent. According to Bull (1984) by 1980 the 1944 version of universal free meals had been abandoned. It exists only for the poor. Thus, 'the last ten years have seen a *persistent worsening* of the combined poverty/inequality problems in all its connections with educational systems' (Hughes 1984). Poverty is being reinforced by separate treatment. It is no longer a goal to eradicate it. The laws of an economic necessity based upon competitive struggle, the survival of the fittest, make this an idealistic and impractical dream. One tightens the belts of the poorest.

Through institutionalised structures of discrimination based on race, class, sex, religion, age, individuals learn the character-forming lessons of inequality. All those at the bottom have to do is look around to see that life is hard; and all those who are at the top have to do is look around to see that life is pleasant. The two rarely meet except as mediated through the entertainments media. What each knows of the other is largely presumptive. Occasional riots, reported muggings, violent thefts and so on may give pause for thought, may temper decisions. Despite the obvious inequalities, the obvious discriminations, the obvious brutality inflicted on the poorest, any violent reaction from the poorest condemns them as the dangerous-Others, condemns them as ungrateful for all the benefits schooling, unemployment benefit, National Health Service has heaped upon them. Just lay-abouts, all of them!

The violent imagination is conceived out of such experiences of violation and the images of violation which reinforce, or school these. The images turn upon a dialectic, not only of image shaping experience and experience shaping image but of the ambiguity of images. Those who benefit from violations may interpret their acts as proofs of virility, of strength, of being fit, of being manly. The economic system is founded upon the image of struggle, of the rationality of desire and the pursuit of profit at the expense of a competitor. However, such images may be returned in a form found disconcerting to the rulers through the violence of the mob, the gang. The hardness of the law enforcers becomes matched by the hardness of the law breakers; each finds their manliness, their proof of hardness, in the acts they commit. The mythic images are

179

of male-conceived violence. Social reality becomes structured according to the myths.

How can we get them to see another way? How can we get them to see that violence does not pay? Schooling was thought by many to be the answer. Yet the ambiguity of the images of teacher authority, of teaching by compulsion, subverts in the minds of many the very good intentions of the teacher. Schooling itself becomes a violation when the individual does not want to be there, or is compelled to attend to matters of absurd irrelevance to his or her life, a life which may be one of brutalisation.

The chances that school offers are frequently defined in terms of a chance to get out, to climb up the social ladder, a chance to compete. That is the liberal ideal of providing opportunity. If the opportunity is not taken then it is not the fault of the society which made that chance available. They have only themselves to blame. However, the chance to compete only ensures the continuance of failure, those who fail in the competition; to win, there must be losers. What is the point of a competition without winners and losers? Struggle, the competitive survival of the fittest, these are the images which say: those at the top must be the fittest, must be the best, the most honourable, the most intelligent, the hardest workers. To prove it you only have to look and see.

To break the circularity of image reflecting image and success justifying success in the competitive struggle is perhaps the last right of the losers. A violent lashing out is one course of action. Another is through cooperation with others to build a community of individuals who can say 'No!' to those who would master them.

A teacher has a choice between schooling and education. It is not entirely an either/or situation. As argued in chapter 8, the two stances when appropriately employed may well be complementary. But the last right of the individual is to say 'No!' There comes a point when the individual's doubt concerning the direction of his or her life, the relevance of the instruction provided by the teacher, must take precedence over timetabling necessity.

Children are born into structures not of their making. Much of what comes to be known about the world, its contents, the ways one is expected to behave in it, and what one's place in it is, is told to the child by others (who themselves have largely been told by others). Reality for the individual is largely presumptive. Thus what is known about the world is as much imagined as real. Education reinforces the right of critical reflection upon a world which is largely unknown but largely imagined. If Kuhn (1970) is right and scientists view the world through a paradigm of what it ought to be then to learn a new paradigm is to learn a new way of seeing where old facts are transformed or discarded to fit new imaginations of the world. The imagination of the scientists becomes schooled in order that the community of scientists all see the same thing. All hypotheses become framed within this new way of seeing which define the criteria of what is to count as objective, sure, real, true, hard and fast. Laing (1976) analysed the families of schizophrenics and showed how parents use the technique of mirroring to prove to children that they are like this rather than that. They test the hypothesis in the mirror of images provided by the parent to see that the parent is right all along. The mirror is the paradigm, the way of seeing through which the expert (parent, scientist, teacher) attempts to school the imagination of the Other. The Other is rendered naive, absurd, childish until he or she sees the same way as the expert. There are, of course, a multiplicity of mirrors ranging from what any group considers as commonsensical to those which are the hallmarks of professionalism.

The stance of the educator is to suspend all such mirrors with the statement 'these may be true, but I reserve the right to suspend judgment. And in this suspension of judgment I will look at these phenomena from alternative angles in order to see if from different perspectives they remain the same, change shape, or disappear altogether. And then I reserve the right to make a judgment. And later, if I want, I reserve the right to review the position again, and again, and again.'

However, society which prepares for some future imaginable war cannot afford to eradicate the potential for committing violence by its members. The images of violence of whatever kind therefore retain some association with heroism. It is all in the history books. In war no act is too horrific that it will not be committed by some hero: the unimaginable has happened. The bombs have been dropped, the bodies burnt, the soul tortured. And it is all good entertainment. The war machines are just children's toys to be given at Christmas, the festival of love.

But these are just the last rights of the individual.

Bibliography

Aiken, H. D. (1956), *The Age of Ideology*, New York, Mentor.

Aries, P. (1962), *Centuries of Childhood*, London, Cape.

Arnold, M. (1973), *Culture and Anarchy*, Cambridge University Press, first published 1932.

Avery, G. (1967), *School Remembered: An Anthology*, London, Gollancz.

Bachelard, G. (1969), *The Poetics of Reverie. Childhood, Language and the Cosmos*, trans. by D. Russell, Boston, Beacon Press.

Bain, A. (1879), *Education as Science*, London, Kegan Paul.

Ball, S. J. (1981), *Beachside Comprehensive: A Case Study of Secondary Schooling*, Cambridge University Press.

Bandura, A., Ross, D., and Ross, S. (1963), 'Imitation of film-mediated aggressive models', *Journal of Abnormal and Social Psychology*, 67, 601-7.

Bereiter, C., and Engleman, S. (1966), *Teaching Disadvantaged Children in the Preschool*, Englewood Cliffs, N.J., Prentice-Hall.

Berkowitz, L. (1972), 'Frustrations, comparisons, and other sources of emotional arousal as contributors to social unrest', *Journal of Social Issues*, 28, 1, 77-91.

Berne, E. (1968), *Games People Play: The Psychology of Human Relationships*, Harmondsworth, Penguin.

Bernstein, B. (1970), 'Education cannot compensate for society', *New Society* February 26, 344-7.

Bishton, D. and Homer, B. (1978), *Talking Blues*, AFFOR, 173 Lozells Rd, Lozells B19 1RN.

Bolt, C. (1971), *Victorian Attitudes to Race*, London, Routledge & Kegan Paul.

Brabazon, Lord (1887) (second edition), *Social Arrows*, London, Longmans, Green and Co.

Bray, R. A. (1911), *The Town Child*, London, Fisher Unwin.

Bristol, I. M. (1984), 'Multicultural education: Avon's calling?' *Multiracial Education*, 12, 2, 8-14.

Britain, A. (1977), *The Privatised World*, London, Routledge & Kegan Paul.

Brogden, A. (1981), ' "Sus" is dead: but what about "Sas"?', *New Community*, 9, 1.

Brown, N. O. (1966), *Love's Body*, New York, Vintage Books.

Bull, D. (1984), 'Education: burdening the family', *Poverty* no. 58, August, 11-18.

Burridge, K. (1979), *Someone, No One. An Essay on Individuality*, Princeton University Press.

Burt, C. (1944) (4th edition), *The Young Delinquent*, London, first published 1925.

Campbell, J. (1964), *The Masks of God: occidental mythology*, Souvenir Press.

Campbell Stewart, W. A. (1979), 'Progressive education – past, present and future', *British Journal of Educational Studies*, 27, 2.

Carby, V. H. (1982), 'Schooling in Babylon', in: CCCS, *The Empire Strikes Back. Race and Racism in 70s Britain*, London, Hutchinson in association with the Centre for Contemporary Cultural Studies, University of Birmingham.

Carthy, J. D. and Ebling, F. J. (1964) (eds), *The Natural History of Aggression*, New York, Academic Press.

CCCS (1981), *Unpopular Education. Schooling and Social Democracy in England since 1944*, London, Hutchinson in association with The Centre for Contemporary Cultural Studies, University of Birmingham.

CCCS (1982), *The Empire Strikes Back. Race and Racism in 70s Britain*, London, Hutchinson in association with the Centre for Contemporary Cultural Studies, University of Birmingham.

Clarricoates, K. (1980), 'The Importance of Being Ernest . . . Emma . . . Tom . . . Jane . . .', in: R. Deem (ed.), *Schooling for Women's Work*, London, Routledge & Kegan Paul.

Cloward, R. A. and Ohlin, L. E. (1960), *Delinquency and Opportunity. A Theory of Delinquent Gangs*, New York, Free Press; London, Routledge & Kegan Paul.

Coard, B. (1971), *How the West Indian Child is made Educationally Subnormal in the British School System*, London, New Beacon Books.

Cohen, A. K. (1955), *Delinquent Boys: The Culture of the Gang*, New York, Free Press; London, Collier-Macmillan.

Comstock, G. et al. (1978), *Television and Human Behavior: The Key Studies*, Santa Monica, Rand.

Cooley, C. H. (1956), *Social Organisation*, Chicago, Free Press.

Dale, R. (1979a), 'From endorsement to disintegration: progressive education from the Golden Age to the Green Paper', *British Journal of Educational Studies*, 27, 3.

Dale, R. (1979b), 'Progressive education and politics', *British Journal of Educational Studies*, 27, 3.

Davies, L. (1979), 'Deadlier than the male? Girls' conformity and deviance in school', in: L. Barton and R. Meighan (eds), *Schools, Pupils and Deviance*, Nafferton Books.

Deem, R. (1980) (ed.), *Schooling for Woman's Work*, London, Routledge & Kegan Paul.

Bibliography

Dewey, J. (1938), *Experience and Education*, New York, Collier.
Dollard, J. et al. (1939), *Frustration and Aggression*, Institute of Human Relations, Yale University; also (1944), London, Routledge & Kegan Paul.
Dumont, R. V. and Wax, M. L. (1969), 'Cherokee school society and the intercultural classroom', *Human Organisation*, 28, 3, 217-26.
Elliot, G. (1972), *Twentieth Century Book of the Dead*, Harmondsworth, Penguin.
Empson, W. (1966), *Some Versions of Pastoral*, Harmondsworth, Penguin.
Eysenck, H. J. and Wilson, G. D. (1973), *The Experimental Study of Freudian Theories*, London, Methuen.
Faraday, A. (1974), *The Dream Game*, London, Temple Smith.
Fiddy, R. (ed.) (1983), *In Place of Work. Policy and Provision for the Young Unemployed*, Barcombe, Falmer.
Fidler, G. C. (1980), 'The Liverpool labour movement and the school board: an aspect of education and the working class', *History of Education*, 9, 1, 43-61.
Freeman, A. J. (1914), *Boy Life and Labour: The Manufacture of Inefficiency*, London, King.
Freeman, M. D. A. (1983), *The Rights and Wrongs of Children*, London, Francis Pinter.
Freire, P. (1972), *Cultural Action for Freedom*, Harmondsworth, Penguin.
Freud, S. (1963 edition), *Civilization and its Discontents*, translated by J. Riviere, revised and newly edited by J. Strachey, London, Hogarth Press and the Institute of Psycho-Analysis.
Friedman, N. L. (1967), 'Cultural deprivation: a commentary on the sociology of knowledge', *Journal of Educational Thought*, 1, 2, 88-99.
Fromm, E. (1974), *The Anatomy of Human Destructiveness*, London, Cape.
Fryer, P. (1984), *Staying Power. The History of Black People in Britain*, London and Sydney, Pluto Press.
Fuller, M. (1984), 'Black girls in a London comprehensive school', in: M. Hammersley and P. Woods (eds), *Life in School. The Sociology of Pupil Culture*, Milton Keynes, Open University Press.
Furlong, V. J. (1976), 'Interaction sets in the classroom: towards a study of pupil knowledge', in: M. Stubbs and S. Delamont (eds), *Explorations in Classroom Observation*, London, Wiley.
Garfinkel, H. (1967), *Studies in Ethnomethodology*, Englewood Cliffs, N.J. Prentice-Hall.
Gelles, R. J. and Strauss, M. A. (1979), 'Violence in the American family', *Journal of Social Issues*, 35, 2, 15-39.
Gerth, H. and Mills, C. Wright (1954), *Character and Social Structure. The Psychology of Social Institutions*, London, Routledge & Kegan Paul.
Glaser, B. G. and Strauss, A. L. (1967), *The Discovery of Grounded Theory. Strategies for Qualitative Research*, Aldine, Atherton.

Goodman, P. (1961), *Growing Up Absurd*, New York, Gollancz.

Goodman, P. (1971), *Compulsory Miseducation*, Harmondsworth, Penguin.

Grace, G. (1978), *Teachers, Ideology and Control. A Study in Urban Education*, London, Routledge & Kegan Paul.

Graves, R. (1959), *The White Goddess: A Historical Grammar of Poetic Myth*, London, Faber.

Hamilton, L. W. (1846), *The Institutions of Popular Education*, Leeds, James Y. Knight; London, Hamilton, Adams & Co.

Hargreaves, D. H. (1967), *Social Relations in a Secondary School*, London, Routledge & Kegan Paul.

Hargreaves, D. H. (1981), 'Schooling for delinquency', in: L. Barton and S. Walker (eds), *Schools, Teachers and Teaching*, Barcombe, Falmer.

Hargreaves, D. H. (1982), *The Challenge for the Comprehensive School. Culture, Curriculum and Community*, London and Boston, Routledge & Kegan Paul.

Hargreaves, D. H., Hestor, S. K., and Mellor, F. J. (1975), *Deviance in Classrooms*, London and Boston, Routledge & Kegan Paul.

Harris, M. (1968), *The Rise of Anthropological Theory*, New York, Crowell; London, Routledge & Kegan Paul.

Hatton, S. F. (1931), *London's Bad Boys*, London, Chapman & Hall.

Heer, F. (1974), *Challenge of Youth. Revolutions of Our Time*, London, Weidenfeld & Nicolson.

Hendrick, H. (1980), 'A race of intelligent unskilled labourers: the adolescent worker and the debate on compulsory part-time day continuation schools, 1900-1922', *History of Education*, 9, 2, 159-73.

Henriques, J. (1984), 'Social psychology and the politics of racism' in: J. Henriques, W. Hollway, C. Urwin, C. Venn, and V. Walkerdine (eds), *Changing the Subject. Psychology, Social Regulation and Subjectivity*, London, Methuen.

Heward, C. (1981), 'Growing up in a Birmingham Community, 1851-1871', in: J. Hurt (ed.), *Childhood, Youth and Education in the late Nineteenth Century*, History of Education Society Conference Papers, 1980.

Hirschi, T. (1969), *Causes of Delinquency*, Berkeley, University of California Press.

Hole, J. (1860), *'Light, More Light!' Or the Present State of Education amongst the Working Classes of Leeds and How it Can Best Be Improved*, reprinted by The Woburn Press 1969.

Hollway, W. (1984), 'Fitting work: psychological assessment in organisations', in: J. Henriques, W. Hollway, C. Urwin, C. Venn, V. Walkerdine (eds), *Changing The Subject. Psychology, Social Regulation and Subjectivity*, London, Methuen.

Holt, J. (1969), *How Children Fail*, Harmondsworth, Penguin.

Holt, J. (1974), *Escape from Childhood: The Needs and Rights of Children*, Harmondsworth, Pelican.

Honderich, T. (1976), *Three Essays on Political Violence*, Oxford, Basil Blackwell.

Houston, S. H. (1969), 'A sociolinguistic consideration of the Black English of children in north Florida', *Language*, 45, 3, 599-607.

Hughes, J. (1984), 'The inequality of impoverished education', *Poverty*, 58, 11-18.

Hull, C. (1984), 'Pupils as Teacher Educators', mimeo CARE, University of East Anglia.

Hull, C. & Rudduck, J. (1980), 'Introducing innovation to pupils', paper read at AERA, Boston, USA.

Hull, C. and Rudduck, J. (1981), *The Effects of Systematic Induction Courses for Pupils on Pupils' Perception of an Innovation*, Final Report to the Social Science Research Council, No. HR 684811 British Library.

Humphries, S. (1981), *Hooligans or Rebels? An Oral History of Working Class Childhood and Youth 1889-1939*, Oxford, Basil Blackwell.

Hunt and Hunt (1970), in: J. Middleton (ed.), *From Child to Adult: Studies in the Anthropology of Education*, New York, The National History Press.

Husband, C. (ed.) (1982), *'Race' in Britain*, London, Hutchinson.

Husserl, E. (1970), *The Crisis of European Sciences and Transcendental Phenomenology. An Introduction to Phenomenological Philosophy*, trans. D. Carr, Evanston, North Western University Press.

Hyndman, M. (1978), *Schools and Schooling in England and Wales. A Documentary History*, New York, Harper & Row.

Isaacs, S. (1930), *Intellectual Growth in Young Children/with an appendix on children's 'why' questions by Nathan Isaacs*, London, Routledge & Kegan Paul.

Jacoby, R. (1975), *Social Amnesia. A Critique of Conformist Psychology from Adler to Laing*, Boston, Beacon Press.

Jamdaingi, L., Phillips-Bell, M. & Ward, J. (eds) (1982), *Talking Chalk. Black Pupils, Parents and Teachers Speak about Education*, Birmingham, AFFOR.

Johnson, R. N. (1972), *Aggression in Man and Animals*, Philadelphia, London, Toronto, W. B. Saunders Co.

Kapo, R. (1981), *A Savage Culture. Racism - A Black British View*, London and Melbourne, Quartet Books.

Keddie, N. (1971), 'Classroom Knowledge', in: M. F. D. Young (ed.), *Knowledge and Control*, London, Collier-Macmillan.

Kohl, H. (1971), *36 Children*, Harmondsworth, Penguin.

Kohl, H. (1974), *Half the House*, New York, Dutton.

Kohl, H. (1977), *On Teaching*, London, Methuen.

Konopka, G. (1966), *The Adolescent Girl in Conflict*, Englewood Cliffs, N.J., Prentice-Hall.

Kozol, J. (1967), *Death at an Early Age*, New York, Houghton Mifflin.

Kropotkin, Prince P. A. (1904), *Mutual Aid: A Factor of Evolution*, London, Heinemann.

Kuhn, T. (1970), *The Structure of Scientific Revolutions* (second ed.), vols I and II. *Foundations of the Unity of Science*, University of Chicago Press.

Lacey, C. (1970), *Hightown Grammar*, Manchester University Press.

Laing, R. D. (1976), *The Politics of the family and other essays*, Harmondsworth, Penguin.

Landau, S. F. (1981), 'Juveniles and the Police', *British Journal of Criminology*, January.

Levin, D. M. (1968–69), 'Induction and Husserl's theory of eidetic variation', *Philosophy and Phenomenological Research*, 29, 1–15.

Lewis, H. R. and Streitfeld, H. S. (1970), *Growth Games*, London, Abacus.

Ling, R. (1984), 'A suspended sentence: the role of the L.E.A. in the removal of disruptive pupils from school', in: J. F. Schostak and T. Logan (eds), *Pupil Experience*, London and Sydney, Croom Helm.

Ling, R. and Davies, G. (1984), *A Survey of Off-Site Units in England and Wales*, Social Education Research Project, Centre for Advanced Studies in Education, occasional publication No. 2, Birmingham Polytechnic.

Locke, J. (1880), *Some Thoughts Concerning Education*, London, National Society's Depository, first published 1693.

Lorenz, K. Z. (1966), *On Aggression*, trans. M. Latzke, London, Methuen.

MacDonald, B. (1970), 'Briefing decision-makers: the evaluation of the humanities curriculum project', in: Hamingson (ed.) (1973), *Towards Judgement*, CARE Occasional Publication No. 1, University of East Anglia.

Mackenzie, W. J. M. (1975), *Power, Violence, Decision*, Harmondsworth, Penguin.

Macpherson, C. B. (1973), *Democratic Theory. Essays in Retrieval*, Oxford, Clarendon Press.

McWhirter, L., Young, V. and Majury, J. (1983), 'Belfast children's awareness of violent death', *British Journal Social Psychology*, 22, 81–92.

Matza, D. (1964), *Delinquency and Drift*, New York, London, Wiley.

Mause, L. de (ed.) (1974), *The History of Childhood*, New York, Psychohistory Press.

Mead, G. H. (1934), *Mind, Self and Society*, University of Chicago Press.

Measor, L. (1984), 'Gender and the sciences: pupils' gender-based conceptions of school subjects', in: M. Hammersley and P. Woods (eds), *Life in School. The Sociology of Pupil Culture*, Milton Keynes, Open University Press.

Mehan, H. and Griffin, P. (1980), 'Socialization: the view from classroom interactions', *Sociological Inquiry*, 50, 3–4, 357–92.

Merton, R. K. (1957), *Social Theory and Social Structure*, New York, Free Press.

Midgley, M. (1984), *Wickedness. A Philosophical Essay*, London and Boston, Routledge & Kegan Paul.

Milgram, S. (1974), *Obedience to Authority: An Experimental View*, London, Tavistock.

Miller, J. B. (1958), 'Lower class culture as a generating milieu of gang delinquency', *Journal of Social Issues*, 14, 5-19.

Moore, B. (1978), *Injustice. The Social Bases of Obedience and Revolt*, London, Macmillan.

More, H. (1799), *Strictures on the Modern System of Female Education etc.*, vol. II, 1830 edition, London, T. Cadell.

Morris, D. (1967), *The Naked Ape*, London, Cape.

Morris, R. J. (1983), *Treating Children's Fears and Phobias: A Behavioural Approach*, Oxford, Pergamon.

Neill, A. S. (1973), *Neill, Neill 'Orange Peel': A Personal View of Ninety Years* (revised edition), London, Quartet.

Nisbet, R. (1976), *The Social Philosophers*, London, Paladin.

Nunn, Sir P. (1945), *Education: Its Data and First Principles*, 1st edn 1920, London, Arnold.

O'Brien, M. (1981), *The Politics of Reproduction*, London and Boston, Routledge & Kegan Paul.

Ong, W. J. (1981), *Fighting for Life. Contest, Sexuality and Consciousness*, Ithaca and London, Cornell University Press.

Ortega y Gasset, J. (1957), *Man and People*, New York, Norton & Co.

Parsons, T. (1951), *The Social System*, New York, Free Press.

Perls, F., Hefferline, R. F. and Goodman, P. (1973), *Gestalt Therapy. Excitement and Growth in the Human Personality*, Harmondsworth, Penguin, first published 1951.

Pizzey, E. (1982), *Prone to Violence*, London, Hamlyn.

Phillips, D. P. (1980), 'Airplane accidents, murder, and the mass media: towards a theory of imitation and suggestion', *Social Forces*, 58, 1001-24.

Phillips, D. P. (1982), 'The impact of fictional television stories on U.S. adult fatalities: new evidence on the effect of the mass media on violence', *American Journal of Sociology*, 87, 1340-59.

Phillips, D. P. (1983), 'The impact of mass media violence on U.S. homicides', *American Sociological Review*, 48, 560-8.

Phillips, M. (1981), 'Rage that shattered Thatcher', *New Statesman*, July 17.

Platt, A. M. (1977) (second edition), *The Child Savers. The Invention of Delinquency*, The University of Chicago Press.

Rawls, J. (1971), *A Theory of Justice*, Oxford University Press.

Renvoize, J. (1979), *Web of Violence. A Study of Family Violence*, Penguin.

Ricoeur, P. (1970), *Freud and Philosophy: An Essay on Interpretation*, trans. by D. Savage, New Haven and London, Yale University Press.

Robottom, J. (1976), 'A history of violence', in: N. Tutt (ed.), *Violence*, HMSO, Social Work Development Group.

Ross, P. (1984), 'Altered states of consciousness and the psychology of the self', in: Schostak, J. F. and Logan, T., *Pupil Experience*, London, Croom Helm.

Rousseau, J. J. (1974), *Emile*, trans. B. Foxley, London, Dent.

Rudduck, J. and May, N. (1983), *Sex Stereotyping and the Early Years of Schooling*, A report of a project conducted in Norfolk schools and funded by the EOC, CARE, University of East Anglia.

St John Brooks, C. (1982), 'The myth of St. Saviour's', *New Society*, March 4.

Sartre, J. P. (1976), *Critique of Dialectical Reason*, trans. A. Sheridan-Smith, ed. J. Ree, London, Verso.

Sax, S. and Hollander, S. (1972), *Reality Games. Games People Ought to Play*, New York, Popular Library.

Scarman, The Rt Hon. The Lord (1981), *The Brixton Disorders*, Cmnd 8427, London, HMSO.

Schaff, A. (1970), *Marxism and the Human Individual*, based on a translation by O. Wojtasiewicz, New York and London, McGraw-Hill.

Schostak, J. F. (1983a), 'Race, riots and unemployment' in: R. Fiddy (ed.), *In Place of Work. Provision and Policy for the Young Unemployed*, Barcombe, Falmer.

Schostak, J. F. (1983b), *Maladjusted Schooling. Deviance, Social Control and Individuality in Secondary Schooling*, London and Philadelphia, Falmer.

Schostak, J. F. (1983c), 'Making and breaking lies in a pastoral care context', *Research in Education*, 30, 71–93.

Schostak, J. F. (1984), 'A Day In The Life ... A Study of Pastoral Care', Affective Curriculum Conference, St Hilda's, Oxford, September.

Schostak, J. F. and Logan, T. (eds) (1984), *Pupil Experience*, London and Sydney, Croom Helm.

School of Barbiana (1969), *Letter to a Teacher*, Harmondsworth, Penguin.

Schutz, A. (1976), *The Phenomenology of the Social World*, trans. by George Walsh and Frederick Lehnert, London, Heinemann.

Sevenhuijsen, S. and de Vries, P. (1984), 'The women's movement and motherhood', in: A. Meulenbelt, J. Outshoorn, S. Sevenhuijsen and P. de Vries, *A Creative Tension. Explorations in Socialist Feminism*, London and Sydney, Pluto Press.

Sharpe, R. and Green, A. (1975), *Education and Social Control*, London, Routledge & Kegan Paul.

Silver, P. and H. (1974), *The Education of the Poor. The History of a National School 1824–1974*, London, Routledge & Kegan Paul.

Sivanandan, A. (1983), Editorial, 'British racism: the road to 1984' *Race and Class*, 25, 2.

Smith, M. (1977), *The Underground and Education. A Guide to the Alternative Press*, London, Methuen.

Smith, M. P. (1983), *The Libertarians and Education*, London, George Allen & Unwin.

Spender, D. (1982), *Invisible Women. The Schooling Scandal*, London, Writers and Readers Cooperative.

Stanworth, M. (1981), 'Gender and schooling. A study of sexual divisions in the classroom', *Explorations in Feminism*, No. 7, Women's Research and Resources Centre, London.

Bibliography

Stenhouse, L. et al. (1982), *Teaching about Race Relations; Problems and Effects*, London, Routledge & Kegan Paul.

Stinton, J. (1979), in: (ed.) Writers and Readers Publishing Cooperative, *Racism and Sexism in Children's Books*, London.

Swinburne, A. J. (1911), *Memories of a School Inspector. Thirty-five Years in Lancashire and Suffolk*, published by the author, London.

Szasz, T. S. (1973), *The Manufacture of Madness*, London, Paladin.

Taft, D. R. and England, R. W. (1942), *Criminology*, New York, Macmillan.

Tattum, D. P. (1982), *Disruptive Pupils in Schools and Units*, Chichester, Paladin.

Thrasher, F. M. (1927), *The Gang. A Study of 1,313 Gangs in Chicago*, University of Chicago Press.

Tinbergen, N. (1951), *The Study of Instinct*, Oxford, Clarendon.

Toch, H. (1972), *Violent Men. An Inquiry into the Psychology of Violence*, Harmondsworth, Penguin.

Tragesser, R. S. (1977), *Phenomenology and Logic*, Ithaca and London, Cornell University Press.

Tredgold, A. F. (1925), 'Delinquency in children' in: E. S. Chesser (ed.), *Health and Psychology of the Child*, London, Heinemann.

Troyna, B. (1984), 'The product being sold is racial harmony: a case study in social advertising and race relations', *Multiracial Education*, 12, 2, 24–33.

Von Hentig, H. (1967), *The Criminal and his Victim*, New York, Anchor Books.

Wallbank, M. V. (1979), 'Eighteenth century public schools and the education of the governing elite', *History of Education*, 8, 1, 1–19.

Waller, W. (1932), *The Sociology of Teaching*, New York, John Wiley; London, Chapman & Hall.

Walvin, J. (1982), *A Child's World. A Social History of English Childhood 1800–1914*, Harmondsworth, Penguin.

Wardle, D. (1974), *The Rise of the Schooled Society. The History of Formal Schooling in England*, London and Boston, Routledge & Kegan Paul.

Westley, W. A. (1953), 'Violence and the police', *American Journal of Sociology*, 59, 34–41.

Willis, P. (1977), *Learning to Labour*, Farnborough, Saxon House.

Wilson, E. O. (1978), *On Human Nature*, Cambridge and London, Harvard University Press.

Wolfgang, M. E. and Ferracuti, F. (1967), *The Subculture of Violence. Towards an Integrated Theory of Criminology*, London and New York, Tavistock.

Woods, P. (1978), 'Negotiating the demands of school work', *Curriculum Studies*, 10, 4, 309–27.

Wright, D. R. (1984), 'What do pupils learn about race?', *Education Journal*, 6, 1.

Wright, J. (1984), 'Resisting "special education"', *Multiracial Education*, 12, 2, 3–7.

Wrong, D. H. (1961), 'The oversocialised conception of man in modern sociology', *American Sociological Review*, 26, 2, 183-93.

Zastrow, C. (1979), *Talk to Yourself Using the Power of Self-Talk*, Englewood Cliffs, N.J., Prentice-Hall.

Name index

192

Subject index